Chicago on foot

Chicago on

foot

**WALKING TOURS
OF
CHICAGO'S ARCHITECTURE**

Completely Revised, Second Edition

by Ira J. Bach
President, Urban Associates, Inc.

J. PHILIP O'HARA, INC.
Chicago

Picture Credits

Cover montage by Allen Carr.
Architectural Camera, Ltd., 25 left; Daniel Bartush, 82 left; Orlando R.
Cabanan, 114-15, 340; Allen Carr, 6, 11, 15 right, 17, 19, 23, 25 right, 34,
35 left, 38, 42 top, center left, 46 top left, 55, 58, 61, 63 left, 67, 69, 71, 72 right,
87, 95, 98, 100, 101, 108-9, 119, 124, 127 left, bottom right, 139 top right,
bottom, 145, 146, 149, 154-55, 163, 164, 165, 172 left, 196, 198, 201, 246, 268,
274, 287, 288, 289, 295, 297, 300-301, 304, 306, 327, 330, 331, 332, 334, 335,
342, 345, 346, 349, 353 bottom; Chicago Department of Urban Renewal, 89,
206, 253; Chicago Park District, 171, 264; Chicago Plan Commission,
33 top left, 92; Bill Engdahl, Hedrich-Blessing, 79 left, 261; Hube Henry,
Hedrich-Blessing, 15 left, 172-73; Balthazar Korab, 42 bottom left, 131;
Mart Studios, Inc., 117 right; Terry's Photography, 82 right; © 1969 by
Philip A Turner, 2-3, 8, 30, 35 right, 42 right, 46 bottom left, right,
51 bottom left, 52, 63 right, 75, 80, 88-9, 102, 105, 113, 117 left, 123,
127 right top, center, 133, 137, 139 top left, 150, 159, 160-61, 168-69, 175,
181, 184-85, 189, 191, 205, 211, 212, 219, 224, 228, 237, 238-39, 243, 248, 251,
256-57, 269, 276-77, 283, 307, 312-13, 317, 323, 325, 353 top.

J. Philip O'Hara, Inc., 20 East Huron, Chicago, 60611. Published
simultaneously in Canada by Van Nostrand Reinhold Ltd.,
Scarborough, Ontario.

Acknowledgments
We are indebted to Robert W. Heidrich, President of the Frederick Law
Olmsted Society of Riverside, for permission to use a portion of the text
in this book entitled RIVERSIDE—A VILLAGE IN A PARK, published
by the Society in 1970.

Library of Congress Number: 73-6746
ISBN: 0-87955-401-0 cloth binding
ISBN: 0-87955-402-9 paper binding
First Printing F

To Muriel

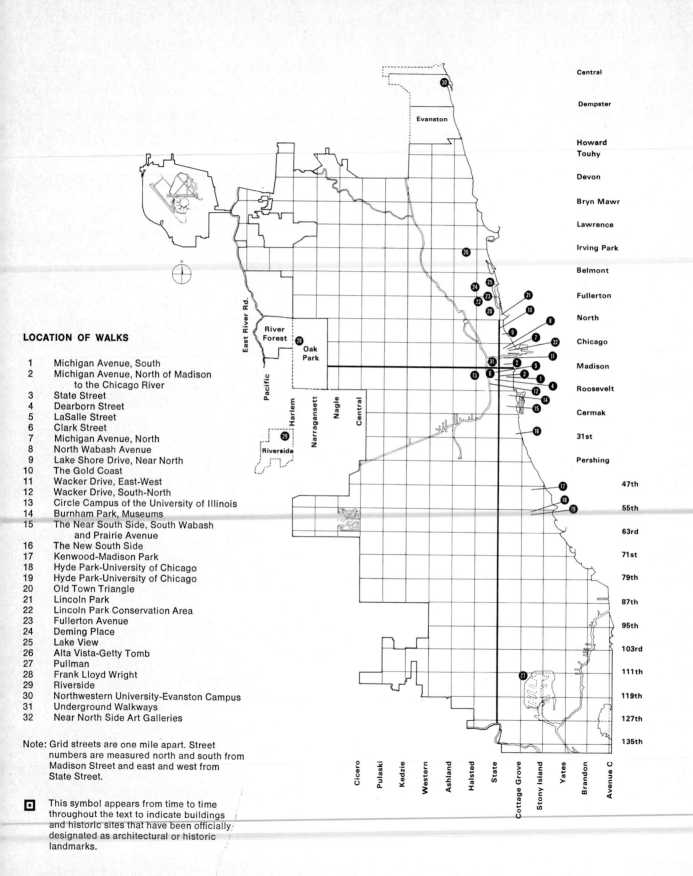

LOCATION OF WALKS

1	Michigan Avenue, South
2	Michigan Avenue, North of Madison to the Chicago River
3	State Street
4	Dearborn Street
5	LaSalle Street
6	Clark Street
7	Michigan Avenue, North
8	North Wabash Avenue
9	Lake Shore Drive, Near North
10	The Gold Coast
11	Wacker Drive, East-West
12	Wacker Drive, South-North
13	Circle Campus of the University of Illinois
14	Burnham Park, Museums
15	The Near South Side, South Wabash and Prairie Avenue
16	The New South Side
17	Kenwood-Madison Park
18	Hyde Park-University of Chicago
19	Hyde Park-University of Chicago
20	Old Town Triangle
21	Lincoln Park
22	Lincoln Park Conservation Area
23	Fullerton Avenue
24	Deming Place
25	Lake View
26	Alta Vista-Getty Tomb
27	Pullman
28	Frank Lloyd Wright
29	Riverside
30	Northwestern University-Evanston Campus
31	Underground Walkways
32	Near North Side Art Galleries

Note: Grid streets are one mile apart. Street numbers are measured north and south from Madison Street and east and west from State Street.

▣ This symbol appears from time to time throughout the text to indicate buildings and historic sites that have been officially designated as architectural or historic landmarks.

Contents

Introduction

An excellent public response to the first edition of this architectural walking tour of Chicago has prompted its updating and revision. What has been a continued source of gratification is its use by the many young foreign and American visitors to the city as well as by Chicagoans themselves.

Leading many group walks has been a pleasant dividend for me, but I now yield to the Chicago School of Architecture Foundation, with its dedicated staff of young docents, who conduct many walks throughout the year for the benefit of the Glessner House.

The non-architectural walks have been eliminated in this new edition while two highly significant architectural walks have been added. The nineteenth-century "new town" of Riverside has been added along with the Evanston campus of Northwestern University. Both walks well deserve to be included as part of a series of those of architectural importance.

The walks proposed here have been selected to present Chicago as a great cosmopolitan city as well as a collection of local community areas, all tied together by an intricate web of transportation that makes them accessible to the pedestrian for a closer view.

Since Chicago is a vast outdoor museum of great architecture created in about one hundred years, the major focus of the walks is architectural. From 1883 to 1893 the "Chicago School of Architecture" came into being. During that decade a whole galaxy of buildings appeared, reaching the unprecedented heights of twelve, fourteen, sixteen, and twenty-three stories. The architects of the Chicago school employed a new type of construction: *the iron skeleton,* at that time called quite simply "Chicago Construction." They invented a new kind of foundation to cope with the problems of the muddy ground of Chicago: *the floating foundation.* They introduced the horizontally elongated window: *the "Chicago window."* They created the modern business and administration building. And around the turn of the century, the so-called Prairie House came into being here.

Of equal significance is the current work of Chicago architects, often characterized as a continuation of the "Chicago school." The pure forms, horizontally elongated windows, and rugged strength and force are still to be seen in many of today's buildings. Architects of the present, however, have not hesitated to experiment with their own designs and materials. Though Mies van der Rohe's "Glass Houses" on North Lake Shore Drive may be considered the ultimate development of certain trends of the Chicago school, the cylindrical towers of Marina City bear little resemblance. Their concrete slab construction, circular balconies, and pie-shaped rooms hardly follow the tradition of the "Chicago school" of architects. Nor does the facade of the Henry Hinds Laboratory for the Geophysical Sciences Building at the University of Chicago—though the older school of architects would approve the functional origin of the new features.

Complete coverage of buildings worth noting in Chicago cannot possibly be attempted, especially in view of the tremendous pace at which construction is going on. While following the routes proposed here, the pedestrian will many times come across other interesting or beautiful buildings. The frequency with which this may happen is only another tribute to the endless vitality of this tremendous city.

■ This symbol appears from time to time throughout the text to indicate buildings and historic sites that have been officially designated as architectural or historic landmarks. The Commission on Chicago Historic and Architectural Landmarks was created on January 17, 1968 by ordinance of the City Council of the City of Chicago. A predecessor commission, known as the Commission on Chicago Architectural Landmarks, was created in 1957 by Mayor Richard J. Daley. Because broader powers were considered desirable, the legislature and City Council acted to replace the first commission by creating the present one. The new commission now includes the preservation of historical as well as architectural landmarks.

The City of Chicago has been particularly unfortunate in having lost Louis Sullivan's Garrick Theatre in 1963 and Sullivan and Adler's Old Stock Exchange Building in 1972. Efforts to save these buildings failed because of inadequate landmarks preservation legislation. Indeed, ineffective landmarks preservation is widespread in the United States.

The Chicago Chapter Foundation of The American Institute of Architects and The National Trust for Historic Preservation commissioned a study in 1971, *Development Rights Transfers; A Solution to Chicago's Landmarks Dilemma* by John Costonis and Jared Shlaes, May, 1971. The study had to face up to the fact that, though adequate in its definition of criteria and procedures for selecting landmarks and historic districts, existing landmarks legislation does not come to grips with the hard economic problems of preservation.

The recommendations of the study are under consideration and have been submitted to the Commission on Chicago Historical and Architectural Historic Architecture. Briefly, they authorize the owners of a landmark building to transfer the development right of the site to a city landmarks bank for eventual sale to a property owner desiring to enlarge the bulk of a planned structure.

Under proper planning and zoning controls, the owners of a landmark structure would be compensated for preserving their building and the city and general public would benefit by safeguarding another landmark. Other cities in the U.S.A. are likewise considering similar legislation. All agree that some type of financial assistance should be available to owners of landmark buildings.

Chicago is famous too for one of the first comprehensive city plans produced on this continent. The pedestrian will become aware of the planning, especially on the lakefront. In 1909 Daniel H. Burnham and Edward H. Bennett enunciated policies that have been instrumental in shaping the city of today. They established, among other things, the city's shoreline for public use only, by recommending the extension of lakefront parks, and set the pattern for the city's system of forest preserves, linked by highways.

Chicago's street system is the conventional grid, laid out with major streets at mile and one-half mile spacing. There are also a number of diagonal streets, some of them tracing old Indian trails, which bisect the junctions of major streets of the grid pattern, forming six-spoked intersections—creating some of the city's most difficult traffic problems.

More recently, a number of expressways have been built in Chicago. These carry traffic to and from the central business district and also serve large volumes of north-south and east-west crosstown traffic. The new roads have considerably shortened travel time within the city and have tied the various parts of the metropolitan area more tightly together. They have also helped to improve public transportation by the installation of rapid transit lines in the median strip of the Eisenhower, Dan Ryan and Kennedy expressways.

The street numbering system in Chicago follows the compass, with the east-west division marked by State Street, and the north-south directions divided by Madison Street. The city is about 25 miles north and south, and about 15 miles east and west.

Since all of the city's topography is flat, walking—which is said to be one of the best forms of exercise—will not be strenuous. The routes outlined here are well lighted and well patrolled at night, although most of them are designed for daytime.

Instructions for each walk on "How to get there" assume that downtown Chicago—the Loop—is the starting place. Since bus-routes and bus numbers change from time to time, the safest way will be to phone the CTA for precise instructions before starting out—or at least ask the bus driver whether the number you are here told to take will still carry you to your destination.

This book makes no attempt to advise on places to stay or eat. The city abounds with good hotels and restaurants, lists of which can be obtained from the Chicago Convention and Tourism Bureau (332 South Michigan).

In the preparation of the second edition, I want to thank the many persons who have taken the time to communicate to me additional information or corrections that might be useful now. I particularly want to acknowledge and thank Lewis W. Hill, Commissioner of the Department of Development and Planning, for the base maps used in the texts; Robert Heidrich and Patricia Raney for their assistance on the work of Olmsted and the Town of Riverside; Carl W. Condit, Hugh Duncan, and J. Carson Webster for their critical statements in *Chicago's Famous Buildings* (University of Chicago Press, 1969), Frederick Koeper in *Illinois Architecture* (University of Chicago, 1968), which have set a pattern of excellence in reviewing the Chicago School of Architecture; William Kerr, Vice President, Northwestern University, and Mrs. Marjorie Perkins for their help on the buildings and campus of Northwestern University; Calvert W. Audrain, Director Physical Planning, University of Chicago, for advice on the University of Chicago campus; Michael Shymanski and Norbert Pointner of the Beman Committee for their able assistance on Pullman; William McLenahan, Director, and John Hern, staff member, of the Commission on Chicago Historical & Architectural Landmarks for their aid; Mary Reidy, for her editorial guidance, and Allen Carr, for his excellent photography; and once again my dear friend Marshall Holleb, without whose companionship and wit I might have given up walking long ago.

IRA J. BACH
Chicago, March 1973

IRA BACH knows Chicago intimately. His unquenchable curiosity has led him through miles of walks in the city and its suburbs. He has acquired a deep familiarity with everything from the small details on the facade of the Rookery to Pullman's extraordinary "company town" on the far south side. As the Executive Director of the Chicago Dwellings Association, he reorganized that agency to develop and expand middle income housing in Chicago. Earlier he served the city as Commissioner of City Planning and Secretary of the Chicago Plan Commission, and before that as Executive Director of the Chicago Land Clearance Commission, in which capacity he was in charge of the slum clearance and redevelopment programs that resulted in Lake Meadows, Michael Reese, Prairie Shores, and Hyde Park-Kenwood. He has lectured at a number of universities throughout the country, and from 1958 to 1963 was visiting critic in City Planning at Yale University. In 1969 he resigned his position with the Chicago Dwellings Association to become president of Urban Associates, Inc. CHICAGO ON FOOT is his view, as planner, architect and citizen of the city he knows so well.

Architectural walks

Walk-1

Buckingham
Memorial Fountain.

1. Grant Park
   E. of Michigan Ave.
   Roosevelt Rd. to Monroe St.

2. Conrad Hilton Hotel
   720 S. Michigan Ave.

3. Sheraton-Blackstone Hotel
   S. Michigan & E. Balbo

4. Pick-Congress Hotel
   520 S. Michigan Ave.

5. Sculpture of Equestrian Indians
   —Buckingham Fountain
   E. of Congress Plaza
   & Michigan Ave.

6. Auditorium Building—Roosevelt
   University
   430 S. Michigan Ave.

7. Fine Arts Building
   410 S. Michigan Ave.

8. The Chicago Club Building
   81 E. Van Buren St.

9. Continental National American Center
   310 S. Michigan Ave.
   55 E. Jackson Blvd.
   325 S. Wabash Ave.

10. McClurg Building
    218 S. Wabash Ave.

11. Railway Exchange Building
    80 E. Jackson Blvd.

12. Orchestra Hall Building
    220 S. Michigan Ave.

13. Borg-Warner Building
    200 S. Michigan Ave.

14. Art Institute of Chicago
    Michigan Ave. at Adams St.

15. Peoples Gas Company Building
    122 S. Michigan Ave.

16. Lake View Building
    116 S. Michigan Ave.

17. Illinois Athletic Club
    112 S. Michigan Ave.

18. Monroe Building
    104 S. Michigan Ave.

19. Mid-Continental Plaza
    Wabash Ave. between Monroe &
    Adams

20. University Building
    79 E. Monroe St.

21. Gage Building
    18 S. Michigan Ave.

22. Chicago Athletic Association
    12 S. Michigan Ave.

23. Willoughby Tower
    8 S. Michigan Ave.

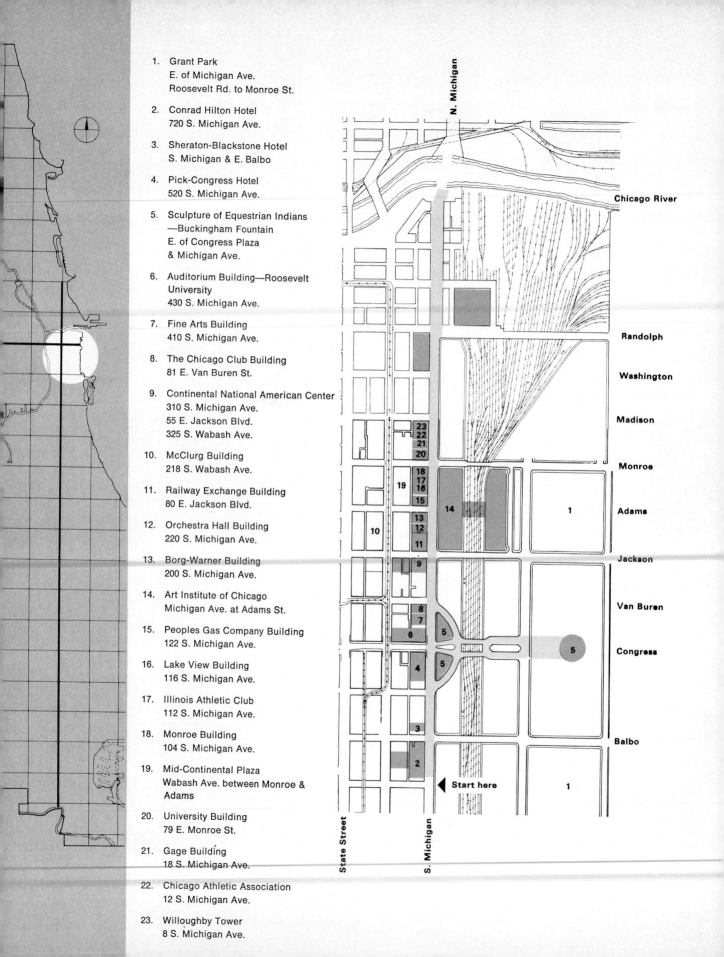

Walk · 1

MICHIGAN AVENUE : SOUTH

WALKING TIME: About 2 hours.   HOW TO GET THERE: Take a southbound CTA "shuttle"
bus, No. 149 (Michigan-State-Wacker—reduced fare service) on State Street (2 blocks west of
Michigan). Get off at Balbo Street (700 S). Cross Michigan Avenue, and you are in Grant Park.

Chicago's skyline is one of the most exhilarating sights in the
world. Day or night the view is magnificent—from an airplane
approaching the city, from a boat on Lake Michigan, from a car
on the Outer Drive, or from the footpaths in Grant Park.
It is always impressive.

Michigan Avenue stretches along Lake Michigan from the ancient
Illinois Central railroad station, several blocks south of Balbo,
to the recently constructed 80-story Standard Oil Building and
the 40-story Prudential Building, at Randolph Street to the north,
before other streets intervene to bar the view of the lake. From
the Conrad Hilton Hotel, just south of Balbo, to the Chicago
River, three blocks north of the Prudential—the distance
covered by this walk—Michigan Avenue is rich with sculpture,
gardens, and fountains.

Grant Park—Extending from Roosevelt Road
(12th Street) to Monroe Street (100 S).

Grant Park was no accident. Daniel Burnham designed it as part
of the Chicago Plan of 1909. First, the lake was filled from
Michigan Avenue out to what is now the Outer Drive, to provide
the necessary land space. The park was planned as an immense
green expanse following loosely the pattern of Versailles. In
the spring, when the park's hundreds of small trees and shrubs
are in bloom, this is a place of incomparable beauty.

And in the midst is the magnificent seated Lincoln, last work of
Augustus St. Gaudens. Chicago is the fortunate possessor of
this monument because of a $100,000 bequest for a Lincoln statue
from John Crerar, the man who also willed the city the John
Crerar Library. (St. Gaudens was also the sculptor of the standing

5

Lincoln statue at the entrance to Lincoln Park. See Walk No. 21, Lincoln Park. Don't look for a statue of *Grant* in Grant Park; that's in Lincoln Park instead!)

The area that now is occupied by the Monroe Street parking lot and the Illinois Central railroad tracks, between Monroe and Randolph, will eventually be decked over and landscaped, thus completing Burnham's original plan for the park.

Conrad Hilton Hotel—720 South Michigan.
Architects: Holabird and Roche (1927)

Start your walk from the Conrad Hilton Hotel, on the southwest corner of Balbo and Michigan. Here you will be in the world's largest hotel (previously the Stevens), which contains about 3,000 rooms. It is 25 stories high with a four-story tower and two to five basements, supported on rock foundations. With its many restaurants, grills, bars, meeting rooms, and spacious ballroom, the Conrad Hilton is almost continuously being used throughout the year as headquarters for national conventions and conferences. (Hotel tours can be arranged by advance reservation with the service manager. For information phone WA-2-4400, and ask for the bell captain.)

Sheraton-Blackstone Hotel—Michigan and Balbo.
Architects: Marshall and Fox (1910)

Just north of the Hilton, on the *northwest* corner of Michigan and Balbo, is the Sheraton-Blackstone Hotel, many times a political headquarters during national nominating conventions. It offers a rather pleasing exterior of French Renaissance architecture. At the time it was built, in fact, it won a gold medal for excellence of design.

Pick-Congress Hotel (formerly the Congress)—
520 South Michigan.
Architects: Clinton J. Warren (1893);
Holabird and Roche (1902 and 1907);
Holabird and Root (1956)

The Pick-Congress Hotel stands opposite the Congress Plaza Drive. In contrast with the Sheraton-Blackstone's exterior, it has a facade of rugged gray limestone suggesting the influence of Henry Richardson. Its "Peacock Alley" off the main lobby was

Pick-Congress Hotel.

6

once one of the city's gathering places for outstanding social events. In the most recent renovation a section of the ground floor, on the north side, was opened up and arcaded, to allow the widening of Congress Street into Congress Parkway. (The south side of the Auditorium Building, across the street to the north, underwent the same kind of change.)

Buckingham Memorial Fountain—Designed by Bennett, Parsons, and Frost of Chicago and Jacques Lambert of Paris (1926)

Flanking Congress Plaza—across Michigan Avenue in Grant Park —are two American Indian equestrians with drawn bows, created by the Yugoslavian sculptor Ivan Mestrovic. Of heroic scale, they make a sweeping entrance to the enormous Buckingham Fountain, just to the east. This fountain, modeled from one of the Versailles fountains, is said to be the largest in the world—about twice as large as its model. It has a great central stream with 133 jets of water, some of which reach about two hundred feet in the air. Each night from 9:00 to 9:30 during its active season (May through September) the Fountain is illuminated, with shifting colors played on it throughout the half hour. It has become a popular rendezvous day and night for visitors to Chicago.

The Buckingham Fountain was donated to the city of Chicago in 1927 by Miss Kate Buckingham in memory of her brother Clarence.

◳ **Auditorium Building**—430 South Michigan. Architects: Adler and Sullivan (1889); Architect for Restoration of Auditorium Theatre: Harry Weese (1967)

The Auditorium Building, on the northwest corner of Michigan Avenue and Congress Parkway—now owned by Roosevelt University—is one of Chicago's most famous cultural and architectural landmarks. Its construction was a triumph of the partnership of Louis Sullivan, with his inspired architectural imagination, and Dankmar Adler, with his extraordinary engineering genius.

The Auditorium Theatre, originally surrounded by hotel and office space, has long been justifiably renowned for its large, well-equipped stage and its perfect acoustics.

7

Auditorium building.

The Chicago Landmarks Commission citation of 1959 reads:

> In recognition of the community spirit which here joined
> commercial and artistic ends, uniting hotel, office building, and
> theatre in one structure; the inventiveness of the engineer
> displayed from foundations to the perfect acoustics; and the
> genius of the architect which gave form and, with the aid of the
> original ornament, expressed the spirit of festivity in rooms
> of great splendor.

Disaster threatened the building in 1929, however, when the
Chicago Opera Company, which had used the Auditorium Theatre
for many years, moved to the newly completed Civic Opera
Building; and it became a certainty with the economic depression
of the 1930's. By 1940 the Auditorium Building was bankrupt

8

and the theatre was closed. From 1942 to 1945 the building was used as Chicago headquarters for the United Service Organization. In 1946 it was purchased by Roosevelt University (then Roosevelt College), and hotel rooms and offices were converted as needed for its new purpose.

The Auditorium Theatre was fortunately left untouched at this time, though all movable contents had been sold at auction soon after bankruptcy was declared. Unable to raise the enormous amount of money needed to restore the theatre, Roosevelt University nevertheless appreciated its value. In 1958 the University established a nonprofit organization, the Auditorium Theatre Council, which in nine years succeeded in raising the $2,250,000 required for restoration. After 26 years of darkness, the Auditorium Theatre opened once again on October 31, 1967, with the New York City Ballet performing to an audience of 4,200.

The University's administration is to be congratulated on having proceeded on a vast and costly restoration and remodeling program of the entire Auditorium Building. The great lobby facing Michigan Avenue has been restored, including a portion of the mosaic tile flooring, marble wainscoting and chandeliers. The grand staircase is once again the graceful and delightful Sullivan brainchild.

The lobby was one of the showpieces of the Auditorium Hotel when it opened in 1889 and still exhibits many of the great architectural elements designed by Louis Sullivan and Dankmar Adler. The original mosaic tile floor was made of tile tesserae laid in multi-colored design motifs. The central columns in the lobby are faced with an imitation marble called scogliola and contain utility plumbing and electrical connections for the upper stories. There is a six-foot dado around the lobby of Mexican onyx. Originally the lighting was in rosette clusters of filament bulbs and there were stencilled patterns on the ceiling bays and on the undersurfaces of each of the beams. The restoration when completed, including new light fixtures, will be as faithful as possible to the original lobby design and color scheme.

Naturally, the upper floors that contain classrooms were modernized for safety but pleasantly designed and planned. The Michigan Avenue stairways have been restored to the original gold leaf ornament on the balustrades; and the stained-glass windows were restored with artificial lighting behind. This stairway now faces the new Walter Heller Center instead of the former light well.

Because Roosevelt University "campus" consists primarily of the former Auditorium complex, any expansion had to be within or adjacent to the confines of the property. This planning dilemma was turned into a challenge that was met head on by the architects and planners.

First, the tower that formerly divided the hotel and office building was remodeled and modernized. This was once the tallest tower in the city and as a result, many visitors climbed the 95 feet from the 10th floor to the top. Originally, the tower had 7 floors and now it has 8, and the new 16th floor houses the air conditioning, heating, and other mechanical equipment for the tower offices of the Labor Education Division and the Walter E. Heller College of Business Administration, the English and psychology departments. Within the main building facing Michigan Avenue, there were 16 classrooms, 30 offices, and 5 laboratories remodeled.

A fantastic piece of architectural squeezing was accomplished by constructing the Walter E. Heller Center within the former light and ventilation court. An 11-story and mezzanine structure, 100 feet long and 25 feet wide, was the answer. This structure now houses classrooms, laboratories, business office, and language laboratory. The connections at each floor to the main building are unobtrusive.

The Herman Crown Center built on a land site 80 feet by 180 feet on Wabash Avenue just north of the Auditorium is indeed a well-planned and well-conceived "child" of Louis Sullivan. The simple concrete facade with the typical Chicago school windows relates well to its parent building next door. The interior design carries the spirit of Sullivan into the later twentieth century, to Roosevelt University's credit.

For tours of the University call 341-3623, weekdays only. Tours of the Auditorium Theatre may be arranged by calling 922-2110. Groups of 25 preferred: general admission, $2; students, $1.

Fine Arts Building—410 South Michigan.
Architect: S. S. Beman (1884)

Next to the Auditorium is the Fine Arts Building, for years a center of musical and dramatic events and at one time—along with the Auditorium and Orchestra Hall—the performing arts center of Chicago. The facade is rugged and is a good companion for the Auditorium. The interior contains two theatres and high-ceilinged upper floors with studios and recital halls—from which sounds of hopeful artists can be heard scaling the heights.

The Chicago Club Building—81 East Van Buren Street.
Architects: Burnham and Root (1885)

This building was occupied by The Art Institute until 1892. At that time the present main building of The Art Institute was completed permitting the sale of this ornate structure to The Chicago Club. The building fronts 90 feet on Van Buren Street and 75 feet on Michigan Avenue. It is 95 feet high, including four stories and basement, and is made of steel, Connecticut brownstone, and brick. The Italian Romanesque style of the exterior lends dignity to this section of Michigan Avenue.

Cross Van Buren Street heading north and as you pass 332 South Michigan Avenue Building, it should be noted that the Chicago Convention and Tourism Bureau occupies the 20th floor. Much information is available to anyone interested in Chicago as a conference and convention center.

Continental National American Center—
Building Number 1: 310 South Michigan Avenue.
Architects: Graham, Anderson, Probst and White (1924)
Building Number 2: 55 East Jackson.
Architects: C. F. Murphy and Associates (1962)
Building Number 3: 325 South Wabash.
Architects: Graham, Anderson, Probst and White (1972)

The three CNA buildings are connected and demonstrate the growth and progressive attitude of this large corporation. Building Number 1, of inconsequential design, is representative of the architecture of the 1920's. Building Number 3, designed by the same architectural firm some 50 years later, reflects the strength of the sleek steel-and-glass structures of today. Its

Fine Arts building

11

45-story steel structure stands high above its two predecessors and is virtually the tallest building in the southeast portion of the Loop. The steel-and-glass facade is of the Chicago school of architecture. The facade has a deep sculptured appearance. Here the ¼-inch-thick steel plates that sheath the building reflect the shape of the structural members. The windows, which are twice as wide as those in the adjacent building, are set back and free from all metal surrounds. The window mullions are bold, the structural columns exposed on the exterior clearly express the large uninterrupted interior spaces. The two later buildings designed by different architectural firms are painted a rich red color which helps unite them and bring color into the downtown area. The corporate headquarters are in building Number 3.

Before you turn back to Michigan Avenue, cross to the north side of Jackson Boulevard at Wabash Avenue and walk across Wabash to the west side of the street to 218 South Wabash Avenue—the McClurg Building.

McClurg Building—218 South Wabash.
Architects: Holabird and Roche (1900)

This landmark building was completed in 1900 and is 9 stories on pile foundations. The famous Chicago windows can be seen along with the terra-cotta facing of the facade. It is an excellent early example of a simple, straightforward, steel-cage design for an office building.

Return to Jackson Boulevard and cross to the east side of Wabash Avenue and walk back to Michigan Avenue. On the corner is the Railway Exchange Building.

Railway Exchange Building—80 East Jackson Boulevard.
Architect: D. H. Burnham and Company (1904)

The building is 17 stories with a white terra-cotta facing. There is one basement and the structure rests on hardpan caissons. Daniel Burnham maintained his office here on the top floor during preparation of The Plan of Chicago, completed in 1909. His planning associate, Edward Bennett, also worked with him there. Bennett's son maintains an architectural office in the same suite.

Orchestra Hall Building—220 South Michigan Avenue.
Architect: D. H. Burnham and Company (1905)
Architect for Restoration of Orchestra Hall:
Harry Weese (1969)

The building is 10 stories with one basement. The hall, home of the world-famous Chicago Symphony Orchestra, occupies most of 9 stories. The orchestra was founded by Theodore Thomas in 1898 and the Orchestral Association, a not-for-profit citizens organization, is the owner of the property. The facade is composed of Indiana limestone and red brick in a style derivative of the Italian Renaissance. The names of Bach, Mozart, Beethoven, Schuman, and Wagner are made a part of the design over the entrance.

Borg-Warner Building—200 South Michigan Avenue.
Architects: A. Epstein and Sons (1960)

This steel-cage building was the first contemporary structure on Michigan Avenue. It replaced the old Pullman Building that was erected in 1884. A famous restaurant known as The Tip Top Inn occupied the entire top 10th floor, a precursor of the proliferation of rooftop eating places. S. L. Beman was the architect.

Art Institute of Chicago—Michigan Avenue at Adams.
Architects: Shepley, Rutan, and Coolidge (1892);
For McKinlock Court: Coolidge and Hodgson (1924);
For North Wing: Holabird and Root (1956);
For Morton Wing: Shaw, Metz and Associates (1962)

Now cross Adams and then Michigan to view one of Chicago's most prized possessions, its Art Institute—the entrance guarded by two large, sculptured lions. So overpowering, in fact, are the lions that most people fail to see the statue of George Washington that is standing in the central arch at the top of the entrance steps.

The original part of the building is French Renaissance in spirit, a style considered appropriate for art museums at the time but quite at variance with the trend of the Chicago school. In the center of McKinlock Court, which is classical rather than Renaissance, is a fountain with sea creatures sculptured by

13

Carl Milles—a duplicate of one in his native Sweden. Here in the open air, lunch is served on clear summer days.

The Art Institute houses a theatre and an art and drama school, in addition to its art collections. A section of special interest to architects is the Burnham Library of Architecture Gallery, created to provide space for exhibits from the Burnham Library Collection—established in 1912 in memory of the great architect and city planner, Daniel H. Burnham.

Among the Institute's especially noted art treasures are an unusually large collection of French Impressionist paintings, a superb variety of works by the Spanish master El Greco and his fellow countryman Goya, a room of paintings by Rembrandt, and an extensive collection of Oriental art. The building's latest addition, Morton Wing, contains a permanent exhibit of contemporary painting and sculpture.

Open daily 10:00 A.M. to 5:00 P.M. Thursday 10:00 A.M. to 8:30 P.M. Sundays and holidays 1:00 P.M. to 6:00 P.M. Voluntary admission fee (suggested $1.00 for adults and 50¢ for children). Admission to the Thorne Room, 25¢.

Under Michigan Avenue, north and south of the Art Institute, are two of the city's largest underground parking facilities with space for 4,000 cars.

Peoples Gas Company Building—
122 South Michigan Avenue.
Architects: D. H. Burnham and Company (1911)

Back on the west side of Michigan, this gray granite building is 20 stories, with two basements on hardpan caissons. The exterior walls on the two street fronts, above the monolithic granite columns, are supported on steel cantilever girders.

Just to the south of the main entrance of the building is the entrance to the offices of the Chicago Association of Commerce and Industry at 130 South Michigan. Questions pertaining to the various aspects of the growth of the Chicago metropolitan area can be answered by a well-informed staff. Booklets on some categories are available at nominal prices.

Left, Continental National American building. *Top right*, Bronze lion in front of the Art Institute. *Bottom right*, Gage building and the Chicago Athletic Club.

15

Lake View Building—116 South Michigan Avenue. Architects: Jenney, Mundie and Jensen (1906)

This building was originally known as the Municipal Court Building. It was first built as a 12-story structure to which five stories were added in 1907. The facade has three bays for windows with white terra-cotta as the exterior material.

Illinois Athletic Club—112 South Michigan Avenue. Architects: Haynes and Barnett of St. Louis, Missouri (1908)

This private club was completed in 1908 and is 12 stories with two basements on hardpan caissons. The facade is Indiana limestone with a base of gray granite. Step to the curb and look up to the sculptured frieze just under the cornice. The figures portray mythological characters in action.

Also note the three heroic figures at the second-floor level. One male gladiator is being urged to combat by two female figures. These friezes add lustre to the facade and to this section of Michigan Avenue.

Monroe Building—104 South Michigan Avenue. Architects: Holabird and Roche (1912)

This building is 16 stories with a beige-colored, granite facade in a simplified eclectic Gothic and Italian Romanesque design. It not only has a pleasing appearance, but a well-planned series of office floors. Note the way the fluting is carried up the full length of the building.

Mid-Continental Plaza—Wabash Avenue between Monroe and Adams. Architects: Alfred Shaw and Associates, Inc. (1972)

Walk one-half block west to a 55-story structure where the eye follows the vertical lines of the aluminum skin over the steel and concrete columns. There is a secondary horizontal series of lines that mark the floors and add rhythm to all three facades. The interior ground floor has been well planned for large pedestrian movements from the garage, street, elevators to upper floors, and pedestrian underpass to the Palmer House across Wabash Avenue.

This building in the heart of the Loop has been well-conceived
for the convenience of the public and tenants and, in addition,
provides automobile parking for guests of the Palmer House.
It has a striking lobby with grey marble floors and walls that set
off the aluminum escalators. The setting is one of efficiency
and order.

University Club—79 East Monroe Street.
Architects: Holabird and Roche (1909)

Located at the northwest corner of Monroe and Michigan, this
Indiana limestone, Tudor Gothic design structure is 14 stories,
with one basement on pile foundations. If you step to the curb on
Michigan Avenue, you can see the great cathedral dining hall
which occupies two stories of the top floors.

▣ Gage Building—18 South Michigan.
Architects: Holabird and Roche; architect for the
decorative facade: Louis Sullivan (1898)

Back on the west side of Michigan, just beyond Monroe Street,
you come to the Gage Building. Referring to Louis Sullivan's
facade on this building—the only part of the structure that he

Mid-Continental Plaza.

17

designed—the Architectural Landmarks Commission in its citation speaks of "the imaginative use of original ornament." Although the 2 buildings to the south of it, at 30 and 24 South Michigan, which were completely the work of Holabird and Roche, seem more modern in their lack of ornament, they do not equal the high quality of design in the Gage Building.

The entire citation from the Architectural Landmarks Commission reads:

> In recognition of the fine relations established between piers, windows, and wall surfaces; the excellence of proportions throughout; and the imaginative use of original ornament.

Chicago Athletic Association—12 South Michigan Avenue. Architect: Henry Ives Cobb (1893)
Addition at 71 East Madison Street.
Architects: Schmidt, Gorden and Martin (1906)

The building at 12 South Michigan Avenue was completed in 1893 after experiencing a disastrous fire. It is 10 and 11 stories, with one basement, on spread foundations. The adjoining addition at 71 East Madison is 12 stories with three basements, steel columns, and rock caissons. Step to the curb on Michigan Avenue and note the fascinating way in which Cobb designed the facade in a Venetian Gothic theme. Note that the top two floors contain a great two-story dining hall. Limestone and red brick are the materials used.

Willoughby Tower—8 South Michigan Avenue. Architect: Samuel N. Craven (1929)

Replacing the 8-story Willoughby Building, this 36-story structure on caissons has a gray granite base with an Indiana limestone facade on Michigan Avenue as well as on Madison Street.

This marks the end of Walk 1 but if you have the strength and desire to continue on Michigan Avenue, turn to Walk No. 2 and cross to the north side of Madison Street. Or else, return here at another time.

Madison Street divides the city into north-and-south street numbers as does State Street for east-and-west street numbers.

Entrance to the main
reading room of the
Chicago Public
Library with its
elaborate mosaics
and coffered ceiling.

1. Tower Building
   6 N. Michigan Ave.

2. 30 North Michigan Avenue Building

3. Pittsfield Building
   55 E. Washington St.

4. Chicago Public Library
   78 E. Washington St.

5. John Crerar Library Building
   86 E. Randolph St.

6. Prudential Building
   Randolph St. E. of Michigan Ave.

7. Standard Oil Building
   Randolph St. E. of Michigan Ave.

8. Maremont Building
   168 N. Michigan Ave.

9. Carbide and Carbon Building
   230 N. Michigan Ave.

10. Old Republic Building
    307 N. Michigan Ave.

11. 333 North Michigan Avenue Building

12. One Illinois Center
    111 E. Wacker Dr.

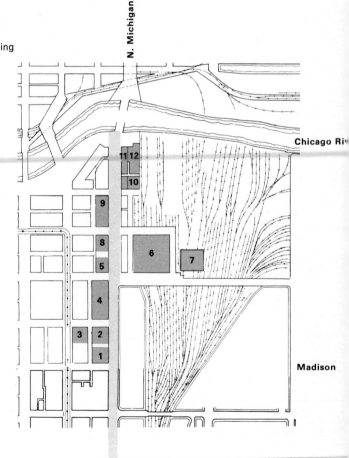

Walk · 2

MICHIGAN AVENUE : NORTH OF MADISON TO THE CHICAGO RIVER

WALKING TIME: About 2 hours.   HOW TO GET THERE: Walk on State Street to Madison, go two blocks east to Michigan Avenue and start at the northwest corner.

Tower Building—6 North Michigan Avenue.
Architect: Richard E. Schmidt (1899)
Architects for addition: Holabird and Roche (1916)

This building was formerly known as the Montgomery Ward and Company Building with a frontage of 86 feet on Michigan Avenue and 163 feet on Madison Street. The building of steel-frame construction is 12 stories with a tower and one basement on wood-pile foundations. Four stories were added later, thus reducing the original scale of the tower.

The street facade of the lower three stories is of carved Georgia marble. The upper part of the facade is an umber-colored brick. The Tower was remodeled in 1955 by architects Loebl, Schlossman and Bennett. A. Montgomery Ward who occupied the original tower office was victorious for all Chicagoans in obtaining an opinion from the Supreme Court of Illinois that no building other than the Art Institute be permitted in Grant Park.

30 North Michigan Avenue Building—
Architect: Jarvis Hunt (1914)

This was originally named the Michigan Boulevard Building when it was 15 stories high. Five stories were added in 1923, making it 20 stories with two basements on rock caissons. The exterior design is a modified Gothic. The base is granite and the facade is terra-cotta. Many medical offices are located here.

21

Pittsfield Building—55 East Washington Street.
Architects: Graham, Anderson, Probst and White (1927)

This structure is located just west of the 30 North Michigan
Building and is 21 stories with a 17-story tower. A black granite
base and gray limestone facade gives this structure a pleasing
effect. Medical personnel are the principal occupants of the
building.

Chicago Public Library—78 East Washington.
Architects: Shepley, Rutan, and Coolidge (1897)

Extending a full block along Michigan Avenue, from Washington
to Randolph, is the main building of the Chicago Public Library.
Though not at all in the style of the Chicago school of that time,
it is an impressive example of revivalist architecture, not only
on the outside but throughout the interior as well. The broad
marble staircases and the many beautifully colored mosaics that
decorate both the walls and the ceilings are a magnificent sight
for any period. The lighting fixtures and mosaics are the work
of Louis Tiffany.

The blue Bedford stone, granite, and limestone exterior with
large arches and columns is not unlike a Roman gateway. The
colonade is Ionic, with solid piers interspersed. The frieze bears
the names of historic authors. The Washington Street entrance
is treated in the Roman style with coffers and ornament, while
the Randolph Street entrance is in the Grecian style with
Doric columns and entablature. A stone balustrade surmounts
the walls. An enormous Soldiers Memorial Hall occupies the
entire second floor north with Civil War mementos.

Here are the central stacks and reading rooms of the city's
entire library system, which consists of more than 50 branches
and a total of over three million items—phonograph records,
musical scores, pictures, and slides, as well as books and
periodicals.

A new central library is being planned for another location. The
library board has taken action to remodel the present structure
into a popular library and cultural center.

Open daily 9:00 A.M. to 9:00 P.M. Saturdays 9:00 A.M. to
5:30 P.M. closed Sundays and holidays.

Now cross Randolph Street

John Crerar Library Building—86 East Randolph Street.
Architects: Holabird and Roche (1920)

Although the library itself in 1968 was moved to the campus of
the Illinois Institute of Technology, the gray limestone building
occupies a prominent corner on Michigan Avenue and probably
will be maintained as a commercial office building. The
structure is 16 stories with one basement on rock caissons.

Prudential Building—East Randolph Street.
Architects: Naess and Murphy (1958)

Cross over to this 40-story building which occupies a square
block of choice property facing on Grant Park. Unlike buildings
of the Chicago school of architecture, the Prudential of gray
Bedford limestone presents the appearance of a huge monolith.
The Prudential's trademark, the Rock of Gibraltar, is used as
the theme for a sculptured west wall of the east wing. There is
an observation tower which has a very commanding view of the
city if the weather is clear.

Left, John Crerar Library building.
Right, Chicago Public Library.

23

Standard Oil Building—East Randolph Street.
Architects: Edward D. Stone and the Perkins and
Will Partnership (1974)

Just east of the Prudential Building is the new Standard Oil
Building, containing the corporate headquarters of the Standard
Oil Company of Indiana. This 80-story, steel structure with a
light-gray marble exterior finish is one of the world's tallest.
Facing Grant Park on the south, it can be seen for miles around.

The slender structure occupies 25 percent of the site. The tower
design is based on the tube principle. The design incorporates
an outside wall of five-foot windows separated by five-foot
triangular sections which are part of the building frame. This
permits the bulk of mechanical services such as utilities and air
conditioning to be supplied through the triangular sections. This
design permits flush window walls inside the structure.

Facing Grant Park, the tower is 194 by 194 feet and set back 140
feet from Randolph. The tower rises 80 stories above street
level to a height of 1,136 feet. The gross area of the tower is
2.7 million square feet.

Maremont Building—168 North Michigan Avenue.
Architects: Marshall and Fox (1916)
Architect for Remodeling: Casriel Halperin (1964)

Cross back to the west side of Michigan Avenue. This structure
was originally known as the Federal Life Building. With one
basement on caissons, this building rises 12 stories. When the
exterior and base were remodeled in 1964, the base was created
of white marble.

The 8-foot metal sculpture by Theodore Roszak in the lobby
fascinates and puzzles viewers who are no more enlightened
when they read the title "206—H and R." The actual title is
"Invocation-Variation #3," and was executed by this eminent
modern sculptor in nickel, silver, and stainless steel. The work is
the third in a series called "Invocation" which represents an
ambitious attempt to translate and interpret fundamental ideas
concerning the meaning of life.

Carbide and Carbon Building—230 North Michigan Avenue. Architects: Burnham Brothers (1929)

This structure is 40 stories with two basements on rock caissons. It is distinguished for the gold and black terra-cotta tower, black terra-cotta facade and black granite and gold base. The gold, of course, is painted on the terra-cotta and metal. The Burnham brothers were the sons of the distinguished architect and city planner Daniel H. Burnham.

Cross now to the east side of Michigan Avenue to the Old Republic Building and note the building directly east that is part of the Illinois Central Air Rights Development discussed at the end of this walk.

Old Republic Building—307 North Michigan Avenue. Architects: Vitzhum and Burns (1925)

This building is 24 stories on hardpan caissons. The original name of the structure was the Bell Building. The base is a beige-colored granite and a light-gray, terra-cotta facade—typical of the commercial school of architecture of the 1920's—otherwise undistinguished.

Left, One Illinois Center and 333 North Michigan Avenue building. *Right*, The tower of the Carbide and Carbon building.

333 North Michigan Avenue Building.
Architects: Holabird and Root (1928)

This building is representative of the distinguished work of this equally distinguished firm of architects for the golden period of the late 1920's. The building can be seen from the full length of Michigan Avenue north of the Chicago River. The entrance was remodeled in 1969, but the balance of the building retains that fascinating design quality of the 1920's—sometimes referred to as "Art Moderne." The elevator doors carry sculptured figures in relief of Edgar Miller. The building's base is a gray marble and the entire facade is a gray limestone.

One Illinois Center—111 East Wacker Drive.
Architect: Ludwig Mies Van der Rohe (1970)

The Building

One Illinois Center is an office tower consisting of 29 office floors and a lobby floor on a landscaped plaza overlooking the Chicago River and Lake Michigan. Lobby escalators lead below-plaza level to a concourse bordered by retail shops and restaurants. Below the concourse are three levels of parking for over 300 cars. The building contains approximately one million square feet of rentable office space and 35,000 square feet of retail shops. The structure is reinforced concrete. The curtain wall is dark bronze aluminum and bronze-tinted glass.

The Complex

One Illinois Center is the first building planned as an integral part of Illinois Center, the complex also known as the Illinois Central Air Rights Development, constructed on air rights over the Illinois Central railroad yards. Illinois Center's business and residential towers and parks, with below-plaza shopping concourse and parking facilities, will be developed on 83 acres of land over 15 years. The Center will extend east of Michigan Avenue to the lake, and south of the Chicago River to Randolph Street. The residential area is to the east.

A daytime population of about 80,000 will work and shop in 9 million square feet of office space and 1.24 million square feet of retail space. About 35,000 residents will live in the Center's 19.5 million square feet of apartment area.

Four circulation levels will carry vehicular and pedestrian traffic within and through the complex. The lowest level will accommodate commercial vehicles. The intermediate level will serve through traffic from the Loop to the Outer Drive. Slightly above this level will be an all-weather pedestrian walkway with shops, continuing the concourse level as it exists in One Illinois Center. On the plaza itself, the only vehicular traffic will be local traffic serving the complex. A north-south distributor subway will serve this area with a station adjacent to Two Illinois Center. It will connect with the Hancock Building on the north, McCormick Place on the south and the Chicago Circle Campus of the University of Illinois on the west.

Two Illinois Center is a twin of One Illinois Center, by the same architect, to be completed in 1973. Below the plaza, its concourse and parking will be an extension of the levels provided under One Illinois Center. The buildings will function as a unified development. Two Illinois Center is built partially over the lower and intermediate levels of East South Water Street. A third structure directly east is the Hyatt House Hotel, designed by A. Epstein and Sons, Inc. This 1,000-room hotel of brick and glass will be completed in 1974.

This walk ends here at the Michigan Avenue Bridge. Note that both Michigan Avenue and Wacker Drive are two-level drives and the bridge is a double decker. The bridge pylons have commemorative sculpture concerning the early history of Chicago including the Fort Dearborn Massacre. Plaques and plates on nearby structures and sidewalks locate the site of Fort Dearborn.

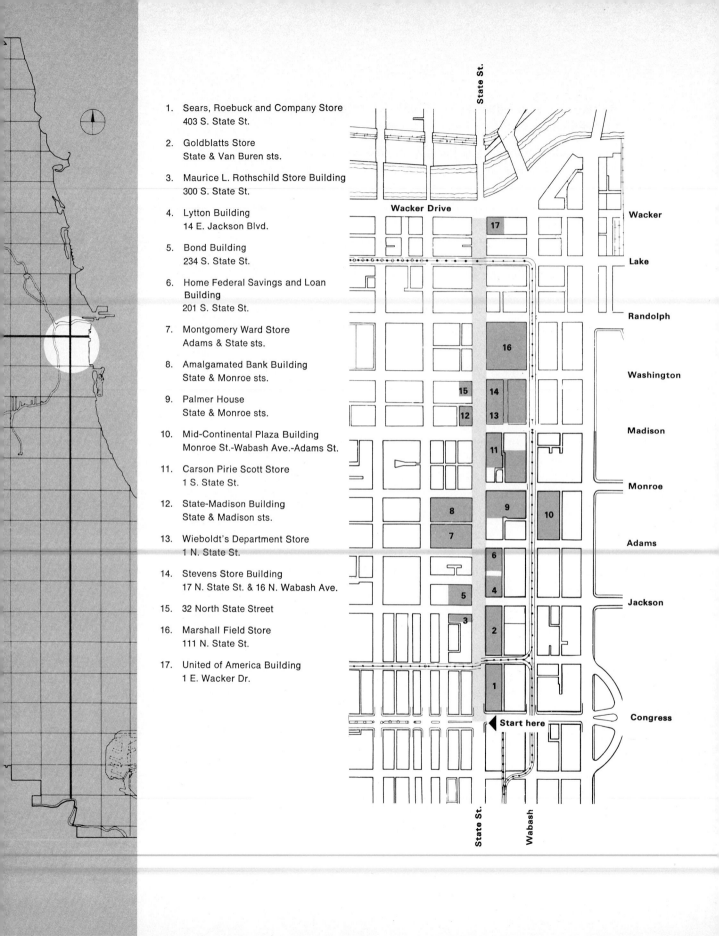

1. Sears, Roebuck and Company Store
   403 S. State St.

2. Goldblatts Store
   State & Van Buren sts.

3. Maurice L. Rothschild Store Building
   300 S. State St.

4. Lytton Building
   14 E. Jackson Blvd.

5. Bond Building
   234 S. State St.

6. Home Federal Savings and Loan
   Building
   201 S. State St.

7. Montgomery Ward Store
   Adams & State sts.

8. Amalgamated Bank Building
   State & Monroe sts.

9. Palmer House
   State & Monroe sts.

10. Mid-Continental Plaza Building
    Monroe St.-Wabash Ave.-Adams St.

11. Carson Pirie Scott Store
    1 S. State St.

12. State-Madison Building
    State & Madison sts.

13. Wieboldt's Department Store
    1 N. State St.

14. Stevens Store Building
    17 N. State St. & 16 N. Wabash Ave.

15. 32 North State Street

16. Marshall Field Store
    111 N. State St.

17. United of America Building
    1 E. Wacker Dr.

Walk · 3

STATE STREET

WALKING TIME: About 1 hour.   HOW TO GET THERE: Walk to Congress Parkway, 7 blocks south of Randolph; or take any southbound CTA bus on State Street south of Randolph, and get off at Congress (500 S). (Check with the driver to be sure the bus will not leave State before it reaches Congress.)

State Street—"That Great Street," as the city's commercial promoters enjoy calling it!—boasts the biggest strip of major department stores of any street in America. As a part of Chicago's central business district, State Street offers economic advantages provided nowhere else in the entire Midwest. It is a market for buyers and sellers from all over the nation and the world, and this fact alone would give it special distinction. But, in addition, State Street displays some architectural gems along the way as it stretches through the Loop from the Congress Parkway to Wacker Drive—the extent of this walk.

Although State Street itself is not predominantly a theatre and entertainment strip, it becomes at night Chicago's Great White Way, as a result of its unusually large and brilliant lights.

Nowhere in the nation is there such a concentration of retail department stores. Starting at the south end with Sears Roebuck and Company, we see one large store after another. The main entrances on State Street are augmented by the former carriage entrances on the side streets as well as on Wabash Avenue. The linear relationship of the buildings makes it convenient for the shopper to go on foot from store to store—or be driven to the nearest side street.

◧ Sears Roebuck Store—403 South State Street. Architect: William LeBaron Jenney (1891)

Starting the walk at Congress, you come first to the Sears Roebuck Store, located on the east side of State and extending a whole block—from Congress north to Van Buren. In its early days this was known as the Leiter Building II. Levi Z. Leiter, once a partner of Marshall Field, had already done business on his own at another location. The first Leiter Building, also designed by

29

Jenney, stood at the corner of Wells and Monroe streets and later became the Morris Building. Although the present Sears Roebuck store was originally constructed for still another company, Leiter took it over after a very short time. Just under the cornice of the State Street facade remains this inscription: L. Z. LEITER, MDCCCXCI.

This 8-story building, with 3 facades of white Maine granite, was designed by one of the pioneers in the Chicago school of architecture, William LeBaron Jenney. He had produced the first example of typical Chicago construction in his Home Insurance Building of 1885 (no longer standing), and he continued the development of the Chicago school in the second Leiter Building. Jenney allowed the steel skeleton, only recently introduced at that time, to determine the outward characteristics of the building—its division into enormous square sections, each filled with many large windows.

A plaque attached to the building on the State Street side quotes a citation from the "Chicago Dynamic Commission," dated October 27, 1957 (two months before the Architectural Landmarks Commission was formed):

> Bold, vigorous and original design expresses the light and open character of this building. One of the nation's most impressive early works of commercial architecture.

Goldblatts Store—State and Van Buren streets. Architects: Holabird and Roche (1912)

Cross over now to the northeast corner of State and Van Buren streets to the Goldblatt department store chain, central office, and store building. The store building was first known as Rothschild's and then as a subsidiary of Marshall Field and Company as the Davis Store. The building is 10 stories, with three basements and has wide, spacious windows that fit into the Chicago window category.

Maurice L. Rothschild Store Building—300 South State Street. Architects: Holabird and Roche (1906)

This building occupying this excellent corner location is no longer the Rothschild store. It was originally constructed to 8 stories and two basements on rock caissons. In 1928 four

Opposite, The Sears, Roebuck store, formerly the Leiter Building II.

stories were added together with an adjacent addition at 308 South State Street. A gray granite base and light-gray terra-cotta complete the exterior.

Lytton Building—14 East Jackson Boulevard.
Architects: Marshall and Fox (1913)

This building contains the Lytton Store at the northeast corner of Jackson and State. The building is 19 stories with three basements on caissons—a graceful, well-designed structure for its time.

Bond Building—234 South State Street.
Architects: Friedman, Alschuler and Sincere (1949)

This building replaced the old Hub Store Building (now Lytton's). The building is 6 stories over one basement on 62-foot wood piles. The State and Jackson facades are faced with granite. The framing is of structural steel to the second floor and reinforced concrete above. Morris Lapidus of New York City was the associate architect.

Home Federal Savings and Loan Building—
201 South State Street.
Architects: Skidmore, Owings, and Merrill (1966)

State Street has few new buildings or skyscrapers. It remains principally a street lined with multistory buildings of moderate height, occupied by stores of long-established companies selling wearing apparel, jewelry, and the endless assortment of the department stores.

The principal exception is the Home Federal Savings and Loan Building, on the southeast corner of Adams and State. In this handsome new structure the vertical lines are accented by the stainless steel mullions. The entire building is enveloped in dark glass panels.

To make way for this building, the Home Federal Savings and Loan Association demolished an earlier one of considerable architectural merit—the Republic Building designed by Holabird and Roche, dating back to 1905.

Montgomery Ward Store—Adams and State.
Architects: William LeBaron Jenney (1890-91);
Perkins and Will Partnership (1963)

Montgomery Ward and Company now occupy the building at the
northwest corner of Adams and State, previously known as the
Fair Store. This 11-story structure, extending along Adams from
State to Dearborn, is the largest of 3 large buildings designed
by Jenney and completed in 1891. Even larger than the Sears
Roebuck store, it covers a floor space of some 55,000 square feet.
Again Jenney used the principle of the steel skeleton as his
design, although here he used more ornamentation than in the
Sears building. In 1963 the whole store was remodeled from plans
by the Perkins and Will Partnership. The rehabilitation work is
well designed and appropriately sympathetic with the original
building; the result is a pleasant exterior and an efficient, warm
interior. (See also comments on Walk No. 4, Dearborn Street.)

Amalgamated Bank Building—
Southwest corner of State and Monroe streets.
Architects: A. Epstein and Sons, Inc. (1972)

This steel gage, 7-story bank building is a remodeled former
department store structure. This is the attractive financial
headquarters for the Amalgamated Clothing Workers Union as
well as a bank for the general public.

Palmer House—State and Monroe.
Architects: J. M. Van Osdel (1875);
Holabird and Roche (1925)

The building on the east side of State at Monroe is the Palmer
House, long one of the most distinguished hotels in Chicago, with
a popular shopping arcade running through the building from
State to Wabash. The Palmer House preceding this building was a
real Chicago pioneer, for it was erected only a few years after
the Great Fire of 1871—a still earlier Palmer House having been
opened just two weeks before the fire and then completely
destroyed. The 1875 building is said to have been the first fireproof
hotel and the first to provide its residents with electric lights,
telephones, and elevators. It was built at a time when the Chicago
school of architects was making great strides in improving the
construction and facilities of hotels and apartment buildings.

Mid-Continental Plaza Building—
Monroe-Wabash-Adams.
Architects: Alfred Shaw and Associates (1972)

If you decide to walk through the Palmer House Arcade, be sure to step out at Wabash and look across the street at this new and powerful office building. This 50-story office building has a sheath of tinted glass and stainless steel that soars for 572 feet. The spandrels, comprising the section between the gray-glass windows and the floors, match the glass and give a striking vertical appearance. There will be a pedestrian walkway under Wabash Avenue connecting with the Palmer House, done as part of the subway construction under Wabash Avenue.

◘ Carson Pirie Scott Store—1 South State Street.
Architects: Louis Sullivan (1899, 1904);
Daniel H. Burnham and Company (1906);
Holabird and Root (1960)

At State and Madison, the intersection that is famed as the "World's Busiest Corner," stands the most *notable* of Chicago's department stores architecturally, and the one always most *noticed* by the infrequent visitor to State Street—the Carson Pirie Scott Store.

What you see today is the result of several stages of construction, so that the total building is probably less unified than it would otherwise have been. Fortunately, however, the architects of 1906 and 1960 had such deep respect for Sullivan's original design that they followed the pattern closely in their additions. Here you have one of the best illustrations of the effectiveness of the horizontally elongated "Chicago window." The ornamentation decorating the windows of the first 2 stories is in pleasant contrast with the clean, unadorned precision of the window lines above them.

Originally occupied by the Schlesinger and Mayer Company, for whom it had been constructed in 1899 and enlarged in 1904, it was purchased later in 1904 by Carson Pirie Scott. The first and easternmost section, of only 3 bays and 9 stories, faced only Madison. The 1904 enlargement was made possible by the demolition of two older buildings next to this site. The addition, which rose 12 stories instead of 9, included 3 more bays on

Ornamental cast iron detail, Carson Pirie Scott building.

Opposite left, Entrance, Carson Pirie Scott. *Right,* the Marshall Field clock at the corner of State and Randolph.

34

Madison and extended around the corner, with 7 bays on State Street. Sullivan was the architect for both the original building and the extension. His love of incorporating ornamentation even in the designs of commercial buildings is expressed here in the intricate intermingling of leaf and flower designs that decorate the main entrance at the corner, as well as the windows of the lower stories. This rich but delicate pattern gives an unusually luxurious effect to an entrance already distinguished by its semicircular shape and its location at the corner of the building.

The third unit, extending the building still farther on State Street, was designed by Burnham in 1906; and the most recent extension of that long facade, by Holabird and Root in 1960, still following Sullivan's original plan. The result is therefore a true Sullivan masterpiece, no matter what other architects were involved before the building reached its present proportions.

In *Space, Time and Architecture*[1] Sigfried Giedion says of this building:

> The front is designed to fulfill its indispensable function, the admission of light. Its basic elements are the horizontally elongated "Chicago windows," admirably homogeneous and treated to coincide with the framework of the skeleton. The whole front is executed with a strength and precision that is matched by no other building of the period.

And Frederick Koeper remarks, "In this design Sullivan has afforded us those dual pleasures of architecture: an involvement with decoration as well as the satisfaction of discipline and order."[2]

State-Madison Building—
Northwest Corner—State and Madison.
Architects: Holabird and Roche (1905-1917)

This building occupies all the land from State Street to Dearborn Street, comprising nearly a half block. It was first occupied by the Boston Store—an operation of the Netcher Family and of the well-known Mollie Netcher who became the matriarch of the family in the 1920's. She was part of the colorful merchant families of Chicago.

The building is 17 stories with three basements and was converted into an office building in 1948.

Wieboldt's Department Store—One North State.
Architects: Holabird and Roche (1900-1901-1905)

Formerly Mandel Brothers Store Building, this structure was built in three main sections and today is divided into two main sections. The Wabash Avenue building is 12 stories and the State Street building 15 stories. Another colorful character of the

1920's was Colonel Leon Mandel who was the titular head of this old Chicago merchant family.

Stevens Store Building—
17 North State Street and 16 North Wabash Avenue. Architects: D. H. Burnham and Company (1912)

The building is 19 stories over two basements on hardpan caissons. The woman's specialty store, Chas. A. Stevens & Co. occupies the lower floors and basements. Small shops and offices occupy the balance of the building.

▣ 32 North State Street (previously the Reliance Building)
Architect: Charles Atwood, of Daniel H. Burnham and Company (1894-95)

In the next block, on the northwest corner of State and Washington, is an Architectural Landmark once known as the Reliance Building. The dark limestone base contrasts markedly with the glass and white terra-cotta of the towering, 15-story structure above.

Speaking of the Reliance Building, Giedion comments that ".... although its glazed white tiles have become encrusted with dirt, its airiness and pure proportions make it a symbol of the Chicago school." And pointing out that the Reliance was built nearly 3 decades before Mies van der Rohe envisioned his glass-and-iron skyscraper as a kind of fantasy, in 1921, he continues: "But it may be that this Chicago building is something more than an incentive for fantasy: an architectonic anticipation of the future."[3]

The citation by the Architectural Landmarks Commission reads:

> In recognition of the early and complete expression, through slender piers, small spandrels, and the skillfully restrained use of terra-cotta with large areas of glass, of the structural cage, of steel that alone supports such buildings.

Marshall Field Store—111 North State Street.
Architects: Daniel H. Burnham & Company (1892, 1904, and 1907)

The walk up State Street should include the interior of the

Marshall Field and Company Store. You can walk through from State to Wabash or from Washington to Randolph, for the building occupies the entire block. At the Washington and Randolph ends of the store are open courts, surrounded by grilled railings at each floor and covered by skylights. The skylight at the south end of the store (Washington Street) is a slightly arched dome of colored mosaic at the level of the fifth floor ceiling. The other (Randolph Street) is a plain glass skylight at the top of the building. The Randolph Street court is a perfect setting for the enormous Christmas tree that delighted Marshall Field customers for years.

The original Marshall Field store was built at the corner of State and Washington. This was the site of 3 previous buildings that had been used by the Field and Leiter partnership—the first of which had been destroyed by the Chicago fire a few years after it was erected. The rest of this famous store was constructed in two sections—in 1904 and 1907; and the Marshall Field men's store, at the southwest corner of Wabash and Washington was added in 1914.

United of America Building—1 East Wacker Drive. Architects: Shaw Metz and Associates (1962)

Continuing the State Street walk, you cross Randolph, the movie theatre section of the Loop, and come to the last building of this tour—the marble-faced tower of the United Insurance Company of America, which was once the tallest marble-faced commercial structure in the world. The strongly vertical lines of this 41-story structure contrast sharply with the circular towers of Marina City just across the river. (Marina City is featured as the last stop of Walk Number 4, Dearborn Street.) From a restaurant at the top of the United of America building, diners have a panoramic view of the city.

United of America building.

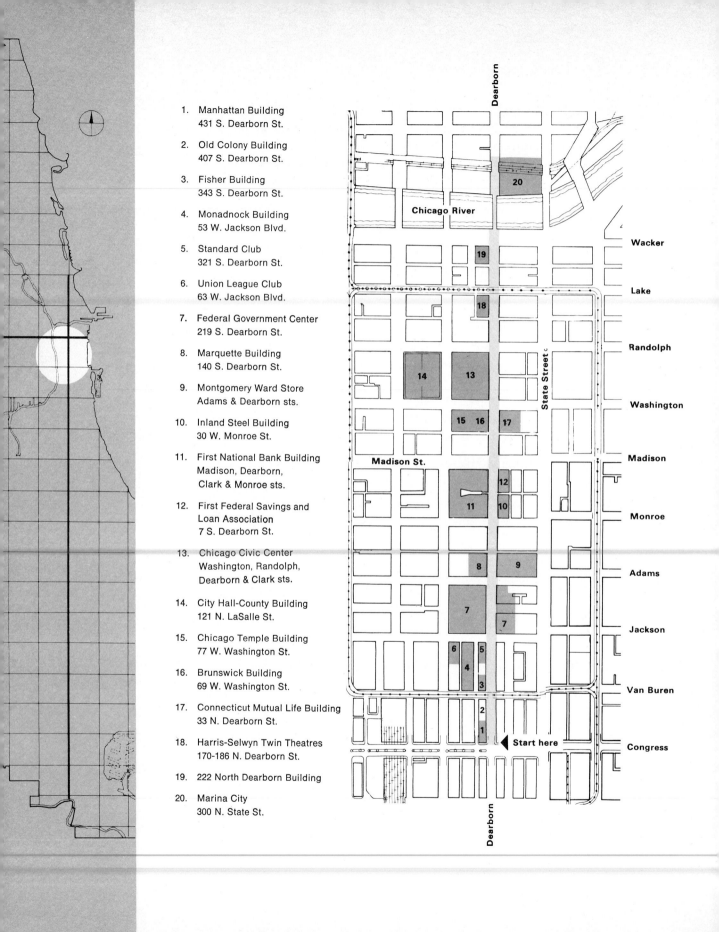

1. Manhattan Building
   431 S. Dearborn St.

2. Old Colony Building
   407 S. Dearborn St.

3. Fisher Building
   343 S. Dearborn St.

4. Monadnock Building
   53 W. Jackson Blvd.

5. Standard Club
   321 S. Dearborn St.

6. Union League Club
   63 W. Jackson Blvd.

7. Federal Government Center
   219 S. Dearborn St.

8. Marquette Building
   140 S. Dearborn St.

9. Montgomery Ward Store
   Adams & Dearborn sts.

10. Inland Steel Building
    30 W. Monroe St.

11. First National Bank Building
    Madison, Dearborn,
    Clark & Monroe sts.

12. First Federal Savings and
    Loan Association
    7 S. Dearborn St.

13. Chicago Civic Center
    Washington, Randolph,
    Dearborn & Clark sts.

14. City Hall-County Building
    121 N. LaSalle St.

15. Chicago Temple Building
    77 W. Washington St.

16. Brunswick Building
    69 W. Washington St.

17. Connecticut Mutual Life Building
    33 N. Dearborn St.

18. Harris-Selwyn Twin Theatres
    170-186 N. Dearborn St.

19. 222 North Dearborn Building

20. Marina City
    300 N. State St.

Dearborn

Chicago River

Wacker

Lake

Randolph

State Street

Washington

Madison St.

Madison

Monroe

Adams

Jackson

Van Buren

Start here

Congress

Dearborn

Walk · 4

DEARBORN STREET

WALKING TIME: About 1½ hours.   HOW TO GET THERE: Take any southbound CTA bus on State Street south of Randolph, and get off at Van Buren (400 S). Walk west across Plymouth Court, to Dearborn (36 W), which runs parallel to State Street.

Manhattan Building—431 South Dearborn. Architect: William LeBaron Jenney (1890)

This walk offers a virtual history of the modern skyscraper, which had its beginnings here in Chicago—one of the results of the tremendous architectural development that rebuilt the city after its almost total destruction by fire in 1871.

Located at the south end of the walk—in fact one block farther south than Van Buren—is the Manhattan Building, famed as the first 16-story building in the world. (Though only 12 stories when first built, 4 more were added a few years later.) Designed by the man who has often been called the father of the steel skyscraper, William LeBaron Jenney, the Manhattan is now the oldest tall office building to have used skeleton construction throughout. The second Rand McNally building, designed by Burnham and Root in the same year, also used skeleton construction throughout but was demolished in 1911.

Although the design of the Manhattan Building is not first-rate, it gives a not unpleasing effect.

Old Colony Building—407 South Dearborn Street. Architects: Holabird and Roche (1893)

This building is 210 feet high, with 17 stories and a basement. It fronts on three streets—Dearborn, Van Buren, and Plymouth Court. It is built with tower bays at the corners and presents a well-designed appearance. The first four stories are of light-blue Bedford stone and the upper part pressed brick and white terra-cotta. The building has received an architectural award as noted by a plaque at the entrance.

41

◘ Fisher Building—343 South Dearborn.
Architects: Daniel H. Burnham and Company (1896)

North of Van Buren, on the same side of Dearborn, stands the
Fisher Building, an Architectural Landmark. The steel frame
skeleton, which was also used here, is by no means disguised by
the rather elaborate Gothic ornamentation. The architect for
this building was the Burnham who is world-famous for his
Chicago city plan. His frequently quoted admonition, "Make no
little plans; they have no magic to stir men's minds," seems to
have been heeded by Chicago architects, and Dearborn
Street is one of the results.

◘ Monadnock Building—53 West Jackson.
Architects: North half, Burnham and Root (1891);
south half, Holabird and Roche (1893)

Across the street from the Fisher Building, between Van Buren
Street and Jackson Boulevard, is another Architectural Landmark,
the Monadnock, internationally famed as the world's largest
office building at the time of construction and still known as the
highest commercial building (16 stories rising 197 feet high)
with outside walls of wall-bearing construction. Some of the walls
at the base are said to be 15 feet thick to support the tremendous
weight. Even the north half of the building, however—the only
part that has outside walls of masonry only—did use steel
for the interior columns and floor supports; and the south half,
built two years later, used some vertical steel in the outer walls.

Originally this building had 4 separate entrances to 4 separate
sections, each named after a New England mountain, according to
the fancy of the 4 branches of the New England family that
owned it. The main entrance, still the most impressive, was at 54
West Van Buren, but when construction of the elevated railroad
tracks and station darkened Van Buren, Jackson became the
more desirable street. Following these changes, the Monadnock's
management transformed its "back door," at 53 West Jackson,
into the main entrance. In the late 1890's it was decided to call the
entire building merely the Monadnock, dropping the other 3
mountain names, though continuing to operate the four sections
separately as A, B, C, and D. Finally, in the 1920's, all
division into 4 parts was abandoned.

Left, top and center, The Fisher
building, details. *Bottom,* Arcade
of U.S. Courthouse. *Right,* Monadnock building.

43

The Monadnock's files tell of an early test of the building's ability to withstand Chicago's winds despite its unusual height and lack of wind braces. When a near-hurricane, with winds reaching the velocity of 88 miles an hour, struck Chicago a few years after the Monadnock was completed, experts in engineering rushed to the building with some trepidation and conducted a pendulum experiment from the top floor. A plumb bob that was swung down through the stairwell to the lobby floor, to measure the structure's vibrations at the height of the storm, marked a small pattern not more than ⅝″ by ⅜″—an experiment that reassured everyone who had feared what high winds might do to this building!

The citation of the Monadnock Building as an Architectural Landmark reads:

> In recognition of its original design and its historical interest as the highest wall-bearing structure in Chicago. Restrained use of brick, soaring massive walls, omission of ornamental forms, unite in a building simple yet majestic.

Standard Club—321 South Dearborn Street. Architect: Albert Kahn, Detroit, Michigan (1926)

This 10-story, elegant, private club building was constructed in 1926 and follows a general design pattern of Italian Renaissance. Bedford limestone and pressed brick are the materials used on both the Dearborn Street and the Plymouth Court facades.

Union League Club—65 West Jackson Boulevard. Architects: Mundie and Jensen (1926)

Just to the west of the Monadnock Building is this 22-story, club building of a granite base and pressed-brick facade. In the style of the late Italian Renaissance, this club still maintains a separate entrance for the ladies. This private club was once famous as the citadel of the Republican Party of Chicago.

The Federal Governmental Center—219 South Dearborn. Architects for the Federal Center, of which this is the first building completed: Ludwig Mies van der Rohe; Schmidt, Garden, and Erikson; C. F. Murphy Associates; A. Epstein and Sons. (1964)

Crossing Jackson Boulevard on Dearborn, going north, means

jumping from the late nineteenth century to the middle twentieth. On the east side of Dearborn stands a spectacularly modern 27-story structure of steel and glass, the Everett Dirkson Building. This is one of a complex of three buildings in Chicago's new Federal Center. The Center extends from Jackson Boulevard north to Adams Street, occupying both sides of Dearborn to Clark. An office building of over 40 stories is at the south end of the complex, and a post office is in a low-rise building. All 3 structures face a large open plaza—the entire design being a strong statement of the genius and influence of the great architect Mies van der Rohe.

A stabile by Alexander Calder, 53 feet in height, made of carbon steel and painted a special shade of red will be placed at the northeast corner of the Federal Center Plaza, making Dearborn Street a great area of plazas, architecture and sculpture—a standard for other cities to follow.

As you continue north on this walk, you will see two more great plazas surrounded by first-rate buildings. This current trend toward more open space around city skyscrapers is in marked contrast with the canyon effect so often developed in the past. Dearborn Street is indeed a street of overwhelming architecture, in space as well as in time.

Marquette Building—140 South Dearborn.
Architects: Holabird and Roche (1894)

At the northwest corner of Dearborn and Adams is the Marquette Building. The influence of Louis Sullivan can be noted in the ornamental design, which marks off the bottom 2 stories and the top 3, distinguishing these clearly from the rest. The wide windows and the obvious response of the pattern to the skeleton structure are characteristic of the Chicago school.

You will want to go inside this building to see the mosaics of scenes from Chicago history that decorate the mezzanine balcony.

Directly across the street from the Marquette is the recently remodeled Montgomery Ward Store (previously the Fair Store), seen from its State Street side on Walk Number 3.

Montgomery Ward Store—Adams and Dearborn.
Architects: William LeBaron Jenney (1890-91);
Perkins and Will Partnership (1963)

Directly across the street from the Marquette is the recently
remodeled Montgomery Ward Store (previously the Fair Store),
seen from its State Street side on Walk Number 3. (See also
comments for that walk.) In the remodeling, the original
wide-span windows so characteristic of the Chicago school of
architecture have been retained, but the old facade has been
completely covered with a new skin of attractive light-colored
stone. The interior is most inviting, with all the advantages
of a modern structure.

◩ **Inland Steel Building**—30 West Monroe.
Architects: Skidmore, Owings, and Merrill (1957)

One block to the north, at the northeast corner of Dearborn and
Monroe Streets, is the Inland Steel Building, appropriately
constructed of stainless steel and glass. In the lobby is a
stunningly unique piece of wire sculpture by Richard Lippold.

This 19-story building was one of the first to use only *external*
steel columns for support, also one of the first to build a separate
structure (to the east) for elevators and stairs, and to use steel
and glass as the chief building materials. The result is a
striking, first-rate design.

First National Bank Building and Plaza—
Between Monroe and Madison, Dearborn and Clark.
Architects: Perkins and Will Partnership and
C. F. Murphy Associates (Building 1969, Plaza 1973)

Directly across the street is the second of three great plazas in the
Loop—that of the First National Bank of Chicago. The first
object to capture the eye is the building itself. The sweeping lines
of this "A"-shaped, 60-story structure creates an exhilerating
sight. The steel frame has a light-gray, granite skin. The granite
there is carried out, not only on the sidewalks and plaza, but
in the two-story banking room and mezzanine as well.

The upper floors contain not only the offices of the bank but
distinguished works of art from all over the world. This excellent
collection was made under the direction of Katherine Kuh,
former Curator of Modern Art at the Art Institute of Chicago.

Left top, Inland Steel building.
Bottom, Chicago Civic Center pla-
za and Picasso sculpture. *Right,*
First National Bank Building.

47

The main banking room and mezzanine contain hundreds of counters and desks for servicing the many customers who use its facilities. The splendid height and scale of the room remove any feeling of overcrowding or chaos. The lighting attached to the ceiling has been combined with the air conditioning and consequently is on continuously. The same system is used throughout the entire building.

The exciting two-level plaza covering a half-city block has restaurants, landscaping and soon to be realized great art form. A major work of Marc Chagall is being created for the people of Chicago and will take form soon on an opened landscaped terrace of this First National Plaza in the center of the Loop—only a stone's throw from Picasso's colossus in the Civic Center Plaza.

The massive architectural mosaic measuring 70 feet long, 14 feet high and 10 feet wide, will have more than 3,000 square feet of bright ceramic murals, especially designed for Chicago by the world-renowned artist, who will also personally supervise each step of its realization.

The "Chicago Chagall" will occupy an open terrace in the center of the plaza, and will overlook an illuminated fountain of changing water columns in a park-like setting of trees, plants and flowers.

The design is a gift by Chagall to the people of Chicago. It has been described as part sculpture, part mural and part architecture—in every way unique. The donors for the cost of construction were Mr. and Mrs. William Ward Prince of Chicago.

A large number of vehicles are accommodated at underground levels which are accessible by tunnels under Clark Street from spiral ramps and a port-of-entry located across the street.

From the existing subway under Dearborn Street, a station provides direct access to lower levels of the building. In addition, in the future, underground pedestrian walkways will connect the building to the Civic Center and other structures to the north, and also to the Federal Center to the south. Finally, a new distributor subway has been proposed under Monroe Street at the south edge of the site. This subway will provide direct access to commuter railroad stations and garages, to Chicago Circle Campus, to the near north side, and to McCormick Place.

The architects have stated that the form of the bank building evolved quite naturally from the space-need program. From a broad banking base, where the lower floors accommodate all the bank's equipment and staff, the tower tapers upward in a sweeping curve to narrower tenant floors. Thus, form follows function. The bank's address is No. 1—1st National Plaza. The bank has constructed a second building across the street, that is described in the walk on Clark Street. Its address is No. 2—1st National Plaza. For tours of the bank building and plaza, call 732-6202 or inquire at the Information Desk in the main banking floor.

Before crossing north at Madison, look back across Dearborn to the former Tribune Building.

First Federal Savings & Loan Association—7 South Dearborn. Architects: Holabird and Roche (1902) Architects for South Wing: Holabird and Root (1958)

Here is another first, but this time it is a savings and loan association, the largest in terms of funds on deposit in Chicago. The structure originally housed *The Chicago Tribune* before the move to its present location on North Michigan Avenue.

The structure is 17 stories high and reputed to be the first in Chicago with two basements (another first).

Chicago Civic Center—between Washington and Randolph, Dearborn and Clark. Architects: C. F. Murphy Associates; Loebl, Schlossman, and Bennett; Skidmore, Owings and Merrill (1964)

One block north, on the west side of Dearborn, is the great plaza of the Chicago Civic Center, a focal point of city and county government activity. This immense open space offers the visitor an exciting visual treat and a chance to sit and rest in the midst of otherwise crowded city streets. With fountain, flags, and trees, the plaza is dominated overwhelmingly by the huge Picasso sculpture in Cor-Ten steel. The design of "Chicago's Picasso" was a gift to the city from the sculptor himself, and the original model is in Chicago's Art Institute. Like most of Picasso's creations for many years, this was the subject of much controversy. There was disagreement about whether it represents the great head of a woman, the soaring wings of an enormous bird, a strange composite animal, or—as one facetious newspaper columnist would have it—the head of Picasso's pet basset hound! Controversy aside, however, this is a powerful work of art. It has been erected in an especially appropriate setting, which allows viewers to walk around it freely and consider it from all angles and various distances—from each of which it presents a different effect.

The *Civic Center Building*, 31 stories of offices and courtrooms, covers the north half of the plaza. This too was highly controversial at first, especially before the steel of its walls had oxidized to its present russet brown. Cor-Ten steel was chosen as the material for the building, as well as for the Picasso, because it requires no upkeep and becomes more beautiful as it ages. (A special virtue of Cor-Ten steel is its resistance to *atmospheric* corrosion, so that it is not worn away by weathering, even though its color is changed.)

The power and the scale of this contemporary structure are overwhelming; the older, smaller buildings around the plaza come into focus only later, though many were most impressive when erected. They are a phenomenon of contrasts, one with another. The horizontal bays are 89 feet wide which makes this distinguished building one of great strength and vigor.

City Hall-County Building—121 North LaSalle.
Architects: Holabird and Roche (1907, 1911)

One of these older buildings, dating back more than half a century, is the City Hall-County Building—really 2 duplicate buildings, the county building on the east having been completed several years before its city twin. They are built on sturdy classic revivalist lines with heavy Corinthian columns across the facade. Together they cover an entire block to the west of the Civic Center. Tours may be arranged in advance by calling the Mayor's Office of Inquiry and Information (744-3370).

Chicago Temple Building—77 West Washington.
Architects: Holabird and Roche (1923)

To the south, across Washington, is the Chicago Temple

Left top, Brunswick building. *Bottom*, City Hall-County building. *Right*, Connecticut Mutual Life building.

Marina Towers.

Building, standing 550 feet high, in Gothic revival style, including an elaborate spire. This provides space for offices and a downtown Methodist church. Except for a short time after the Great Fire of 1871, this site has been occupied continuously by a downtown church for more than 100 years.

Brunswick Building—69 West Washington. Architects: Skidmore, Owings, and Merrill (1964) Partner in Charge: Myron Goldsmith

Next to the Chicago Temple is the massive Brunswick Building. Though only recently constructed, the heavy concrete wall surfaces of the Brunswick are reminiscent of the Monadnock Building. From the lower concourse of this building you can reach other downtown buildings by an underground walkway. (See Walk No. 31.)

Connecticut Mutual Life Building—33 North Dearborn. Architects: Skidmore, Owings, and Merrill (1966)

Just across Dearborn Street from the Brunswick is an utterly different type of building, the Connecticut Mutual, a glass structure standing light and lean on its steel frame. Though this was designed by the same firm of architects as the Brunswick, the two buildings are in striking contrast with each other. They are a tribute to the versatility of the architects' inventiveness and illustrate the wide variety of modern building materials and forms.

Harris-Selwyn Twin Theatres—170-186 North Dearborn. Architects: Crane & Franzheim (1923)

Now occupied by the Michael Todd and the Cinestage that show motion pictures, these twin theatres represent the best of their time. The exterior design is English Renaissance of the Edwardian period when many similar small theatres were built in London. The exterior skin is a white terra-cotta. The interiors of both houses are intimate and warm. The wood paneling and spacious proscenium arches of both auditoriums created just the right climate for good, live performances and appreciative audiences.

222 North Dearborn Building.
Architects: C. F. Murphy Associates (1969)

As you leave the twin theatres, continue north across
Lake street. On the west side of Dearborn is the
building erected for the Blue Cross - Blue Shield groups.
This all-beige-colored concrete structure has a rugged, heavy
quality; it gives an effect of tremendous mass, especially in
the upper section extending by cantilever construction
beyond the lower part.

Marina City—300 North State Street.
Architects: Bertrand Goldberg Associates (1964)

Although the official address of Marina City is State Street,
you have an excellent view of these twin towers from Dearborn
and Wacker Drive. This exciting, world-famous complex has
included its many functions in a highly concentrated space—
apartments, garages, restaurants, offices, bank, television
theatre, ice-skating rink, and marina. The parking space is
a continuously rising circular slab throughout the first 18
stories of each tower, the apartments taking up the rest of
the 62 stories of each. The cantilevered balconies of the
apartments give these cylindrical towers their scalloped
forms. Apartments are pie-shaped.

Marina City marks a departure from the glass-and-steel skeletons
that have been so popular in recent years. This tallest concrete
building in Chicago, 62 stories rising more than 580 feet in the
air, uses virtually no structural steel. These are towers of slab
construction, circular discs resting on columns. Marina City also
demonstrates excellent application of core-and-cantilever
construction, which was first used by Frank Lloyd Wright.

A model apartment may always be seen at Marina City, and a
trip to the open-air observatory at the top is available Saturdays
and Sundays when the weather permits. (Since the observatory
is not roofed or glassed in, no visits are permitted after the first
snowfall of the year.)

To enter Marina City, you cross the Dearborn Street drawbridge,
with plaques worth reading. They summarize the history of the
bridge and quote the citation presented to it as the "Most
beautiful steel bridge movable span," by the American Institute
of Steel Construction in 1963-64.

Walk-5

Lower LaSalle Street
and the Board of
Trade building.

1. LaSalle Plaza
   180 N. LaSalle St.

2. State of Illinois Building
   160 N. LaSalle St.

3. Bismarck Hotel Office and
   Theatre Complex
   LaSalle & Randolph sts.

4. 30 North LaSalle Building

5. American National Bank Building
   33 N. LaSalle St.

6. One North LaSalle Street Building

7. Northern Trust Company
   50 S. LaSalle St.

8. Harris Trust and Savings
   111 W. Monroe St.

9. Midwest Stock Exchange and
   Central National Bank
   120 S. LaSalle St.

10. LaSalle Bank Building
    135 S. LaSalle St.

11. Exchange National Bank Building
    134 S. LaSalle St.

12. The Rookery
    209 S. LaSalle St.

13. Continental Illinois National Bank
    and Trust Building
    231 S. LaSalle St.

14. 208 South LaSalle Street Building

15. Federal Reserve Bank
    230 S. LaSalle St.

16. Board of Trade Building
    141 W. Jackson Blvd.

Walk · 5

LA SALLE STREET

WALKING TIME: 1 to 1½ hours.   HOW TO GET THERE: Walk west on Randolph to
La Salle Street (140 W), 3 blocks west of State Street.

Be sure to take this walk on a weekday during business hours,
when the rhythm of Chicago at work is best felt.
LaSalle Street in the Loop is the Wall Street of the Midwest.
From Randolph, the street looks like a canyon, with skyscraper
office buildings and banks along each side and the 45-story
Board of Trade Building like a towering mountain at the south.
Here, in the 4-block area between Madison and Jackson, are
clustered Chicago's major banks; here are found both old and
new stock exchange buildings; and here, at the end of the 4
blocks, stands the overpowering Board of Trade Building with
the statue of Ceres at its top. Activities inside some of these
buildings send political and economic waves across the country,
affecting in fact the world economy.

This walk starts at the southwest corner of LaSalle and Lake
streets.

LaSalle Plaza—180 North LaSalle Street.
Architects: Harry Weese and Associates (1972)

This plainly rugged and distinguished 38-story reinforced
concrete building has a two-story lobby. The trees and brick
plaza give LaSalle Street a new human scale in this cavernous
thoroughfare. This handsome structure is truly in the tradition
of the Chicago school.

State of Illinois Building—160 North LaSalle Street.
Architects: Burnham Brothers (1924)

This building is 20 stories with one basement and was
originally known as the Burnham Building until its purchase by
the State of Illinois in 1946. The building contains many branch
offices of the state government.

Bismarck Hotel Office and Theatre Complex—
Southwest Corner—LaSalle and Randolph streets.
Architects: Rapp and Rapp (1926)

This well-planned complex contains an office building, theatre and hotel. The hotel lobby and Walnut Room are well designed and worth a visit.

On the east side of LaSalle, between Randolph and Washington, looms the bulky, massive *City Hall-County Building* with its heavy pillars, designed under the old belief that government buildings should be monumental in size and style. (See Walk No. 4.) The interior has been renovated and modernized. The mosaic tile in the lobby has been well preserved. Tours are available through the Mayor's Office of Inquiry and Information, Room 100. (Telephone: 744-3370)

30 North LaSalle Building
(The old Stock Exchange Building).
Architects: Adler and Sullivan (1894)

I regret to report that this stunning, historical, and distinguished building was destroyed in 1972. Although the Chicago Historical and Architectural Landmarks Commission recommended the building in 1971 as an architectural landmark, the City Council, which under the law must approve such actions, did not do so. It will be replaced by a high-rise office building.

Some of the ornaments will be used in the new wing of the Chicago Art Institute, where the entrance arch will be rebuilt, along with the old trading room.

While the building was being demolished, a well-known architectural photographer Richard Nickel was tragically buried in rubble and killed while trying to salvage some of Sullivan's ornamentation.

American National Bank Building—
33 North LaSalle Street.
Architects: Graham, Anderson, Probst and White (1929)

This building was originally known as the Foreman National Bank Building. It is 38 stories with two basements on rock and hardpan caissons. A granite base and Bedford limestone comprise

Entrance to 30 North LaSalle (old Chicago Stock Exchange).

the exterior materials. The lower floors, occupied by the bank, were completely remodeled in 1971 in the Williamsburg style.

One North LaSalle Street Building.
Architects: Vitzthum and Burns (1930)

This Bedford limestone building is 49 stories on rock caissons. The majority of tenants are law firms as are those in the American National Bank Building, both buildings representing the powerful growth of the banking business just prior to the Great Depression.

Northern Trust Company—50 South LaSalle.
Architects: Frost and Granger (1906, 1930)
Architects for newest section:
C. F. Murphy Associates (1967)

At the northwest corner of Monroe and LaSalle is the Northern Trust Company and its new, adjoining structure to the west, which extends almost to Wells Street. At Wells there is a refreshing change from LaSalle's city canyon—an open space landscaped with fountains, providing a drive-in section for hurried or late customers.

Harris Trust and Savings Bank—111 West Monroe Street. Architects: Shepley, Rutan and Coolidge (1915)
Second Building: Skidmore, Owings and Merrill (1957)
Third Building: Skidmore, Owings and Merrill (1974)

The original 20-story building is now framed by two stunning additions. The first is to the east and is at the southwest corner of Monroe and Clark streets and the second at the southeast corner of Monroe and LaSalle streets. All three buildings are connected at the banking floor levels and constitute a complex of buildings one block in length.

An unusual feature of the building farthest east is its recessed floor halfway up, which holds mechanical equipment usually found on the roof or in the basement. The stainless-steel mullion and the tall, narrow window pattern are especially effective.

Building Number 3 extending from the original building on the east to LaSalle Street is 38 stories. The address is 105 South LaSalle and opened in 1973.

Midwest Stock Exchange and Central National Bank—
120 South LaSalle Building. Architects: Graham, Anderson, Probst and White (1926-29)

In the second block beyond Madison is the building now used by the Midwest Stock Exchange, the financial center of the Midwest—second only to New York's in size and economic significance. More than 500 members of the Exchange represent security firms doing business in all parts of the country. The Central National Bank, however, occupies most of the lower floors of this building.

The building, which also provides space for various other financial concerns, faced many difficulties in its early years, for it was completed just at the beginning of the depression of the '30's.

Visitors' gallery open daily 9:00 A.M. to 2:30 P.M. Closed Saturdays and Sundays.

LaSalle Bank Building—135 South LaSalle Street. Architects: Graham, Anderson, Probst and White (1934)

At the end of the east side of the block is the LaSalle Bank Building, formerly known as the Field Office Building. The structure was carried out in two sections—one on Clark Street and the second facing LaSalle Street. The building is 23 stories with a 19-story tower and three basements on rock caissons.

This is the site of the famous Home Insurance Building (demolished in 1931) which was the world's first skeleton steel-and-iron building, designed in 1884 by the father of such construction William Le Baron Jenney.

Exchange National Bank Building—134 South LaSalle Street. Architects: Shepley, Rutan and Coolidge (1908)

This Florentine type of Italian Renaissance structure was formerly known as the Corn Exchange Bank Building, located at the northwest corner of Adams and LaSalle streets. It has 17 stories and is constructed on rock caissons. The Exchange National Bank maintains an excellent photography exhibit. Local and internationally famous photographers' works are kept on display.

LaSalle Bank building.

61

◘ The Rookery—209 South LaSalle Street.
Architects: Burnham and Root (1886);
Frank Lloyd Wright (1905)

Just across Adams Street is an Architectural Landmark—an extraordinary building called The Rookery. This quaint name is a heritage from the temporary city hall located here from 1872 to 1884, which had been nicknamed The Rookery because it seemed to be the favorite gathering place of downtown pigeons! The city hall had been built around an iron water tank, the only remnant of the previous occupant of this site—a city reservoir building serving the south side of Chicago, which was destroyed in the Fire of 1871. While the temporary city hall was here, Chicago's first public library stored its books in the old water tank—surely the only library in the world to have been housed in such a container.

The present Rookery, one of the oldest precursors of the modern skyscraper, is distinguished in its own right. Its sturdy yet ornamental exterior is partly of skeleton structure, partly wall-bearing, and the building as a whole has the appearance of enormous vitality. The powerful columns, alternating with piers, arches, and stonework, which characterize the exterior, make a dramatic contrast with the lobby inside, which is unique in its elaborate but delicate ornamentation. The glass-and-iron tracery of the domed skylight above the second floor of the lobby court (though now painted over) harmonizes with the extensive grille work used below around the first- and second-floor balconies and along the sides of the two-part suspended stairway at the west side. The main stairway, unconnected with this one, starts at the second floor and runs to the top of the building. A cylindrical staircase, it projects beyond the west wall of the building, requiring an additional, semicircular tower to enclose it. With elevators for regular upward travel, this main stairway is still considered useful as a possible fire escape.

The gold-and-ivory decorations of the court are the work of Frank Lloyd Wright, who remodeled this part of the building in 1905.

Opposite, overall view and details of the Rookery.

62

The citation from the Landmarks Commission reads:

> In recognition of its pioneering plan in providing shops and offices around a graceful and semi-private square and further development of the skeleton structural frame using cast iron columns, wrought iron spandrel beams, and steel beams to support party walls and interior floors.

Continental Illinois National Bank and Trust Building—231 South LaSalle Street. Architects: Graham, Anderson, Probst, and White (1923)

In the giant, block-square building of the Continental Illinois National Bank and Trust Company, you have revivalist architecture again. The "classic" design is said to have been taken from some early Roman baths. Inside, you take an escalator to the enormous open banking floor, where tall Ionic columns stress again the pseudo-classic style.

The Continental Illinois claims to be Chicago's oldest bank, the result of many mergers and changes of name dating back to 1857. It became officially the Continental Illinois National Bank and Trust Company, with a national charter, in 1932.

Across the street from the Continental Illinois, at 230 South LaSalle, is the Federal Reserve Bank of Chicago, ornamented with Corinthian columns (architects, Frost and Granger, 1922). A second tower to the west was designed by C. F. Murphy and Associates, 1960.

Cross over to the west side of the street and back north a few feet.

208 South LaSalle Street Building. Architects: D. H. Burnham and Company (1914)

This building, formerly known as the Continental Bank Building, is 20 stories with two basements on rock caissons. A huge monolith extends west to Wells Street, from Adams to Quincy. It has a Bedford limestone facing throughout and adds to the canyon-like quality of LaSalle Street.

Now directly southward to another bank building at 230 South LaSalle Street.

Federal Reserve Bank—230 South LaSalle Street.
Architects: Graham, Anderson, Probst and White (1922)
Architects for addition: C. F. Murphy and
Associates (1960)

This bankers' bank for the entire Midwest has three basements
on rock caissons and faces on LaSalle, Jackson, and Quincy. The
original structure's entrance on LaSalle Street has Roman
Corinthian columns and pediment. All facades are of a light
Bedford limestone. The addition faces on Jackson and Quincy
and is 25 stories.

Board of Trade Building—141 West Jackson Boulevard.
Architects: Holabird and Root (1929)

The focal point of this entire walk has been the Board of Trade
Building, with its commanding location at the foot of LaSalle
Street, on Jackson Boulevard. From Randolph this towering
structure seems to block LaSalle Street at its southern end, but
at Jackson you discover that LaSalle merely jogs a bit to the left
and continues southward beyond the Board of Trade. At the
top of the 45 stories in this building stands—appropriately—
a statue of Ceres, Greek goddess of grain, a 32-foot figure
topping the 526-foot skyscraper.

Step into the lobby and enjoy the interior "art deco" design by
Gilbert Hall, former chief designer of Holabird & Root. The
school of design known as "art deco" flourished briefly from the
mid-1920's to the outbreak of World War II. The style was
forceful, direct, emphasizing rectilinear rather than voluptuously
curving lines. It was an upbeat, inspiring type of art, featuring
sunrays, rainbows, large leafy plants and well-muscled young
people at work or at some athletic pursuit.

The lobby, upper lobby, trading room, elevator doors and lighting
fixtures are exceptionally high caliber "art deco." The
contrasting of the black and light color marbles is fascinating
and pleasant to view. If you are fortunate to be here before 1:00
on a weekday, you will be admitted to the visitors' gallery of
the Trading Room.

The enormous room of the grain exchange, which is the largest in the world, is on the second floor. Since this "Pit" rises for several floors, it can be well observed from the visitors' gallery on the fifth floor. (Open daily 9:30 A.M. to 1:00 P.M. Closed Saturdays, Sundays, and holidays.) To the uninitiated, the sights and sounds of trading in this Pit seem like bedlam. Fortunately, however, visitors are given a leaflet explaining the rules of the game, which indeed is a game full of economic consequences everywhere. Here are several "pits," each a circle of traders interested in buying or selling a particular commodity—wheat, soybeans, soybean oil and meal, oats, rye, and several other commodities, such as cotton, lard, and beef. Shouts and hand signals in the bidding are clear to those involved, and the constantly changing prices are recorded on a big board immediately for all to see. Messengers run back and forth between the bidders with messages telephoned or wired from firms or individual customers from all parts of the world. The men trading here represent more than 1400 members of the Board of Trade. Traders, messengers, and staff of the exchange are distinguished by the color of the jackets they wear. The Board of Trade is indeed a tremendous marketplace, although the actual commodities that change hands here are miles away.

The Board of Trade Observatory, at the top of the building, provides one of the highest viewpoints in Chicago. (Open daily Monday through Friday 9:30 A.M. to 1:15 P.M. Films at 9:45, 10:30, 11:30 and 12:30. Free admission.)

Walk-6

St. Peter's Church.

1. Chicago Temple Building
   77 W. Washington St.

2. Chicago Title and Trust Company
   Building
   111 W. Washington St.

3. St. Peter's Church and Friary
   110 W. Madison St.

4. The Chicago Loop Synagogue
   16 S. Clark St.

5. Two First National Plaza
   20 S. Clark St.

6. Harris Trust and Savings Bank
   111 W. Monroe St.

7. Bell Savings and Loan Association
   Building
   79 W. Monroe St.

8. Edison Building
   72 W. Adams St.

9. Bankers Building
   105 W. Adams St.

10. Continental Illinois
    National Bank
    and Trust Company
    105 W. Adams St.

11. Trans Union Building
    Clark St. & Jackson Blvd.

Walk · 6

CLARK STREET

WALKING TIME: 1 to 1½ hours.   HOW TO GET THERE: Walk west on Washington Street to Clark Street (77 west) 2 blocks west of State Street.

This walk starts at the southeast corner of Washington and Clark streets just opposite the Civic Center Plaza.

Chicago Temple Building—77 West Washington. Architects: Holabird and Roche (1923)

We encountered this unique Methodist Church and office building on Walk Number 4 but this time we will also visit two additional religious structures—a Roman Catholic Church and an Orthodox Jewish Synagogue. These three major churches representing the Protestant, Catholic, and Jewish faiths are located within a one-block radius, making it convenient for Loop workers to worship during daytime hours.

The Temple Building has 21 stories plus an 8-story spire and basement on rock caissons. The gray Indiana limestone, French Gothic style structure offers an interesting pattern of intricate design as against the bold, plain design of the Brunswick Building to the east.

Chicago Title and Trust Company Building—111 West Washington Street. Architects: D. H. Burnham and Company (1913); Holabird and Root (1947)

Now cross to the west side of Clark Street to a building that houses nearly all of abstract and real estate property insurance for metropolitan Chicago and many other regions of the U.S.A.

Known as the Conway Building when it was first constructed, the structure was purchased and remodeled in 1947 under the

The spire of the Chicago Temple building.

69

direction of Holabird and Root. At that time, the interior court was filled to a height of 6 stories. An indoor pedestrian walkway system connects with the adjacent American National Bank Building and One North LaSalle Street Building.

This white terra-cotta building is 21 stories and is completely modernized and commands a strategic location near City Hall-County Building and the Civic Center. Probably more business deals are made in its lobby than in all the offices above.

St. Peter's Church and Friary—
110 West Madison Street.
Architects: K. M. Vitzthum and J. J. Burns (1953)

Now walk south on Clark to Madison and turn west to St. Peter's.

St. Peter's Church in Chicago is a 5-story, marble-covered Roman basilica, consisting of the main church, two chapels on the second floor, and living quarters on the other three floors for the Franciscan priests in charge. The facade is overwhelmingly dominated—as the designers intended it to be—by a gigantic crucifix "Christ of the Loop," 18 feet high, weighing 26 tons. This extraordinarily expressive figure of Christ, the work of the Latvian sculptor Arvid Strauss, hangs above the entrance in front of the only window of the building—a Gothic arch of stained glass. The church, built on the site of the old LaSalle Theatre, was planned as a religious center for Catholic visitors to the city and the many thousands of Catholics who work in the Loop.

The Chicago Loop Synagogue—16 South Clark Street.
Architects: Loebl, Schlossman and Bennett (1957)

As you approach the Loop Synagogue, just a few doors south of Madison, on Clark Street, you will be struck by the unique metal sculpture above the entrance—"The Hands of Peace," by the Israeli sculptor Henri Azaz. Symbolically outstretched hands are surrounded by irregularly spaced letters, in both English and Hebrew, spelling out a Biblical benediction.

From the visitors' balcony inside you can see the interesting, well-conceived plan of this structure, which has made optimum use of the narrow city lot on which it is constructed. The seating arrangement, running at right angles with what is expected,

The metal sculpture "The Hands of Peace," above the entrance to the Chicago Loop Synagogue.

70

achieves a special effect of spaciousness. And the entire wall opposite the street entrance is composed of a gloriously colored stained-glass design on the theme "Let there be light!"—the work of Abraham Rattner of New York.

Two First National Plaza—20 South Clark Street. Architects: C. F. Murphy Associates and The Perkins and Will Partnership (1971)

This is the second structure of the First National Bank complex that faces on the First National Bank Plaza. There are 30 stories above grade, as well as basement levels largely occupied by service ramps and tunnels extending under the plaza level and bank building. (See Walk No. 4)

The exterior columns and spandrels are fireproofed with poured-in-place concrete and faced with pointed steel panels. Enclosures at street level are clear glass in steel frames with bronze doors. Upper floors have solar bronze double glazing in steel frames with plastic thermal break for air circulation.

The granite paving on the sidewalks and interior floor areas at street level match the One First National Plaza. Note the pedestrian walkway through the center of the building that connects with LaSalle Street and The Barrister's Building. This walkway has been in this location for many years and continues the tradition of connecting the "First with the Barristers."

Left, Two First National Plaza. *Right*, Pedestrian passageway to The Barrister's building.

Harris Trust and Savings Bank—

111 West Monroe Street. Architects for Eastern portion of Buildings: Skidmore, Owings and Merrill (1957)
Second Building: Shepley, Rutan and Coolidge (1915)
Third Building: Skidmore, Owings and Merrill (1974)

At the southwest corner of Clark and Monroe is the first of a complex of three bank buildings integrated as one (See Walk No. 5). The third structure is just west of the original Harris Bank Building and will be 38 stories when completed in 1974. This will be a combination bank and office building; the bank will occupy the entire ground floor level from Clark to LaSalle Street. There will be a public plaza of 5,000 square feet at the LaSalle-Monroe corner.

Bell Savings and Loan Association Building—

79 West Monroe. Architect: Jarvis Hunt (1900)
Architects for south addition:
Holabird and Roche (1924)

This 13-story and one-basement structure was formerly known as the Chicago Title and Trust Building and is now the home of the Bell Savings and Loan Association. Up-to-the-minute weather reports are available in the lobby. Also, monthly construction reports covering the Chicago metropolitan area are produced here.

Edison Building—72 West Adams Street.
Architects: D. H. Burnham and Company (1907)

Located at the northeast corner of Clark and Adams, this 18-story structure has two basements and contains the principal offices and control center of this important utility company. Although the executive offices are located nearby in the First National Bank Building, nearly all of the consumer services are located here. There is also a pedestrian walkway connecting the adjacent Marquette Building that contains shops, restaurants, and Edison service facilities.

Bankers Building—105 West Adams Street.
Architects: Burnham Brothers (1927)

Located at the southwest corner of Clark and Adams, this structure was designed by the Burnham Brothers, who followed

73

in their illustrious father's footsteps—Daniel H. Burnham. The building is 41 stories with one basement on rock caissons.

At this point, it should be worth looking across the street to the third great open plaza on this walk—the Federal Plaza (See Walk No. 4).

Note the low post office structure at the corner in contrast with the two tall structures. The excellent site plan has provided a third great Loop plaza.

Continental Illinois National Bank and Trust Company—105 West Adams Street.
Architects: Graham, Anderson, Probst and White (1924)

This is the eastern facade of this huge bank building, realistically promoted as "the big bank with the little bank inside," that is included on Walk Number 5. It was formerly known as the Illinois Merchants Bank Building. After several bank mergers the name was finally changed to the present. The building is 19 stories with two basements on rock caissons.

Trans Union Building—Southwest corner Clark and Jackson. Architects: A. Epstein and Sons, Inc. (1961)

This 24-story building with marble-and-glass facade is the last stop on this walk. There is a two-story lobby of marble, wood, and bronze. The generous set back and plaza show off the building to good advantage.

Trans Union Building.

74

Walk-7

Chicago Water
Tower.

1. Wrigley Building
   400 N. Michigan Ave.

2. Equitable Building
   401 N. Michigan Ave.

3. Sun-Times-Daily News
   Building
   401 N. Wabash Ave.

4. Tribune Tower
   435 N. Michigan Ave.

5. Uptown Savings and Loan
   Association Building
   430 N. Michigan Ave.

6. 500 North Michigan Avenue
   Building

7. Sheraton-Chicago Hotel
   505 N. Michigan Ave.

8. Michigan Terrace Apartments
   525 N. Michigan Ave.

9. Time-Life Building
   Fairbanks Ct. between
   Ohio St. & Grand Ave.

10. McClurg Court Center
    McClurg Ct. between
    Ohio & Ontario sts.

11. Woman's Athletic Club
    626 N. Michigan Ave.

12. 625 North Michigan Avenue
    Building

13. Saks Fifth Avenue Building
    669 N. Michigan Ave.

14. Allerton Hotel
    701 N. Michigan Ave.

15. 737 North Michigan Avenue
    Building

16. Water Tower
    800 N. Michigan Ave.

17. American Dental Association
    Building
    211 E. Chicago Ave.

18. I. Magnin Store Building
    830 N. Michigan Ave.

19. Water Tower Plaza
    Michigan Ave.-Chestnut-
    Seneca-Pearson sts.

20. John Hancock Center
    875 N. Michigan Ave.

21. Continental Plaza Hotel
    Michigan Ave. &
    Delaware St.

22. Fourth Presbyterian Church
    126 E. Chestnut St.

23. Playboy Building
    919 N. Michigan Ave.

24. 900 North Michigan Avenue
    Building

25. Walton Colonnade Apartment
    Building
    100 E. Walton St.

26. Drake Hotel
    Lake Shore Dr. at
    Michigan Ave.

Walk · 7

MICHIGAN AVENUE : NORTH ("THE MAGNIFICENT MILE")

WALKING TIME: About 1½ hours.   HOW TO GET THERE: Take any of the following northbound CTA buses—No. 151 (Sheridan), No. 152 (Addison), or No. 153 (Wilson-Michigan) on State Street; or a No. 76 (Diversey) on Wabash. Get off at the Michigan Avenue bridge, Michigan and Wacker (300 N).

Where Chicago's "Magnificent Mile" begins, just north of the Chicago River, are buildings of contrasting architecture. The development of this part of Michigan Avenue, featuring both revivalist and contemporary styles, might be said to date from the 1920's, when both the street and underground levels of the Michigan Avenue bridge were completed.

Wrigley Building—400 North Michigan. Architects: Graham, Anderson, Probst, and White (1921; annex 1924)

The gleaming white Wrigley Building (named for the family of chewing-gum fame) with its finger-like clock tower rises from the northern edge of the Chicago River. The white terra-cotta with which the building is covered and the powerful floodlights focused on it every night make this always a conspicuous part of the Chicago skyline. Featuring baroque terra-corra ornamentation, the building is an architectural link to Chicago's earlier days. Between the main building and its annex is an attractive small plaza.

Equitable Building—401 North Michigan. Architects: Skidmore, Owings, and Merrill; Alfred Shaw & Associates (1965)

The Equitable Building, representing the architecture of the present, stands like another sentinel on the east side of the Avenue. Set far back from the street, it is approached through a spacious plaza called Pioneer Court, which includes an attractive fountain with the names of early Chicago leaders— its pioneers—inscribed around the base. From Pioneer Court

77

a descending stairway leads to a restaurant and shops below, directly on the river bank.

The building itself, a 40-story structure of metal and glass, is clearly a product of the twentieth century, with a variation in the window arrangement that gives it special character. The slender external "piers" that separate the regular groups of 4 windows each have no supportive value, but they are more than ornamental. Within these "piers" are pipes for pumping hot or cold air into the offices as needed—from machinery located at the top and bottom of the building.

Together the Equitable and Wrigley buildings offer an appropriate gateway to what has been called the Champs Elysées of Chicago—North Michigan Avenue, famous throughout the country for its shops of great prestige, along with distinguished art galleries, restaurants, and clubs.

Sun-Times - Daily News Building—401 North Wabash.
Architects: Naess and Murphy (1957)
(See also Walk No. 8, North Wabash Avenue.)

The gateway to the Avenue is also the newspaper center of Chicago. The Field Enterprise Inc., of the Marshall Field family, operates the *Sun-Times - Daily News*. The building, though not actually on Michigan but along the north bank of the river, presents a striking view to the pedestrian crossing the Michigan Avenue bridge. It is connected with the famous avenue by a plaza located between the towers of the Wrigley building.

For tours through this busy, modern newspaper plant, call 321-3005.

Tribune Tower—435 North Michigan.
Architects: Hood and Howells (1925)

The Tribune Tower, a Gothic revival skyscraper, has long been a Chicago landmark. North Michigan Avenue would not be the same without the Wrigley Building, Water Tower and the Tribune Tower. They are synonymous with the growth and strength of Chicago.

In 1922, the *Tribune*'s publisher, the late Robert R. McCormick, for whom McCormick Place was named, held an international competition for the design of the building. Architects from all

Left, Wrigley building. *Right,* Equitable building.

over the world responded and out of the many designs, the winners selected were Raymond Hood and John Mead Howells, prominent New York architects.

The great Gothic arch entrance is quite impressive as are the various world-wide pieces of stone around the base of the building. Here you will see small pieces of stone from such buildings as Westminster Abbey, Cologne Cathedral, the Arch of Triumph in Paris, the Holy Door of St. Peter's in Rome, and even the Taj Mahal.

You must step across the street or walk back to the Equitable Plaza to see the crowning glory of this unusual building. The great flying buttresses, such as one sees on the exterior of European Gothic cathedrals, are to be seen and seen through. To see the sunlight piercing the buttresses is a remarkable sight and most rewarding to all photographers.

Along the rear of the Tribune Plant Building, located just south of the Tribune Tower, are displayed page ones of various issues of the Tribune with headlines of great national events back into the last century. The Plant was designed by architect Jarvis Hunt in 1920.

The *Chicago Today,* the *Tribune's* sister paper, is housed in an annex just north of the Tower. The Annex is a four-story, Gothic structure with also an Indiana limestone skin. There is a statue of Nathan Hale in the courtyard. It shows the 21-year-old American Revolutionary just prior to his execution by the British.

For tour arrangements, call 222-3232.

Uptown Savings and Loan Association Building—
430 North Michigan Avenue.
Architect: Fred H. Prather (1963)
Architect for Remodeling: Hague Richards (1972)

This white, marble structure is a fine example of a well-planned institution. As a part of the original design, a plaza was conceived that would embrace all of the nations of this hemisphere. The plaza was designed to represent all the flags of each nation, and was named "The Plaza of the Americas." There is a flagpole and flag for each nation, with the exception of Cuba.

80

500 North Michigan Avenue Building.
Architects: Skidmore, Owings and Merrill (1970)

This efficiently designed, travertine marble structure expresses the steel-and-concrete construction it conceals. This handsome structure was expressly designed for office use.

Across the street are the two towers of the Sheraton-Chicago Hotel.

Sheraton-Chicago Hotel—505 North Michigan Avenue.
Architects: Walter W. Ahlschlager (1929) South Tower; Quinn and Christensen (1961) North Tower

The hotel includes two towers and a below-level parking garage. The south tower was once the Medinah Athletic Club and still carries the ornament of its earlier function, including the Oriental turret and onion-shaped dome at the top.

Michigan Terrace Apartments—525 North Michigan Avenue. Architects: Richard A. Raggi and Guenter Malitz (1962)

Here is a fine example of the fine urban center living with amenities that include an indoor swimming pool, lower level garage and restaurant. The building is 33 stories and contains 480 apartments. The exterior is white glazed brick with yellow glazed brick spandrels. The bay windows and tinted glass plus the marble base combine to make an inviting structure.

Next, walk north to Ohio Street and continue east about two blocks to the Time-Life Building.

Time-Life Building—Fairbanks Court between Ohio Street and Grand Avenue.
Architects: Harry Weese and Associates (1971)

The new Chicago Time-Life Building is a 30-story structure that rises to a height of 400 feet with a gross floor area of 700,000 square feet. The building is a rectangular tower three bays wide by 7 bays long. Each bay is 30 feet square. Typical floors begin 87 feet above the sidewalk. The typical floor has no exposed columns.

The structure is concrete with a metal curtain wall of

Left, Tribune Tower.

81

weathering steel which will gradually weather to a deep brown. The windows are of gold, mirrored glass; elevator shafts and lobby walls are covered with granite. The same granite is used in the sidewalk paving and carries through into the floors of the lobby.

Time Incorporated Subscription Services is one of the largest mailing operations in the country. Operations require that the 1800 employees begin at the same time. For this reason, the 12-passenger elevators employ tandem cabs. These two-story cabs are used during peak morning, noon, and evening rush periods. During these periods, persons wishing to go to an odd-numbered floor enter the cabs from the lower elevator lobby and those wishing to go to an even-numbered floor enter from the upper lobby. After the peak has subsided, the system can be switched to normal service in which only the upper half of the two-story cab is used, stopping at each floor in the conventional manner.

The regular bay spacing, exposed structure, and horizontal emphasis of windows reflect the notion that an office building must be a series of equally adaptable floor plans one on top of the other and is in the tradition of the Chicago school, the early office buildings of Louis Sullivan, Carson Pirie Scott & Co. department store, as well as the past period inspired by the late Mies Van der Rohe.

This superbly-designed building is well worth your spending more time here than you originally anticipated.

Now walk one block north to a large city within a city.

McClurg Court Center—McClurg Court between Ohio and Ontario streets. Architects: Solomon, Cordwell, Buenz and Associates (1971)

McClurg Court Center is a fascinating example of the trend in inner-city living towards obtaining maximum security for all the tenants. In this case when a tenant enters the Center, he has at his disposal all the necessities of life that make it unnecessary to step out after dark. Besides covered parking facilities, McClurg Court Center contains 1,028 dwelling units, a 1,250-seat movie theatre, and three tennis courts enclosed in the metal pavilion at the west end of the Center. There are also complete health club facilities, including a swimming pool. There are shops for the convenience of the tenants that service their needs. Concrete walls on towers are sheer walls which restrain the buildings against the wind and offer the viewer a dramatic demonstration of power and strength.

Now walk back to the west side of Michigan Avenue at Ontario. On the way you will pass the CBS Studios and the Museum of Contemporary Art (See Walk No. 32).

Woman's Athletic Club—626 North Michigan Avenue. Architects: Philip B. Maher and Associates (1928)

This low-key, carefully-designed structure is representative of some of the best work by architects in the 1920's. The structure is 9 stories on pile foundations. The Bedford limestone and

Left, Time-Life building. *Right,* 625 North Michigan Avenue building.

pressed-brick exterior articulate the air of quiet elegance of the interior.

At this point you can see the upper portion of the 100-story John Hancock Center. Its sheer size draws the attention of any northbound pedestrian on or near Michigan Avenue.

During the growing season, trees, flowers, and shrubbery give this part of North Michigan Avenue color, texture, and beauty. It is a pleasure to stroll here and view these outdoor attractions as well as the enticing window display of jewelry, books, and wearing apparel. At Christmastime, tiny Italian bulbs strung on the branches of all the trees on the avenue create an air of enchantment. Now, cross to the east side.

625 North Michigan Avenue Building.
Architects: Meister & Volpe Architects, Inc. (1971)

This 27-story, reinforced-concrete, office building was the winner of the 1971 first prize from the Concrete Contractors Association of Greater Chicago.

Included in the building's unusual architectural features is its corner treatment. Structural corner columns were eliminated to provide open corner windows for executive offices.

The exterior of the building is of exposed smooth, formed architectural concrete. Special aggregate, sand, and cement were used to achieve the building's distinctive buff color. The lower portion of the building was sandblasted to give the concrete an even more textured appearance.

Saks Fifth Avenue Building—669 North Michigan Avenue. Architects: First and second buildings, Philip B. Maher and Associates (1925) Remodeling and third building, Holabird and Root (1966)

This North Michigan Avenue branch of this nationally-known department store chain is housed in a complex of three elegant buildings. The two oldest, 671-75 and 669 North Michigan Avenue were originally the Blackstone Shop. The two original structures have undergone numerous remodeling projects. Remodeling of the two original structures was done by the architects of the third, 11-story building, Holabird and Root.

McClurg Center.

85

Allerton Hotel—701 North Michigan Avenue.
Architects: Murgatroyd and Ogden (1924)

This 25-story, famous hotel includes the equally famous Gucci shop. As you walk north you will pass Tiffany's and the Elizabeth Arden Building. Directly east is the striking Knott Hotel and Office Building designed by Joel R. Hillman, completed in 1973.

737 North Michigan Avenue Building.
Architects: Holabird and Root (1927)

This gray limestone building with five stories and penthouse is a real architectural gem. Step into the lobby and enjoy the rich wood paneling and marble interior. The lobby floor is terrazzo and together with the walls, makes a delightful entrance to the upper floor offices. Also, note the small astronomical observatory on the roof, built for the original owner who was an astronomy buff.

Water Tower—800 North Michigan, at Chicago Avenue.
Architect: W. W. Boyington (1867-1869)

At Chicago Avenue, on Michigan, stands one of Chicago's most famous—though by no means its most beautiful—landmarks, the Water Tower. Now closed and empty, this elaborate tower symbolizes Chicago's historic growth. When it was built, 2 years before the Great Fire, this fantastic, pseudo-Gothic creation, with its many turrets rising around the central tower like a section of a medieval castle, was considered a most artistically satisfactory disguise of the standpipe that it concealed.

Its design is far removed from what was developed later in the century by the Chicago school of architects—except that in a sense its form did follow function (or at least originated in function) as those later builders insisted that it should. Within the tower was an iron standpipe 3 feet in diameter and nearly 150 feet high that stored the water supply for the Near North Side. Across the street is the pumping station—still in use!— built of the same material (Joliet limestone) but with less elaborate ornamentation. In 1867 it was noteworthy that the "new" station could pump as much as 18 million gallons a day. Historic notes on the back of a menu for the Water Tower

Cornerstone Centennial Luncheon in March 1967 (sponsored by the Greater North Michigan Avenue Association) pointed out that the 1967 capacity of Chicago's water system was then *3 billion* gallons a day.

Though long ago the Water Tower ceased to be of any use as a standpipe, the city cherishes its presence in the midst of Michigan Avenue traffic. For all its antiquated style of architecture, it seems strangely appropriate here among the more beautiful modern structures around it. By its very contrast in style it is a reminder of Chicago's triumph over the Great Fire of 1871, which destroyed practically everything else in this part of Chicago but was followed by a period of unprecedented building and architectural progress. The tower was designated by the City Council in 1971 as an Historic Landmark.

American Dental Association Building—
211 East Chicago Avenue.
Architects: Graham, Anderson, Probst and White (1966)

In marked contrast with the curiously squatty effect of the historic Water Tower is the slender, stately structure now used as the headquarters of the American Dental Association, a 23-story building just east of Michigan on Chicago Avenue.

American Dental Association building.

87

John Hancock building.

I. Magnin Store Building—830 North Michigan Avenue.
Architects: Shaw, Metz (1958)
Architects for Remodeling: Solomon, Cordwell and Buenz (1971)

The building was originally occupied by Bonwit Teller who moved into the lower floors of the John Hancock Building. A fifth floor was added to the top, and a five-story, 52-foot section was added at the west end of the store building. The fifth floor preserved the vertical street scale, and the slightly projecting panels below the fifth floor strengthen the linear scale of the structure and further lower the apparent building height. A large parking garage and apartment building are immediately adjacent to the west. Across the street to the west and south is the Water Tower Hyatt House and Lewis Towers of Loyola University.

Water Tower Plaza—
Michigan, Chestnut, Seneca, Pearson.
Architects: Loebl, Schlossman, Bennett and Dart (1973)
Associate Architects: C. F. Murphy and Associates

Directly across the street to the east is a new $100 million complex under construction. The plans are for a 76-story combination shopping-office-hotel-apartment complex. The retail portion of the complex will have a large, two-story entrance with mezzanine, providing a Michigan Avenue access for both a new Marshall Field & Company store and a Lord and Taylor store. The two stores will split half of the 600,000 square feet of retail shopping on the 7 shopping floors.

John Hancock Center—875 North Michigan Avenue.
Architects: Skidmore, Owings and Merrill (1969)
Partner in Charge: Bruce Graham

Returning to Michigan Avenue, you will be overwhelmed by the 100-story John Hancock Building, towering more than 1,000 feet in the air. This dominates the vicinity and the skyline much as the Eiffel Tower does in Paris. This characteristic, however, is the only one the two structures have in common. The modern steel building of the John Hancock, surrounded by much open space at its base, is a combination commercial-residential project, with apartments limited to the uppermost 50 stories. Black anodized aluminum and tinted glass are the materials used in the exterior. To cope with Chicago's winds (it is said that the top of the building may sway anywhere from 10 to 15 inches—though those inside would not be aware of it!) the John Hancock has huge cross-bracing steel members that make several giant X's on each side. These produce an interesting ornamental effect as the X's become gradually smaller with the tapering of the building from foundation to top.

The 95th Restaurant occupies the 95th and 96th floors. An observation tower is at the top and is open to the public.

Continental Plaza Hotel—
Michigan Avenue and Delaware Street.
Architects: Alfred Shaw and Associates (1963)

Directly north of the Hancock is this overly stylized hotel containing many shops and restaurants. A new west wing is scheduled for completion in 1973.

Fourth Presbyterian Church—
126 East Chestnut (860 N).
Architects: Ralph Adams Cram (1912);
Parish House: Howard V. Shaw (1925)

Directly across the street, providing a diametric contrast, is the Fourth Presbyterian Church, which is famed for its modified Gothic style. The architect designed many other Gothic revival buildings at that time. The modifications executed here can be seen in such things as the narrowness of the side aisles and the placement of a balcony in the transept space. The buildings, of carved Bedford stone, surround on 3 sides a grass plot, with the 4th side an arcade. The stained glass windows were designed by Charles Connick.

Playboy Building—919 North Michigan Avenue.
Architects: Holabird and Root (1929)
Architects for Remodeling: Ron Dirsmith and
A. Epstein and Sons, Inc. (1972)

Formerly the Palmolive Building, this structure is now part of the Playboy Center that includes the Playboy headquarters offices,

Playboy Towers Hotel, formerly the Knickerbocker, and the new Playboy Club.

Playboy Walk, as the 7500 square-foot lobby arcade is called, is a miniature city for dining or shopping 24 hours a day. Its architecture and design are highlighted by free-form floor areas, molded ceilings in varying heights, lighting changes, mirrored columns, and curving walls faced with oiled-walnut panels. Handmade wire-cut bricks cover uncarpeted walks, and potted plants and trees provide outdoor touches. The result is a pleasant atmosphere designed for pleasure seekers. The crowning glory occurs on the second floor where the Playboy Club is located. It all combines to make a smashing effect.

Fourth Presbyterian Church.

92

The original carved elevator doors by sculptor Edgar Miller have been preserved along with the interior of the cabs. Also, the radically remodeled entrance and lobby come off well. Every item is in low key and reflects an excellent sense of good design on the part of the architects.

Architect Ron Dirsmith designed the Playboy offices in this building. Splendid lighting, colors, and curved wall surfaces with dropped ceilings make each of the several floors of offices unique and quite handsome.

900 North Michigan Avenue Building.
Architect: Jarvis Hunt (1972)

This handsome 9-story apartment building offered elegant surroundings to the tenants of the 1920's. It is still well-maintained and the tenants still enjoy the spacious and well-planned apartments.

Walton Colonnade Apartment Building—100 East Walton Street. Architects: Dubin, Dubin, Black and Moutoussamy (1972)

This is a 256-unit apartment building. Its tower is a 44-story, reinforced-concrete structure which employs a poured-in-place, reinforced-concrete, strut exterior wall system. This exterior is infilled with darkened glass and aluminum fenestration.

The typical floors, rooftop pool and solarium are serviced by three high-speed elevators. Each floor contains 8 dwelling units. Also included are a 7-level parking garage, and a ground-level and lower-level concourse which contain 23,000 square feet of commercial space. The lower-level concourse has an open terraced court as its focal point.

Drake Hotel—Michigan, Walton and Lake Shore Drive. Architects: Marshall and Fox (1920)

This is truly one of the last of the "grand hotels" of this city. It is 13 stories on pile foundations. The exterior is Bedford limestone. The fenestration is generous, affording excellent views for the fortunate guests who face Lake Shore Drive and the Oak Street Beach. The hotel is well-maintained and has retained its air of gracious living. The great fireplace in the center of the lobby is a pleasant sight at all times of the year.

End of the "Magnificent Mile"

The "Magnificent Mile" comes to an end just beyond the Drake Hotel where Michigan Avenue loses its identity by merging with Lake Shore Drive. If the weather permits, take the underpass pedestrian walkway to the Oak Street Beach. Here at Oak Street Beach is a glorious view of Lake Michigan and the pedestrian walkway and bicycle path will take you north with Lake Michigan on your right and many handsome apartment buildings facing you on the left. This is indeed a glamorous section of Lake Shore Drive and is part of the "Gold Coast" of Chicago.

Please note the 1212 Lake Shore Drive Apartment Building—easily the handsomest and most rugged of the new structures on this portion of Lake Shore Drive. Barancik and Conte were the architects and the building was completed in 1970. Also, note the two very attractive reinforced-concrete apartment buildings at 1110 and 1240 North Lake Shore Drive by Hausner and Macsai, architects, completed in 1971. Too, observe the Arthur Aldis House at 1258 Lake Shore Drive. This charming, three-story, Venetian Gothic townhouse was designed in 1906 by architects Holabird and Root. There is a charming Georgian house at the corner.

You are now entitled to a well-earned rest, and it is your privilege now to sit on a bench and enjoy the passing parade.

Walk-8

Marina Towers, IBM building, Sun-Times/ Daily News building.

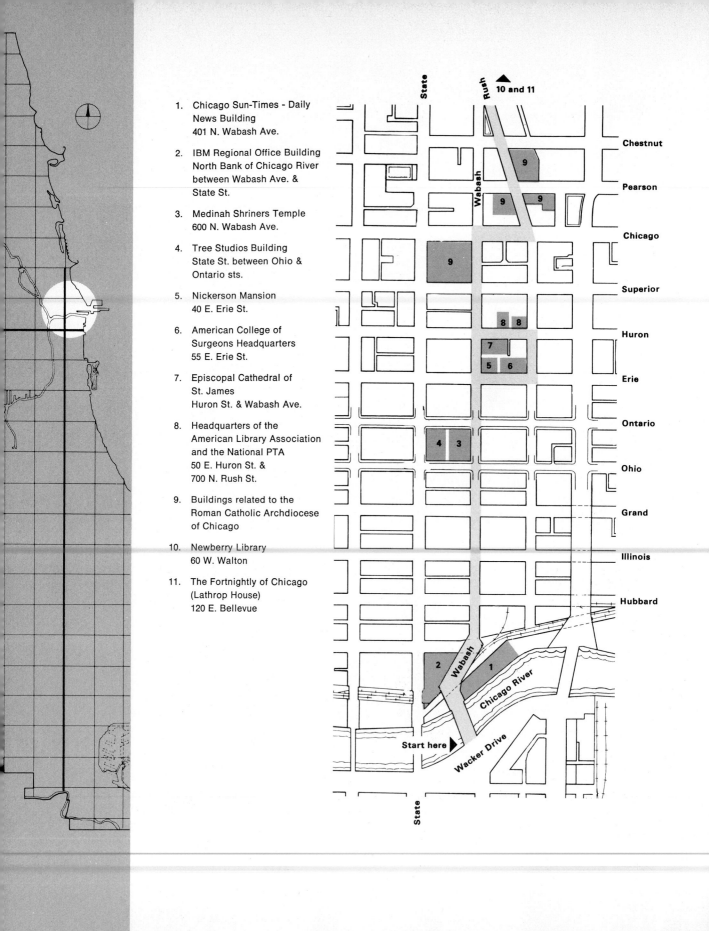

1. Chicago Sun-Times - Daily
   News Building
   401 N. Wabash Ave.

2. IBM Regional Office Building
   North Bank of Chicago River
   between Wabash Ave. &
   State St.

3. Medinah Shriners Temple
   600 N. Wabash Ave.

4. Tree Studios Building
   State St. between Ohio &
   Ontario sts.

5. Nickerson Mansion
   40 E. Erie St.

6. American College of
   Surgeons Headquarters
   55 E. Erie St.

7. Episcopal Cathedral of
   St. James
   Huron St. & Wabash Ave.

8. Headquarters of the
   American Library Association
   and the National PTA
   50 E. Huron St. &
   700 N. Rush St.

9. Buildings related to the
   Roman Catholic Archdiocese
   of Chicago

10. Newberry Library
    60 W. Walton

11. The Fortnightly of Chicago
    (Lathrop House)
    120 E. Bellevue

State

Rush

10 and 11

Chestnut

Wabash

Pearson

Chicago

Superior

Huron

Erie

Ontario

Ohio

Grand

Illinois

Hubbard

Wabash

Chicago River

Start here

Wacker Drive

State

Walk · 8

NORTH WABASH AVENUE

WALKING TIME: 45 minutes.   HOW TO GET THERE: Walk 1 block west of Michigan at Randolph, then turn right on Wabash and walk 3 blocks north, crossing the Wabash Avenue bridge over the Chicago River.

If you are a lucky sightseer, you may arrive at the Chicago River just in time to see one or more of the bridges split in two and rise, permitting tall boats to pass by. These are bascule bridges, or—as they are sometimes called—"jackknife" bridges. Don't be in a hurry; both bridge and boats move slowly!

Chicago Sun-Times - Daily News Building—
401 North Wabash Avenue.
Architects: Naess and Murphy (1957)
(See also Walk No. 7, Michigan Avenue: North.)

This walk starts at the Chicago Sun-Times - Daily News Building on the north bank of the Chicago River at Wabash Avenue. This modern newspaper plant is housed in a long, low building that faces the river the full length of its facade. The horizontal emphasis in the building's architecture is accentuated by this location as well as by contrast with so many skyscrapers on all sides. A pleasant open effect is achieved by the river beside it and the Wrigley Building plaza, which gives it easy access to Michigan Avenue. This landscaped plaza on the east and a pedestrian walkway on the riverside contribute to making the building and its environs a pedestrian's delight.

As you walk inside into the main corridor, you will see the enclosed presses on one side of the building. Through the glass partition you can generally watch one of the many newspaper editions going to press—a fascinating process to the uninitiated.

For a truly exciting view of the Loop, take a short side trip through the Wrigley Plaza and over to the pedestrian walk to Wabash along the north bank of the river. On the way, note the charming small landscaped terrace built and maintained by Field Enterprises. For tours through this busy, modern newspaper plant, call 321-2005.

97

IBM Regional Office Building—The North Bank of the Chicago River between Wabash and State.
Architects: The Office of Mies Van der Rohe and C. F. Murphy Associates (1971)

IBM's new office building was designed to consolidate the offices of the International Business Machine Company's downtown branches in Chicago. The 52-story, steel-and-glass structure, IBM's largest to date, is sheathed in a curtain wall of bronze aluminum and tinted glass. The granite plaza is on a 1.6 acre site overlooking the Chicago River between Wabash Avenue and State Street. The stunning lobby is enhanced by a bust of architect Mies Van der Rohe.

There are 51 floors above the lobby. Of these, 46 are for office space. Two floors contain major computer facilities tied into a network of IBM computers across the country, available to other tenants in the building.

The building's special curtain wall system and heating-cooling system were designed to meet the stringent humidity and temperature requirements of the computer areas. The building's power is all electric.

98

At first glance the building may seem simply pristine or plain. A second glance will reveal the richness of the travertine marble lobby and glass with the gray granite floor of the lobby and plaza. This is truly a great work of architecture. More than that, it is a final statement of one of the twentieth century's most distinguished architect. Chicago is indeed fortunate to have been the home, for over 30 years, of this superb interpreter of the machine age. He used the precision of the machine to make pristine, sculptured monuments to that particular period in time.

Directly north, note the striking garage structure of Cor-Ten steel designed by George Schipporeit in 1972.

Before returning to Wabash, look west across State and see the gigantic home of the American Medical Association.

Medinah Shriners Temple—600 North Wabash Avenue. Architects: Huehl and Schmid (1912)

Now walk north 3 blocks to Ohio Street, and note the very large Medinah Shriners Temple at the northwest corner of Ohio and Wabash. The building with its Moorish style of architecture resembles a mosque, as of course the designer intended. Inside are drill halls, offices, and an auditorium seating about 2,000, which is used for circus performances and other spectaculars as well as for the Medinah drill teams and Shriners band.

Tree Studios Building—State Street, between Ohio and Ontario streets.

Walk west on Ohio to the other half of this block for a glimpse of the Tree Studios building. Though rather drab in outward appearance, this is nevertheless a unique structure, devoted to spacious artists' studios with high ceilings and large window areas. Judge Tree, whose wife was an artist, donated the building. Be sure to walk through the Ohio Street entrance, marked rather oddly "4 - Tree Studios - 6" for a pleasant surprise: on the other side of a small vestibule a door leads you again outdoors, into a delightful, hidden bit of park—with trees, flowers, and benches—which runs the length of the building. Since the park is enclosed on all sides, this gives a special privacy to the studio entrances.

Nickerson Mansion—40 East Erie.
Architects: Burling and Whitehouse (1883)

Return to Wabash and walk north 2 blocks to Erie. The building on the northeast corner, now carrying the dignified commercial sign "Pinnn [sic] Productions," was once one of the most opulent homes in Chicago, the Nickerson residence. This 3-story stone mansion of some 30 rooms was built for the Nickerson family more than 10 years after their previous home on the North Side had been destroyed by the Great Fire of 1871.

For more than 40 years the building was occupied by the American College of Surgeons (see the next stopping place). Nickerson himself, an active financier and one of the founders of the first bank in Chicago to become a national bank, enjoyed it for many years, selling it only in his last years, when he returned east. In his day it was referred to as "Nickerson's Marble Palace," and the richness of the interior certainly merits the name. As you enter the building (visitors are allowed on the first floor), you find yourself in an enormous hall with marble floors and pillars, onyx wall panels, and an alabaster staircase. Handcarved woodwork decorates the entire building. Since Nickerson was an art collector, he used one large room as an art gallery, the contents of which he gave largely to the Art Institute of Chicago when he sold the house.

Fortunately, those who have used the building since Nickerson's day have cherished its original elegance and kept it in good condition. Pinnn Productions, makers of audio-visual materials, distributes an attractive brochure. The soot-begrimed exterior, they say, is irreparable, because the porous building material makes sandblasting useless.

American College of Surgeons Headquarters—55 East Erie. Architects: Skidmore, Owings, and Merrill (1963)

One block farther east, on the southwest corner of Rush and Erie, with main entrance on Erie, is the new building of the American College of Surgeons. From 1919 until the completion of this building in 1963, the College of Surgeons occupied the Nickerson Mansion just described. At 50 East Erie, across the street immediately east of the Nickerson Mansion is the Auditorium used by the American College of Surgeons, the

Detail of massive ornamental facade of the John B. Murphy Memorial.

100

John B. Murphy Memorial. The ground on which the
Memorial Auditorium stands was once the side
yard of the Nickerson Mansion.

Episcopal Cathedral of St. James—Huron and Wabash. Architects: Burling and Bacchus (1856) partially rebuilt after Great Fire (1875) Office Headquarters and Parish House by architects James Hammond and Peter Roesch (1968)

One block farther north, at Huron, is the Episcopal Cathedral
of St. James. This structure is typical of a number of churches built
shortly before and after the Great Fire of 1871, for which
architects followed the Gothic style in a free, somewhat
inventive manner. These churches were often built of local
limestone, called Joliet stone or Lemont limestone, which is seen
in this building. To the east is a stunning office headquarters
and parish house of contemporary design.

Headquarters of the American Library Association and the National PTA

On the north side of Huron are 2 buildings dedicated to
educational purposes. At *50 East Huron* is the headquarters of
the *American Library Association (architects: Holabird and Root,
1961-63)*, built on the site of a much older structure, which had
been used by the ALA since 1945. The earlier building was once

St. James Cathedral reflected in
the windows of the office headquarters and parish house.

101

Cathedral of the Holy Name.

known as the McCormick House. Cyrus H. McCormick II, of the family that won both fame and fortune—as well as occasional labor problems—through the McCormick Harvester plant, is said to have been still living in the house in 1889.

Immediately to the east, at *700 North Rush Street*, is the headquarters of the *National PTA—National Congress of Parents and Teachers (architects: Holabird and Root, 1954)*. Funds to meet the expenses of constructing the National PTA building came largely from individual or PTA donations of anywhere from 10 cents to 10 dollars. "Quarters for Headquarters" was the slogan, and PTA members all across the country contributed whatever they could to provide a home of their own, where the national staff might work in more convenient space and better conditions than had been possible previously in their rented offices. PTA's may well be proud of the result, for the building was cited for excellence of design soon after it was completed.

The sculptured figures on the face of the building, by Chicagoan Milton Horn, symbolize parents' and teachers' responsibilities in educating children. Father, mother, and teacher—each is represented with a child.

Both the ALA and the PTA have recently expanded their quarters by the purchase of property on Rush Street. The PTA now owns the building just north of its 700 North Rush headquarters. And the ALA is already at work in a building at 716 North Rush.

Buildings Related to the Roman Catholic Archdiocese of Chicago

In the next few blocks you will come to a variety of buildings representing the Roman Catholic faith and its Archdiocese in Chicago. (For the Archbishop's residence see Walk No. 10, "The Gold Coast.")

The *Catholic Cathedral of the Holy Name (architects: P. C. Kelly, 1874; Henry J. Schlacks, 1915)* and immediately related buildings occupy the entire block between Wabash and State, Superior Street (732 N) and Chicago Avenue (800 N). School buildings, parish houses, and convent share the block with the church, all built in a similar style—the neo-Gothic used so widely for

103

places of worship. The Cathedral was completely renovated during 1969 under the supervision of C. F. Murphy Associates, architects.

To the north, on the other side of Wabash, is *Loyola University's Downtown Center, Lewis Towers Campus.* The structure that gives this complex of buildings its name is a converted office building on Rush Street (official address, 820 North Michigan Avenue) donated by the late Frank Lewis, Chicago philanthropist *(architects: Schmidt, Garden, and Erikson, 1925).* A newer building on the west side of Rush, connected with Lewis Towers at the 2nd floor by a covered walkway over the street, carries the name "Pere Marquette Campus."

And to the north of Lewis Towers are the imposing buildings of *Quigley Preparatory Seminary,* where youngsters start their training for the priesthood *(architect: Gustav Steinbeck of New York, 1918).* Archbishop James E. Quigley in 1905 had established what was then called Cathedral College. He died before his plans for an expanded school could be carried out, but his successor—Cardinal George Mundelein—fulfilled his aims. Many of the funds came as gifts from children of the Archdiocese, and the school's name was changed to make it a memorial to the man who had originally planned it.

At Quigley Seminary you feel that you are standing before a great French Gothic municipal hall of the 12th century. Various Gothic features combine to give the effect of an authentic medieval structure: the rose window over the chapel entrance, the sculpture on either side, the high-pitched roofs, the buttresses on the Chestnut Street side, and the medieval courtyard. They almost make you expect to see knights in armor ride in on horseback—until you catch a glimpse of the 20th century cars parked inside the courtyard! Whatever Louis Sullivan might have thought of the architecture, this is a most impressive complex of buildings.

Newberry Library—60 West Walton.
Architect: Henry Ives Cobb (1892)
Architect for Remodeling: Harry Weese and Associates (1968)

Newberry Library.

At this point, you are at Wabash Avenue and Chestnut Street and

it is suggested that you continue your walk to see a particularly rewarding structure—the Newberry Library. Continue northward on Rush for one block to Delaware, then two blocks west to Dearborn Street. Now you are at Washington Square on which the Newberry Library faces from the north.

Washington Square is precisely the amount of open space necessary to properly view the Newberry Library. A few other institutional buildings line the east and south perimeters. Together, they form the classic relationship of low structural mass and open space to give the viewer the delightful experience of enjoying architecture in a way that was afforded pedestrians during the Classic and Renaissance periods in Europe.

This library of splendid Spanish Romanesque stands on the site of the Mahlan Ogden house, a wooden mansion that miraculously escaped the Great Fire of 1871 but was later razed to make way for this building. Newberry Library was created by a bequest from Walter Loomis Newberry, an early Chicago businessman.

The Newberry Library houses outstanding collections of reference materials—both bound and unbound matter—that are used by scholars working on advanced research projects in the humanities. Over the years it has purchased entire libraries of individuals in this country and in Europe who had collected books and manuscripts in the field of history, literature, and music. There is an entire section of the library devoted to rare books.

Several collections of Americana are particularly famous, including such unusual materials as grammars in Indian languages and extensive genealogical records.

Before leaving, note that Washington Square, during warm weather, is a resting place for people of the neighborhood and vagrants. Back in the 1920's it served as a forum for any radical or far-out speaker who chose to lend his oratory to the crowds that were gathered each night in anticipation.

If you desire, return to Michigan Avenue by walking east on Oak Street. You will see a variety of stores, shops, galleries, and restaurants, also on Rush Street, for several blocks.

Note the Esquire Theatre at 53 East Oak that was designed by

William and Hal Pereira, Architects, (1937). It was one of the first attempts at producing a modern theme for the motion picture theatre, which up to then had been completely wallowing in "borax" architecture.

Also note the many new high-rise apartment buildings in the vicinity, indicating that many young persons enjoy living in this area.

First, note the narrow but striking triangular concrete apartment building at Oak, State, and Rush streets. It was designed by Joel R. Hillman and completed in 1972.

Next, on the west side of State between Oak and Maple is the stunning concrete tower apartments designed by Ezra Gordon and Jack Levin in 1973. Note the town houses on the roof of the garage as well as the striking entrance complex.

One last building awaits the intrepid walker at this point. Walk from Oak and Rush, one block north to Bellevue and then one block east to the Fortnightly.

The Fortnightly of Chicago (Lathrop House)—
120 East Bellevue.
Architects: McKim, Mead and White (1892)
Architect for Remodeling: Perkins and Will (1972)

This imposing three-story mansion—three windows wide at the center with wide bays on each side—was originally the home of the Lathrop family. The symmetry of the facade, which is in keeping with its eighteenth-century, classic style, is pleasantly relieved by having the entrance set in the left, not the center, of the three central arches. It can be compared with some of the fine nineteenth-century mansions in Boston and New York designed by this leading architectural firm of that period. It is probably the only remaining example in Chicago of the work of McKim, Mead and White.

The mansion has been recently restored and rehabilitated with structural, plumbing, and electrical changes. The entire structure has been modernized and will function as a gathering place for members of the club and their friends.

North Lake Shore
Drive from the Chess
pavilion in the
foreground to Oak
Street beach.

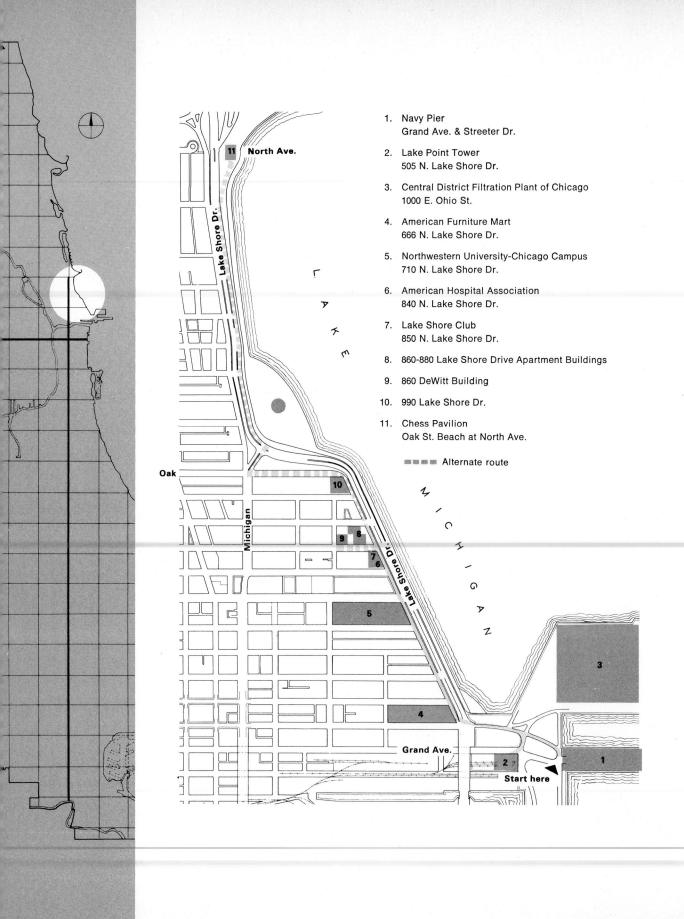

1. Navy Pier
   Grand Ave. & Streeter Dr.

2. Lake Point Tower
   505 N. Lake Shore Dr.

3. Central District Filtration Plant of Chicago
   1000 E. Ohio St.

4. American Furniture Mart
   666 N. Lake Shore Dr.

5. Northwestern University-Chicago Campus
   710 N. Lake Shore Dr.

6. American Hospital Association
   840 N. Lake Shore Dr.

7. Lake Shore Club
   850 N. Lake Shore Dr.

8. 860-880 Lake Shore Drive Apartment Buildings

9. 860 DeWitt Building

10. 990 Lake Shore Dr.

11. Chess Pavilion
    Oak St. Beach at North Ave.

■■■■ Alternate route

Walk · 9

LAKE SHORE DRIVE : NEAR NORTH

WALKING TIME: 1½ hours.   HOW TO GET THERE: Take any of the following northbound
CTA buses—No. 151 (Sheridan), No. 152 (Addison), or No. 153 (Wilson-Michigan) on State
Street; or a No. 76 (Diversey) on Wabash. Get off at Michigan and Grand Avenue (530 N), and
transfer to an eastbound bus No. 65 (Grand Avenue), which will take you to Navy Pier,
which is the end of the line.

This walk starts at *Navy Pier*, just one block to the east and
one block to the north of the Outer Drive/Lake Shore Drive bridge
(which crosses the Chicago River, a strip of land at North Water
Street, and then a strip of water called Ogden Slip).

Navy Pier links Chicago, an international port without a seacoast,
with the rest of the world. Since the opening of the St.
Lawrence Seaway, ships from faraway places change cargo here
during the shipping season—an activity that many find fascinating
to watch. The Pier, stretching nearly a mile out into Lake
Michigan, was built in 1916 as a storage and shipping facility for
lake traffic. In its life of more than half a century it has served
various purposes. During both world wars it was a training center
for the U.S. Navy, and for several years it was the home of the
Chicago branch of the University of Illinois—surely unique
among campuses! Since the University's construction of its new
Circle Campus in Chicago (see Walk No. 13) and its subsequent
departure from Navy Pier, the space here has been used
for convention exhibits and trade shows.

For the sightseer Navy Pier offers unparalleled views of
Chicago's "marine" activity and its spectacular skylines—
both to the south and to the north.

Streeter Drive, a short, curving street at the foot of Navy Pier,
is a reminder that you are on the border of what was once widely
known as *Streeterville*, named after a controversial figure of the
1880's. Just to the north (between Grand and Chicago avenues, St.
Clair and Lake Michigan) lies the part of the city to which
George Wellington Streeter and his wife for more than 30 years
claimed squatters' rights. They called their 180-acre shantytown

the District of Lake Michigan and claimed that neither the laws of Chicago nor those of Illinois had any jurisdiction over it. Other "squatters" whom Streeter persuaded to buy real estate from him gave him substantial backing in his many lawsuits with the city of Chicago. Not until 1918 was this notorious character actually removed from the lakefront land, which had multiplied its value many times during the years of Streeter's occupation.

Though the structures of Streeterville could never have been called architectural achievements, this sea "captain" turned real estate con man deserves more than passing mention. He seems to have been the first to redeem land from Lake Michigan and make a profit on it—a procedure that literally underlies many lakefront skyscrapers today!

The story goes that Streeter and his wife, Maria, started this fantastic real estate project in 1886 after running their excursion boat aground on a sandbar in Lake Michigan somewhat south of Chicago Avenue. Instead of freeing the boat, which they found difficult, they decided to fill up the lake around it instead. And— with the assistance of nearby residents who contributed dirt from construction sites, trash, garbage, and whatever lay at hand —this is exactly what they did. Despite protests from mansion-owners across the Drive, Streeter defied all attempts by the law to oust him from "his" property until someone was killed in one of the numerous confrontations with police. He was then sent to Joliet Penitentiary on a charge of manslaughter. Out on parole 9 months later, he returned to his battle with law and order. Finally, in 1918, court orders were actually carried out: Streeter was removed and the shanties of Streeterville burned to make way for later development.

For all his early success with real estate, Streeter could never have dreamed of the skyline that today has replaced his controversial territory!

Lake Point Tower—505 North Lake Shore Drive. Architects: Schipporeit-Heinrich; Graham, Anderson, Probst, and White (1968)

The most prominent building on the shoreline to the north is Lake Point Tower. This 70-story, cloverleaf-shaped,

Opposite, Four foreign vessels docked at Navy Pier.

113

glass-sheathed apartment building is indeed a beautiful sight. Over 50 years ago (in 1921) a similar building was *designed* by Ludwig Mies van der Rohe in Berlin, but it was never built. The young architects who designed Lake Point Tower, former colleagues of Mies, were obviously influenced by the master. Much of the building's sweep and fluidity, its even sensuous quality, has to do with its hidden columns, all enclosed by the bronze-tinted glass. It is almost mirror-like at times, and in the setting sun's reflection it looks like a golden shaft.

The land under this 900-apartment skyscraper is owned by the Chicago Dock and Canal Company, which controls the entire strip of land and warehouses along the north bank of the Chicago River, including both sides of the Ogden Slip. This ownership extends nearly all the way west to Michigan Avenue. A master plan for the area calls for the eventual construction of several thousand apartment units along with office buildings to be connected to Michigan Avenue by a pedestrian mall.

Central District Filtration Plant of Chicago— 1000 East Ohio Street. Architects: C. F. Murphy Associates and the City Architect (1966)

Out in the lake, just north of Navy Pier, spreads the Central District Filtration Plant of Chicago, largest facility of its kind in

Above, Central District Filtration Plant and Olive Park.

114

the United States—with landscaped grounds and many illuminated
fountains. The sculpture in the lobby of the main building,
by the Chicagoan Milton Horn, represents the history
of the various uses of water.

Visitors to this plant are permitted by appointment only.
Call City Hall 744-4000.

American Furniture Mart—666 North Lake Shore Drive.
Architect: N. Max Dunning
(East portion, 1923; West portion, 1926)
Across Lake Shore Drive you pass two modern hotels—Lake
Tower Inn, at 600 Lake Shore Drive, and Holiday Inn, at 644—and
come to the renowned American Furniture Mart, at 666. This is
one of the two major marts used by leading furniture
manufacturers to display their latest creations, especially during
"market" weeks. (The other of course, is the Merchandise Mart,
also in Chicago. See Walk No. 11, Wacker Drive: East-West.)

Unlike the Merchandise Mart, the American Furniture Mart is
restricted to dealers in furniture—a condition that makes it the
world's largest building given to a single business. Displays by
practically every wholesale furniture dealer in the country
are shown here, and only furniture buyers are
permitted in the building.

115

Northwestern University Chicago Campus—
710 North Lake Shore Drive.
Architects: Holabird and Root (From 1925 on)

An activity center of a completely different kind lies one block
north of the Mart—the Chicago campus of Northwestern
University (bounded by Chicago Avenue, Lake Shore Drive,
Erie and St. Clair sts.). Here are the graduate schools of
medicine, dentistry, business, and law—in various buildings
along the 300 block of East Chicago Avenue, with administrative
offices at 710 North Lake Shore Drive. The Northwestern
Medical Center serves 7 hospitals, including 3 in the immediate
area—Passavant, Wesley Memorial, and the Veterans
Administration Research Hospital—and the Rehabilitation
Institute of Chicago, and a women's and children's hospital. They
are part of the Northwestern Memorial Complex. A walking
tour of this exciting urban campus is most rewarding.

American Hospital Association—
840 North Lake Shore Drive.
Architects: Schmidt, Garden & Erikson (1961-1970)

These two pleasant-looking structures house this enormously
important association.

Lake Shore Club—850 North Lake Shore Drive.
Architect: Jarvis Hunt (1929)

This 18 story club building is a quiet and dignified reminder
of the 20's.

860-880 Lake Shore Drive Apartment Buildings.
Architect: Ludwig Mies van der Rohe, with associate
architects P A C E (Planners, Architects, Consulting
Engineers) and Holsman, Holsman, Klekamp,
and Taylor (1952)

Two blocks north, beyond a city playground, the Armory, and
the headquarters of the American Hospital Association, stand four
apartment buildings designed by Mies van der Rohe. The first
pair of these to be constructed (860-880) have been cited by the
Architectural Landmarks Commission in these words:

> In recognition of an open plan in a multistory apartment building
> where the steel cage becomes expressive of the potentialities
> of steel and glass in architectural design.

116

The second pair, at 900-910 Lake Shore Drive, were built
four years later, in 1956. These buildings reflect the skill of a great
architect, engineer, and innovator. Nicknamed "The Glass
Houses" because they seem to be made almost entirely of glass,
they have been the inspiration for many buildings
all over the world.

860 DeWitt Building—860 North DeWitt. Architects: Skidmore, Owings and Merrill (1966)

Directly west of the 860-880 Lake Shore apartment buildings,
at DeWitt and Chestnut streets, is the 860 DeWitt apartment
building—a handsome structure of reinforced concrete covered

Left, Lake Point Tower. *Right,* 860-
880 Lake Shore Drive, Mies van
der Rohe apartments, with 860 De-
Witt building just behind.

with travertine marble. The contrast between this and "The Glass Houses" is a reminder that modern builders can use old-time building materials—as well as new—with effective results. Always present in the background of this walk is the imposing John Hancock Building with its 100 stories, 2 blocks to the west on Michigan Avenue. (See Walk No. 7, Michigan Avenue: North.)

990 Lake Shore Drive.
Architects: Barancik and Conte (1973)

This stunning concrete structure with metal bay windows presents a powerful punctuation mark at the turn of the drive.

Chess Pavilion—North End of Oak Street Beach.
Architect: Morris Webster (1956)

Around the corner on Lake Shore Drive, as it bends westward after meeting Oak Street, are several palatial apartment buildings that mark the beginning of that section of Chicago referred to as the "Gold Coast." (Walk No. 10 is devoted entirely to the "Gold Coast.")

Note the gracious appearing apartment buildings in this block— all creatures of the 1920's. The 199 East Lake Shore Drive Building is particularly representative of that period as is also the Drake Towers Apartments at 179 East Lake Shore Drive. The Drake, a luxury hotel, stands at the spot where Lake Shore Drive joins Michigan Avenue.

If the weather (and your endurance!) permits, stroll along Oak Street Beach, which you can reach through a pedestrian tunnel at the corner. Such a walk can be exhilarating, with Lake Michigan on one side and the prestigious apartment buildings on the other. The heavy automobile traffic along Lake Shore Drive is in direct contrast with the quiet of the water—or even with its ocean-like turbulence on windy days, which is refreshingly different from the mechanical noises of the city it borders.

The Chess Pavilion at the north end of Oak Street (the south end of Lincoln Park) is a fitting terminal to this walk. This small building is beautiful in its unusual and simple design. The reinforced concrete roof appears to be floating in the air.

Bateman School.

North Ave.

Burton
Place

LaSalle

Clark

Burton Place

Schiller

Banks

State

Goethe

Scott

Astor

Division

Start here

Walk · 10

THE GOLD COAST

WALKING TIME: About 1 hour.   HOW TO GET THERE: Take a northbound CTA bus No. 36 (Broadway) on Dearborn Street, and get off at Division Street (1200 N) and State.

In Chicago the term "Gold Coast" applies to the area bounded by Lake Michigan on the east, LaSalle Street on the west, Oak Street (1000 N) on the south, and North Avenue (1600 N) on the north. The name was given many years ago, indicating of course that this section of the city was peopled by those with most of the city's gold. (Suburbs and country houses were still a thing of the future.)

On the face of the 1000 Lake Shore Drive Building is sculpture —by Bernard Rosenthal, of New York, formerly of Chicago— literally depicting the Gold Coast of Africa.

This walk, however, covers another part of the Gold Coast, starting at State and Division, and moving through Scott Street, Astor Street, and Burton Place. (It seems especially appropriate that the Gold Coast should include a street that carries the glittering name of John Jacob Astor!)

You will be struck by the beauty and tranquillity of this residential area. What is unseen is the struggle to preserve these qualities in the face of change. At one time the section was zoned for single-family residences only, but as land values increased, zoning was changed to accommodate the economic forces. As in Kenwood (see Walk No. 17), most people could no longer afford to maintain such establishments—with rising taxes, increased cost of operation, and the dearth of household help. The choice for many was selling the property to high-rise developers or converting the interior into apartments. Wherever feasible, the latter was attempted. Fortunately, some of the home-owners have been able to keep their property as single-family dwellings.

1209 State Parkway—Just north of Division on the east side of the street is a brick apartment building painted white with glass

121

block windows and small terra-cotta figures in the brickwork. This was built around the time of the 1933-34 Century of Progress in the Art Moderne style of the time. High ceilings, balconies, and terraces give this structure a handsome appearance.

1 East Scott Street.
Architects: Dubin, Dubin, Black and Moutoussamy (1970)

The building's tower is a 24-story, reinforced-concrete structure which employs a poured-in-place, reinforced-concrete strut, exterior wall system. This exterior is infilled with glass-and-aluminum fenestration.

The typical floors and rooftop pool are serviced by three, high-speed elevators. Each floor contains 12 dwelling units.

17-19-21 East Scott Street—At Scott Street (1240 N) turn east and stop at 17, 19, and 21. Note the delightful limestone-and-brick facades. The bay windows and individual entrances give each house a bit of Old World charm.

23 East Scott—An old townhouse handsomely remodeled. The below-grade entrance with the white limestone wall and black columns behind a black iron picket fence give it a modernized 1890 look. The yellow-painted facade of the upper 3 stories is quite striking.

1240-42-44 Astor—Turn north from Scott Street onto Astor (50 E). Here are 3 charming townhouses built around 1890, delightful 3-story structures with bay windows. At 44, the below-grade entrance and curved facade give an 18th-century character to the house.

1250 Astor—A 3-story 1890 townhouse, with limestone facade, imitating an Italian Renaissance design.

1260 and 1301 Astor—At 1260 a 10-story, limestone-faced apartment building in the Art Moderne style of about 1936, and across the street, at 1301, a similar structure. These are 2 of the elegant cooperative apartment buildings that have replaced some of the earlier one-family residences, and they were designed for very much the same kind of home-owner. The Potter Palmers, for instance, took the top 3 floors of 1301 Astor as their Chicago home.

Opposite, Astor Tower Hotel.

Hotels Ambassador—East and West. At Goethe—pronounced "go-thee" with the "th" as in "thin," which may be necessary guidance if you come from outside Chicago—(1300 N) make a short side trip to State Parkway once more. At the corner of Goethe and State Parkway are the Ambassador hotels, home of the noted Pump Room, where so many famous people have dined and danced—or entertained those dining and dancing there.

Astor Tower Hotel—1300 North Astor. And back on Astor is the Astor Tower Hotel, designed by Bertrand Goldberg Associates, 1963—architects for Marina City (see the end of Walk No. 4, Dearborn Street).

1308-10-12 Astor—Three delightful townhouses in sandstone and red brick, with beautiful bay windows at 2nd and 3rd stories.

Playboy Mansion—1340 North State. The famous multimillionaire owner of the Playboy empire, Hugh Hefner, lives just around the corner. Make another short side trip for a view of the outside. (Inside views are more difficult, though in odd-numbered years you may visit the first floor if you find out the exact date of the Inurbia Tour of the Francis W. Parker School—to raise funds for the school.) Hefner's "pad" is a large Georgian mansion complete with swimming pool, art collections, and of course Bunnies!

Court of the Golden Hands—1349-53 Astor. Back on Astor you will see, on the east side of the street, the "Court of the Golden Hands," a charming apartment complex with a delightful courtyard. Each of the 2 golden hands at the entrance seems to be holding an apple. The Georgian facade and marble figure set in a niche make this a memorable sight.

1355 Astor—A well-designed, large-scale English Georgian mansion, constructed about 1910, copied from 18th-century originals.

◨ **Charnley House**—1365 Astor.
Architects: Adler and Sullivan (1892)

This 11-room, 3-story, 1-family residence has fortunately been maintained as such. Although the official architects were Adler and Sullivan, this is understood to be a Frank Lloyd Wright design, drawn up by him for the famous partnership of architects,

for whom he was then working as a young draftsman. The building's compactness contrasts with Wright's later rambling "Prairie House" style but is similar to other early works. Some see Sullivan's touch in the wooden balcony and copper cornice.

What is obviously an extension to the south was built at a later date, to bring the kitchen up from the basement and make the original dumbwaiter service unnecessary. It detracts from the original symmetry of the design.

36-48 Schiller (1400 N)—At Schiller, walk east past the row of townhouses numbered 36 to 48—red brick, 3-story, vine-covered houses, some with bay windows and each with a distinctive subtle design of its own.

1412 Astor—Back at Astor, on the west side, you come to a combination limestone and yellow-brick house. A pediment at the roof line and ornament on the facade give it a Dutch quality.

1427 Astor—Across the street, a 4-story brick house, painted gray, has a handsome, pristine look.

1431 Astor—A curved facade embraces the gray brick of this building, with white Ionic columns supporting a pediment over the porch. This was once the home of Edward L. Ryerson, former chairman of Inland Steel's board of directors.

1435 Astor—Another facsimile of a great Georgian mansion, a style so popular here at the turn of the century. The pilasters at the corners with their Ionic caps give the facade a somewhat heavy appearance. The pleasant ornamentation below the cornice somehow lends an air of authenticity. Black iron picket fences enclose the grounds.

1432 Astor—Back on the west side of the street is a stunning remodeling of a townhouse, converting it into 3 apartments. Limestone and large horizontal glass areas give this daring design a contemporary look. (*Architect, James Eppenstein, 1936*)

1444 Astor—An interesting 4-story apartment building with a limestone facade and bay windows, having some of the appearance of Art Moderne. (*Architects, Holabird and Root, 1936*)

1450 Astor—At 1450, facing Burton Place, is another handsome Georgian townhouse, with limestone base and red brick facade.

Opposite, Charnley House.

125

20 East Burton Place, now the Bateman School—
Architects: Stanford White (1900); David Adler (1927)

At 20 East Burton Place stands another landmark, now used by a private elementary and high school. The building's historical associations are with Chicago's society life. It was built for Mrs. Robert W. Patterson, daughter of Joseph Medill (once mayor of Chicago and *Chicago Tribune* editor), by the ill-fated architect Stanford White. The next owner— Cyrus McCormick—had extensive alterations made in 1927.

This red brick building with marble columns—a mansion of some 40 to 90 rooms (the count varies)—was the scene of some of Chicago's most sumptuous social functions. Here, it is said, slept visiting kings and queens as guests.

The gracious director of the Bateman School, its present tenant, allows visitors the opportunity to enjoy the splendor within— the graceful winding staircase, the 3-inch-thick doors, and the marble bathrooms. A visit inside 20 East Burton Place is a step into the glittering past.

Office of the Greek Orthodox Archdiocese is not far away— in the building at the corner of Astor and Burton Place (1500 N), 40 East Burton.

1518 Astor—A red brick Georgian design with bay windows and a well-proportioned entrance.

1525 Astor—On the east side of the street is the headquarters of the Polish Consulate of Chicago, housed in a handsome red brick Georgian structure, once a townhouse.

1529 and 1539 Astor—Two more charming Georgian houses, of delightful design, with a beautiful garden between them.

Roman Catholic Archbishop's Residence, 1555 North State Parkway—Architect: Alfred F. Pashley (1880)—At the very north end of Astor, facing Lincoln Park, is a large 19th-century, 3-story, red brick, eclectic mid-Victorian mansion. Many chimneys (you will count 19 if you see them all!), several roof peaks, and impressive facades make this building a distinctive landmark. This has been the home of Chicago's Archbishop since the 1880's.

Wrought iron gate in front of the Bateman School. *Opposite,* exterior view and details of Madlener House.

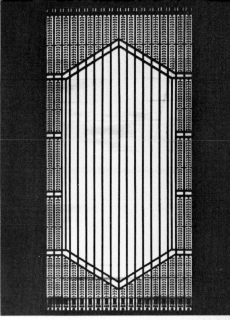

☐ **Madlener House**—4 West Burton Place, now the
Graham Foundation for Advanced Studies in the
Fine Arts. Architects: Richard E. Schmidt (1902);
for interior remodeling: Brenner, Danforth, and
Rockwell (1963)

Walk west on North Avenue to North State Parkway,
then south one block to Burton Place to the home of the Graham
Foundation for Advanced Studies in the Fine Arts, at 4 *West*
Burton Place. This is the noted Madlener House, an Architectural
Landmark, which has been compared with Florentine palaces.
Note the Sullivan-like ornamentation around the door, relieving
somewhat the severity of the design as a whole. Open to the
public by arrangement 9:30 A.M. to 5:00 P.M., Monday through
Friday. Call SU-7-4071.

**Carl Sandburg Village, between the alley east of Clark
and LaSalle, extending from Division to North Avenue.**
Architects: L. R. Solomon and J. D. Cordwell and
Associates (1960 on)

Now walk 2 blocks west of State to Clark Street, along the
western border of the old Gold Coast, for a view of Carl Sandburg
Village. This "village," named of course for Chicago's famous
and well-loved poet Carl Sandburg, consists of high-rise
apartment buildings, townhouses for sale or rent, studios,
gardens, fountains, and shops. A central pedestrian mall
covers the parking areas.

An urban renewal plan referred to as the Clark-LaSalle
Redevelopment Project cleared the slums to which the area had
deteriorated. It is expected that more buildings will
eventually be erected here.

Sandburg Village, although still not totally completed, as you can
see by the stretch of vacant land to the south along the west
side of Clark Street, now totals over 2,000 dwelling units. If you
will now walk a short distance north, you will pass the
Germania Club, set in a private roadway serving it and a high-rise
Sandburg apartment building. The Germania is the former center
of activity where many thousands of families of German
ancestry gathered. Today, as in so many other instances, the
present generation has either moved to the suburbs or no longer

Opposite, Carl Sandburg Village.

128

feels tied. In other words, the membership has dwindled and the building may be sold to the city as part of the urban renewal. The club was constructed in 1889 and designed by architect August Fiedler.

Old Town

At North Avenue look to the west, and two blocks over at Wells Street you will see the center of a half-mile strip known as Old Town. Besides the many restaurants, taverns, book stores, boutiques, museums (yes, museums), there is "Piper's Alley," a completely covered shopping and entertainment mall. Next door is the famous "Second City" where you will find excellent live skits and entertainment along with food and drinks six nights a week. This theatre restaurant is nationally known for its high-quality, satirical performances. Note the exterior ornament that was formerly a part of the facade of the Garrick Theatre Building designed by architects Adler and Sullivan. The building was demolished in 1958 and stood on the north side of Randolph Street opposite the Civic Center. A garage now occupies the site.

Burton Place

One block south of North Avenue, between LaSalle and Wells streets is a one-block stretch of some of the most unusual do-it-yourself type of architecture in all of Chicago. This side street now connects the Wells Street strip with Sandburg Village. Unique and imaginative remodeling and rehabilitation by the owners themselves make Burton Place fascinating. Tile mosaic, glass block, marble, terra-cotta, and old brick, garnered from nearby demolished structures, are some of the materials used in what is obviously self-help work without benefit of architect.

Behind the brick walls you will find patios with marble walks, fountains, sculptured figures, flowers, and trees. A plaque on the wall at 155 Burton Place states that this building was restored in 1927 by Sol Kogen. Kogen was the first owner on Burton Place to attempt rehabilitation by himself. His latent sense of design, although untrained, produced a fascinating and delightful environment for living in the 1920's and 1930's. He was responsible for almost the entire Burton Place rehabilitation.

Opposite, The Latin School of Chicago.

130

131

Now, back to Clark Street and North Avenue on the east side.

The Latin School of Chicago—
Northeast corner of Clark Street and North Avenue.
Architects: Harry Weese and Associates (1969)

The Latin School of Chicago is one of the city's finest progressive private schools. This new structure houses the upper grades and is one block west of the lower-grade school building on Dearborn.

This five-story, concrete frame and brick structure serves an enrollment of 400 pupils. Among the features of the building are an Olympic-size swimming pool at the lowest level, a theatre-auditorium seating 450 on the ground level, a full-service cafeteria with an outdoor terrace for autumn and spring use on the fourth level. There are, of course, classrooms, laboratories, and recreation areas. The urban renewal site and subsequent land use necessitated the inclusion of a rooftop recreation area allowing total reclaiming of the site.

Before urban renewal, this site was occupied by the Plaza Hotel, constructed in 1892 and designed by Clinton J. Warren, architect. The Plaza had bay windows with high-ceilings and generous-sized rooms. The metal grill and open elevator cabs were reminiscent of that era.

Executive House
and Lincoln Tower.

Start here

Chicago River

Wacker Drive

Wacker Drive

N. Michigan Ave.

Wells St.

LaSalle

Clark

Dearborn

State St.

Wabash

1. Stone Container Building
   360 N. Michigan Ave.

2. Lincoln Tower Building
   75 E. Wacker Dr.

3. Heald Square
   E. Wacker Dr., W. of Michigan Ave.

4. Executive House
   71 E. Wacker Dr.

5. Seventeenth Church of Christ Scientist
   55 E. Wacker Dr.

6. North American Life Insurance
   35 E. Wacker Dr.

7. United of America Building
   1 E. Wacker Dr.

8. City Parking Facility, "The Bird Cage"
   11 W. Wacker Dr.

9. 222 North Dearborn Building

10. City of Chicago Central Office Building
    325 N. LaSalle St.

11. Merchandise Mart
    Merchandise Mart Plaza

Walk · 11

WACKER DRIVE : EAST-WEST

WALKING TIME: 1½ hours.   HOW TO GET THERE: Take any of the following northbound CTA buses—No. 151 (Sheridan), No. 152 (Addision), or No. 153 (Wilson-Michigan) on State Street; or a No. 76 (Diversey) on Wabash. Get off at Michigan Avenue and Wacker Drive (300 N).

This walk begins at the intersection of East Wacker Drive and North Michigan Avenue, the spot where once stood Fort Dearborn, one of the military outposts established by President Thomas Jefferson. Plaques on both sides of the street are the only things to remind you of this historic fact. If you stand near the Michigan Avenue bridge and look west, you can see an exciting panorama of today's Chicago along the banks of the Chicago River, where that primitive fort was once the only settlement. The array of contemporary architecture—vertical, horizontal, round, and square—would surely have astonished those early settlers, no matter how ambitious their visions for the future may have been.

The Chicago River, along which you walk, is famed as the river that runs backwards. In order to make it serve more adequately the commercial and sanitary needs of metropolitan Chicago, engineers reversed its current more than 50 years ago, so that it now flows *from* Lake Michigan to the Mississippi River, rather than *into* Lake Michigan as it used to flow. With the recent opening of the St. Lawrence Seaway, the character of the boats seen on the river has changed. In addition to the barges and pleasure boats that always used it, seagoing vessels from distant ports are sometimes anchored here—from England, Denmark, Sweden, Italy, and other far countries.

Wacker Drive, named for Charles Wacker, first chairman of the Chicago Plan Commission, was constructed in 1925, following up the Burnham Plan of 1909. The cluttered old South Water produce market was demolished to make way for this vast improvement.

135

Wacker Drive and North Michigan Avenue, along with the Michigan Avenue bridge, are double-decked, with a seemingly different life going on at the lower level. A double-decked ring road around the Loop had been proposed as part of the Burnham Plan of 1909. But the Wacker Drive segment was the only portion to be completed. (The other two segments—the Eisenhower Expressway and the Outer Drive—have been finished only as upper-level roads.) Traffic on this lower level moves freely.

Stone Container Building—360 North Michigan Avenue. Architect: Alfred S. Alschuler (1923)

The Stone Container Building, at the southwest corner of Wacker Drive and Michigan Avenue, is the first building to be noted on this walk. Formerly the London Guarantee Building, it is especially well known for the replica of a Greek temple on its roof. Obviously, the designers were not following the standards of indigenous art that were developed by the late nineteenth century architects of the Chicago school.

Lincoln Tower Building—75 East Wacker Drive. Architect: Herbert H. Riddle (1928) (Formerly the Mather Tower)

A few hundred feet west is the 24-story Lincoln Tower Building, with its pseudo-Gothic ornamentation in terra-cotta. This narrow structure is distinguished primarily by the fact that it has the *smallest* floor space per story of any commercial building in Chicago!

Heald Square—East Wacker Drive, West of Michigan.

A block west of Michigan Avenue lies Heald Square, with sculptured figures of American Revolutionary War heroes in the center—George Washington, Haym Salomon, and Robert Morris. The square was named for Captain Nathan Heald, ill-fated commandant of Fort Dearborn at the time it was ordered evacuated. He was advised that the Indians would permit safe passage of the soldiers and their families. But as the group of 95 left the fort on August 15, 1812, they were attacked. Only 45 survived.

Incidentally, this is an excellent place from which to view the area—and take pictures if you are a camera fan.

Revolutionary War Heroes in Heald Square.

136

ROBERT MORRIS · GEORGE WASHINGTON · HAYM SOLOMON

137

Executive House—71 East Wacker Drive.
Architects: Milton M. Schwartz and Associates (1960)

Just to the east of Heald Square you will see the stainless steel balconies of the striking high-rise Executive House, designed as a high-quality hotel with special appeal to businessmen—an appeal that has proved highly successful.

Seventeenth Church of Christ Scientist—
55 East Wacker Drive.
Architects: Harry M. Weese and Associates (1968)

To the west of Executive House is a handsome, travertine marble church—semicircular-shaped and topped by a dome. This is the Seventeenth Church of Christ Scientist, constructed in 1968. Entrance to the main auditorium, which has arena-type seating, is through a lower-level foyer.

North American Life Insurance—35 East Wacker Drive.
Architects: Giaver and Dinkelberg, with Thielbar and Fugard as Associates (1926)

South of Heald Square is the former Jewelers Building, now the North American Life Insurance Building. It is topped with a neoclassical temple on each of the four corners, surrounding a huge central tower. Not following any single architectural style, the designers may be said to have used here an *eclectic* design.

United of America Building—1 East Wacker Drive.
Architects: Shaw, Metz, and Associates (1964)

Next to the North American Building is the glistening white marble tower of the United of America Insurance Building. This 41-story structure was once the tallest marble-faced commercial bulding in the world. It is featured as the last stop of another walk—No. 3, State Street.

City Parking Facility, "The Bird Cage"—
11 West Wacker Drive.
Architects: Shaw, Metz, and Dolio (1954)

Just across State Street, at the southwest corner of State and Wacker, is one of the city's parking structures, known to most Chicagoans as "The Bird Cage." Your first view will convince

Opposite, top left, Milton Horn sculpture on facade of parking facility. *Right,* 222 North Dearborn building. *Bottom,* Seventeenth Church of Christ, Scientist.

138

you that the nickname is appropriate. The cables used in the construction give the building its bird-cage appearance. There is a strong contrast between the windowless center portion shielding the elevators (which emphasizes the vertical) and the open wing for parked cars on each side (which strongly emphasize the horizontal). The only ornamentation on the windowless facade is a piece of sculpture by Milton Horn, "Chicago Rising from the Lake." The dark metal of the sculpture contrasts dramatically with the plain white expanse that it decorates. Its sudden projection from the wall may well suggest Chicago's rapid growth.

222 North Dearborn Building.
Architects: C. F. Murphy Associates (1969)

Next, at Dearborn Street, is the former Blue Cross-Blue Shield Building. This heavy, beige-colored concrete structure, with its cantilevered floors, is described in Walk No. 4, Dearborn Street.

◘ City of Chicago Central Office Building (formerly Reid, Murdoch and Company Building)—
325 North LaSalle Street.
Architect: George C. Nimmons (1913)

West of Clark Street, still on the river front, is the City of Chicago Central Office Building, operated by the city of Chicago as a Traffic Court, with offices for city departments. Formerly the Reid Murdoch and Company Building, it was bought by the Monarch Foods Company, who leased it to the city. This is a clean, straightforward structure in red brick—its 320-foot-long facade of 8 stories topped off at the center with a prominent clock tower of 4 more stories. The brick work and contrasting terra-cotta accents give this structure a pleasing effect.

Merchandise Mart—Merchandise Mart Plaza (about 350 North Wells).
Architects: Graham, Anderson, Probst and White (1930)

One block west of the Central Office Building, between Wells and Orleans, where the CTA elevated lines cross the river, looms the massive Merchandise Mart. Although its architectural design is hardly as distinguished or praiseworthy as it was thought to be at the time of construction, this building is nevertheless not to be passed by. For many years the largest building in the world, the Merchandise Mart is still the world's largest wholesale marketing center and one of its 5 largest commercial buildings. Its floor space amounts to about 4 million square feet, where more than 5,000 manufacturers and designers display their products, chiefly furniture and other home furnishings. Twice a year wholesale buyers from all across the country come to Chicago to the home furnishings show that is held here.

Opposite the entrance to the Merchandise Mart on the river side of the plaza stand tall columns with the busts of those who have been selected as the "Merchandise Mart Hall of Fame": Julius Rosenwald, Frank Winfield Woolworth, Marshall Field, John Wanamaker, George Huntington Hartford, and Edward A. Filene, Robert E. Wood and A. Montgomery Ward. Ward's bust was carried out by sculptor Milton Horn and added to the plaza in 1972.

The Mart is owned by the Joseph P. Kennedy family, who bought it in 1945 from the Marshall Field family.

Though not open to the public, the Merchandise Mart offers a 1½ hour guided tour daily, leaving the lobby every 30 minutes, between 9:30 A.M. and 3:30 P.M. Adults, 50¢; children under 12, free. (Closed Saturdays and Sundays.)

1. Union Station
   210 S. Canal St.

2. 222 Riverside Plaza Building
   222 S. Riverside Plaza

3. Mercantile Center
   Jackson & Canal sts. &
   the Chicago River

4. 10 Riverside Plaza Building
   10 S. Riverside Plaza

5. Illinois Bell Telephone and
   American Telephone and
   Telegraph Building
   10 S. Canal St.

6. Chicago and North Western
   Railway Station
   500 W. Madison St.

7. Riverside Plaza Building
   2 N. Riverside Plaza

8. Kemper Insurance Building
   20 N. Wacker Dr.

9. Morton Salt Building
   110 N. Wacker

10. Illinois Bell Telephone
    Building
    225 W. Randolph St.

11. Hartford Plaza Building
    100 S. Wacker

12. 150 South Wacker Drive
    Building

13. U.S. Gypsum Building
    101 S. Wacker Dr.

14. Harris Trust and
    Savings Bank
    Franklin & Monroe sts.

15. The Northern Building
    Wacker Dr. & Adams St.

16. Sears Tower
    Wacker Dr.-Jackson Blvd.-
    Franklin & Adams sts.

17. 300 Wacker Building
    300 S. Wacker Dr.

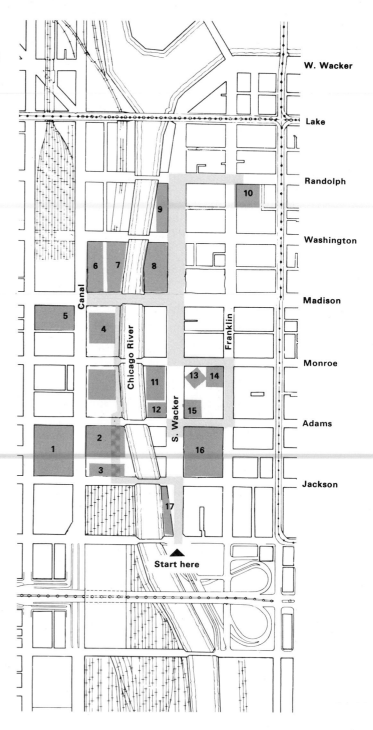

Walk · 12

WACKER DRIVE : SOUTH-NORTH

WALKING TIME: About 1 hour.   HOW TO GET THERE: Walk south to Van Buren Street (400 S), and take a westbound CTA bus No. 126 (Jackson). Get off at Wacker Drive (348 W).

Wacker Drive, which here runs north and south, intersecting Van Buren (and continuing south 2 blocks as far as Harrison) is the same street you followed from east to west in Walk No. 11. The change in direction took place just after the end of that walk, where Wacker Drive follows a bend in the Chicago River and then turns directly south, at Lake Street, to follow the South Branch of the river.

Daniel Burnham, in his plan for Chicago back in 1909, saw Wacker Drive as part of a ring road system surrounding the Loop. Incidentally, Burnham also, in his plans nearly 60 years ago, anticipated the need for a highway comparable to the Eisenhower Expressway. With this plan in mind, the architects constructed the Central Post Office—2 blocks south and across the river from where this walk starts—with a large opening in the center at ground level. Consequently, the Eisenhower Expressway passed through and under the building with a minimum of inconvenience to the Post Office.

This section of the city is sometimes referred to as the Gateway area, since Wacker Drive and the South Branch of the Chicago River are in fact a gateway to the near west. South Wacker Drive, formerly the wholesale garment section of the city, lost hundreds of tenants to the Merchandise Mart when that building was constructed, in 1930 (see Walk No. 11). This change forecast in a way the Drive's redevelopment. The city government and area businessmen are now carrying out a gigantic urban renewal program in this area, extending to the Kennedy Expressway on the west.

143

Union Station—210 South Canal Street.
Architects: Graham, Anderson, Probst and White (1925)

The Union Station formerly covered two square blocks instead of one. The new Riverside Plaza Building lower level serves as the main corridors for entering and departing passengers. The cavernous, high-pillared waiting room still remains. It is one of the few remaining enormous railway terminals still in existence. The closing of the three, south loop railway terminals resulted in bringing several railway lines into Union Station. This concentration of terminal facilities leaves three operating terminals in Chicago. They are the Illinois Central and Northwestern in addition to Union.

222 Riverside Plaza Building—222 South Riverside
Plaza. Architects: Skidmore, Owings and Merrill (1972)

This 35-story building is the third office building to be constructed on air rights as part of the Gateway Center complex. The project's 80,000 square-foot plaza provides all pedestrian and vehicular entrances to the office tower and railroad. Below the plaza, a concourse level accommodates a new passenger terminal area and space for commercial development. The super-structure was a composite structural system consisting of structural steel interior framing and reinforced-concrete, exterior-bearing wall. The exterior of the building has a light-colored architectural concrete finish, complementing the present two steel buildings of the Gateway Center.

The Chicago Mercantile Exchange—
444 West Jackson Boulevard.
Architects: Skidmore, Owings and Merrill (1972)

This distinctive structure designed by a distinguished firm of architects is supported by four huge columns over air rights of the Union Station. Additional columns, criss-cross girders and walls, transfer the entire load of the roof and trading floor to the four main columns to make the column-free interior possible. The exterior dark green, heat-strengthened glass panels help articulate the entire structure.

The visitors' gallery is open on weekdays from 9 A.M. to 1:15 P.M. By all means, go inside and see the exciting trading

floor. The dimensions are 225 feet facing Jackson and 100 feet
facing the Chicago River. The height of the room is 60 feet.
The brokers can be seen trading in such items as live cattle,
pork bellies, eggs, live hogs, Milo hams and Lumber potatoes.

10 South Riverside Plaza Building—10 South Riverside
Plaza. Architects: Skidmore, Owings and Merrill
(still under construction, 1973)

Union Station and its concourse is now giving way to
further development of nearby Gateway Center. The first two
buildings, just north of the station's concourse exit ramp at West
Adams Street, were built on air rights over the tracks leading to
Union Station. They were the first buildings in the continuing
style of the Chicago school of architecture to extend the Loop

The Chicago Mercantile Exchange.

145

business center west of the Chicago River. The tinted glass and russet beams used in the buildings give them the functional exterior framework of the old school.

Surrounded by wide plazas, these two buildings look somewhat squat and bulky, despite their 20-story height—a characteristic dictated by construction over the tracks. The wide architectural spans, similar to those used by the same architects in the Chicago Civic Center, were made possible by the omission of any columns between the center service core and the exterior columns.

From Gateway Center Plaza along the river bank you have a distant view of two markedly different architectural neighbors back on the east side of the river—the Hartford Plaza Buildings, a contemporary expression of the still vibrant Chicago school of architecture, and its sculptured neighbor, the U.S. Gypsum Building, sitting gracefully askew on its site at Wacker and Monroe. You will have a close-up view of the two buildings later in the walk.

Illinois Bell Telephone and American Telephone and Telegraph Building—10 South Canal Street.
Architects: Holabird and Root (1971)

This 25-story building contains 18 floors of equipment plus 7 floors of office space. The architects had a problem designing and planning a structure that called for radiation protection, plus added structural strength to meet high lateral loads. Telephone equipment heat loads required special fan rooms on each floor.

This non-public building expresses itself by the enclosed equipment floor panels. The office floors have glazed infill panels replaceable with a continuation, when necessary, of the equipment floor-panel system.

The exterior colors are smooth buff concrete, matching hammered precast concrete infill panels, solar bronze glazing and bronze anodized aluminum louvers and glazing sections. It is noteworthy that this long-distance equipment building has received two merit awards.

Gateway Center.

147

Chicago and North Western Railway Station—
500 West Madison Street.
Architects: Frost and Granger (1911)

At the north end of Gateway Center Plaza, the massive columns of the Chicago and North Western Railway Station stand stolidly in their classic revival past. The station is one of the busiest commuter centers outside of New York City, and the management has converted the vast waiting room interior into a bright, attractive, and well-planned shopping gallery. A pedestrian way connects the station to the Riverside Plaza Building, which houses the railroad's offices and those of the Northeastern Illinois Planning Commission.

Riverside Plaza Building (formerly Chicago Daily News Building)—2 North Riverside Plaza.
Architects: Holabird and Root (1928)

As you cross the bridge over the river at West Madison Street, you can see the Riverside Plaza Building more fully, sitting sphinx-like as it was designed. With its setbacks and angles, the building is an excellent example of the Chicago skyscraper of that period.

Kemper Insurance Building (formerly Civic Opera House)—20 North Wacker Drive.
Architects: Graham, Anderson, Probst, and White (1929)

Another example of the Chicago skyscraper of the 1920's is the 45-story Kemper Insurance Building, an immense structure erected—at a cost of some $20 million—by Samuel Insull in 1929. Such an investment in that year by even the most sound and upright financier would have been a gamble; in this case it proved a disaster. The subsequent ruin of Insull's financial empire, to say nothing of the dubious methods he had used in building it up, unfortunately wiped out whatever pleasant associations Chicago might have had with the name of a man who loved opera. And the fact that the construction of this building led to the closing of the Auditorium Theatre (see Walk No. 1, Michigan Avenue: South) seemed to many Chicago opera-lovers a cause for resentment rather than gratitude. Herman Kogan has expressed this harsh but understandable judgment of Samuel Insull:

THE CIVIC OPERA HOVSE

More than any one man, he was responsible for the abandonment of the glorious Auditorium as a center of music and opera, because he had built, in an illogical place and with inferior acoustics, his own Civic Opera House at Wacker Drive and Madison Street.[4]

Whatever may be the sentiments toward Insull, however, his building has not gone empty. The current Lyric Opera of Chicago uses its auditorium, seating 3,500 people, just as two other opera companies did before the Lyric was formed. And hundreds of offices became available in the remainder of this mammoth structure.

Morton Salt Building—110 North Wacker Drive. Architects: Shaw, Metz, and Dolio (1961)

Located on the west side of Wacker Drive is the Morton Salt Building, extending from Washington to Randolph and from Wacker Drive to the Chicago River. This Indiana limestone structure, housing the main offices of the Morton Salt Company, affords all its offices and dining rooms a splendid view of the river.

Illinois Bell Telephone Building—225 West Randolph. Architects: Holabird and Root (1967)

The new building of the Illinois Bell Telephone Company, one block east of Wacker on Randolph, makes an effective use of vertical lines of marble and glass, dramatized at night by the interior lighting. This is a first-rate modern building.

Detail: Kemper Insurance building.

149

The exterior colors consist of white marble columns, black granite base, stainless steel trim, black spandrel panels, and smoke gray windows. Before you leave here, stop a moment to enjoy a delightful "rest-pocket" park just to the south of the IBT Building. The small park or plaza has been named Vail Court. The court design includes redwood benches, planters, and a small pool. On a warm day, every seat in this delightful setting is in use.

And just one block beyond this building, at Lake Street, comes the bend in Wacker Drive, where it follows the Chicago River to become the east-west street you traveled in Walk Number 11.

Hartford Plaza Building—100 South Wacker. Architects: Skidmore, Owings and Merrill (1961)

At Wacker Drive and Monroe Street, back south three blocks, are the two conflicting architectural neighbors already mentioned. On the southwest corner is the Hartford Plaza Building—of the Hartford Fire Insurance Company. In this the architects exaggerated the old Chicago school belief that the facade of a building should disclose its interior structural composition. The 21-story concrete skeleton here becomes more than a framework: it serves as sunshades for the interior and gives the building a constantly changing pattern of light and shadow during the day.

150 South Wacker Drive Building. Architects: Skidmore, Owings and Merrill (1971)

The Hartford Plaza has been extended to form a platform for this new 33-story office building by the same owners and architects of the Hartford Plaza Building. The lower concourse connects the two structures, and provides space for a complex of restaurants and shops.

This building's reinforced concrete bearing walls are clad in black granite. From the tenth floor down, alternate columns transfer vertical loads to spandrels of increasing depth to form the major column system at plaza level.

U.S. Gypsum Building—101 South Wacker. Architects: Perkins and Will Partnership (1961)

Directly across the street from the Hartford Fire Insurance

U.S. Gypsum building.

Building, on the southeast corner, is the U.S. Gypsum Building. Its placing on the building lot—at a 45° angle from the street lines—caused some consternation among the adherents of the Chicago school of architecture. Many of them felt this departure from the usual procedure insulted the unity of the buildings that Chicago school architects had developed in the Loop over more than half a century. Many others, however, admired the arrangement and the building itself, designed as a trademark to symbolize the company and the materials the company mines. For example, the triangular character of the plazas and the shape of the building itself (note that each of the 19 stories has 8 corners!) were designed to represent the crystalline mineral in gypsum. Thus the building and its placement were intended to suggest the corporate image of the company that owns it. The soberness of the slate panels and gray glass is offset by the columns of white Vermont marble, which also give the building a sweeping vertical effect.

Harris Trust and Savings Bank—Southwest corner, Franklin and Monroe streets.
Architects: A. Epstein and Sons, Inc. (1973)

Just west of the U.S. Gypsum Building is this 15-story structure that houses the bank's data processing computer support and computer-oriented departments. There is a complete banking facility on the main floor. The structure is a modular design with a tinted-glass and granite-exterior facade.

The Northern Building—Northeast corner, Wacker Drive and Adams Street.
Architects: The Perkins and Will Partnership (1973)

This 30-story structure has an attractive exterior that consists of granite-faced columns with an infill of anodized aluminum that frames the dark glass windows. The floor plan has an off-center utility core that is not visible from the street as is the similar floor plan of the Inland Steel Building.

The ground floor consists of drive-in bank facilities with an interior service area for pedestrians.

Sears Tower—Wacker Drive, Jackson Boulevard,
Franklin and Adams streets.
Architects: Skidmore, Owings and Merrill (1973)

Upon completion in 1974, Chicago's Sears Tower project will be
the largest private office complex in the world. The total
development will contain a gross area of 4.4 million square feet
with 101 acres of floor space. The daily population will
be 16,500 people.

Sears Tower, itself, will be the world's tallest structure,
enclosing 3.9 million gross square feet of floor area rising 109
stories or 1468.5 feet above Chicago City datum. It will occupy
a full city block of approximately 129,000 square feet.

The tower consists of a structural steel frame bolted in place on
the site. The fireproofed frame will be clad in a black aluminum
skin and bronze-tinted, glare-reducing glass. The exterior sloping
plaza will have a granite surface. The space below the plaza
will have three full levels containing facilities for food, including
a cafeteria and tenant storage space.

Provision has been made for a future entrance to the projected
subway station at Franklin Street so that pedestrians will be able
to enter the building directly from the station. Also planned
is a connection to the underground pedestrian walkway system
which may be extended from The Federal Center at Dearborn
and Adams streets, and eventually pass beneath the Chicago
River to connect to the railway stations to the west.

The Sears Tower will be 100 feet higher than the twin towers
of the New York World Trade Center and approximately 325 feet
higher than the roof of the John Hancock Center.

An observation platform near the top of the tower will afford
spectacular views of Chicago and environs.

300 Wacker Building—300 South Wacker Drive.
Architects: A. Epstein and Sons, Inc. (1971)

This unusually long and narrow structure's design was dictated
by a narrow site on the Chicago River. This is a 36-story office
tower of reinforced concrete, with a bronze anodized aluminum
curtain wall with bronze-tinted glass.

Walk-13

Behavioral Sciences
Building.

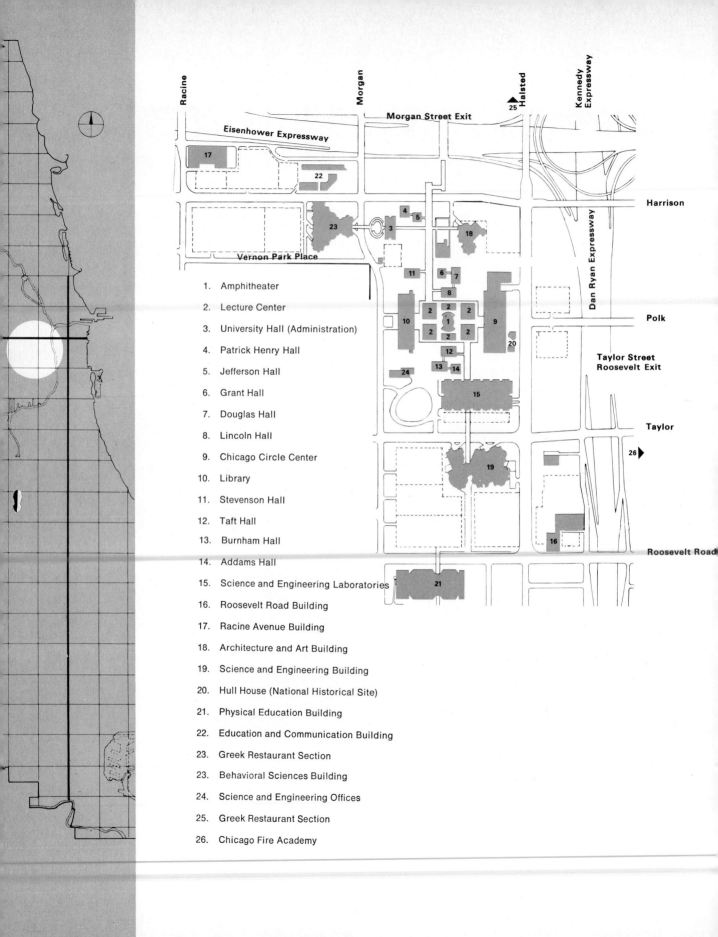

1. Amphitheater
2. Lecture Center
3. University Hall (Administration)
4. Patrick Henry Hall
5. Jefferson Hall
6. Grant Hall
7. Douglas Hall
8. Lincoln Hall
9. Chicago Circle Center
10. Library
11. Stevenson Hall
12. Taft Hall
13. Burnham Hall
14. Addams Hall
15. Science and Engineering Laboratories
16. Roosevelt Road Building
17. Racine Avenue Building
18. Architecture and Art Building
19. Science and Engineering Building
20. Hull House (National Historical Site)
21. Physical Education Building
22. Education and Communication Building
23. Greek Restaurant Section
23. Behavioral Sciences Building
24. Science and Engineering Offices
25. Greek Restaurant Section
26. Chicago Fire Academy

Walk · 13

CIRCLE CAMPUS OF THE UNIVERSITY OF ILLINOIS

WALKING TIME: 1 to 2 hours, depending on how much you "browse" among the buildings.
HOW TO GET THERE: Walk 3 blocks west of Michigan to Dearborn, enter the CTA Dearborn
Street subway, and board a westbound Congress Street train. Get off at the Halsted-Circle
Campus station. Or take any southbound CTA bus on Michigan, Wabash, or State that will
transfer you to a bus No. 7 (Harrison) at Harrison Street (600 S). (Inquire of the conductor.)
The Harrison Street bus will take you to Halsted Street (800 W).

Architects: Skidmore, Owings and Merrill (Walter A. Netsch, Jr.) (Phase I, 1965; Phase II, 1967; Phase III, 1968; Phase IV, 1971) Architects for the Student Union Building: C. F. Murphy Associates.

The modern urban university has emerged to serve space-age students who live with speed, movement, and change. One of the newest of these is the Circle Campus of the University of Illinois, less than a mile southwest of Chicago's Loop. It has replaced the "temporary" headquarters of the University's Chicago undergraduate division, which operated for nearly 20 years (1946-1965) at Navy Pier (see Walk No. 9, Lake Shore Drive). The new location is far more accessible to students from every part of the Chicago area. Featured specifically as a "commuter college," with no resident students, Circle Campus is easily reached by every kind of transportation—commuter railroads bringing passengers to different stations in Chicago, city subway and buses, and of course private cars. (The college provides extensive parking space.)

The name Circle Campus itself reflects the mood of modern traffic, for it comes from the Circle Interchange, where the

157

Eisenhower, Kennedy, and Dan Ryan expressways exchange an unending flow of moving horsepower. But the name alone was not the only contribution of the freeways to the campus. In this constant stream of vehicles the architect, Walter A. Netsch, Jr. (a partner in Skidmore, Owings, and Merrill, who had already designed the Air Force academy in Colorado) must have seen the elements of his campus design—power, dash, energy, freedom of movement, and strength. These ingredients he mixed on his drawing board and fit the entire campus plan around a centerpiece that epitomizes the university concept of all times—communications.

This centerpiece is an open amphitheatre, surrounded by a powerful grouping of buildings in concrete, glass, and brick. Netsch planned this as an open forum, to be used for drama, debate, "outside classrooms," discussions, political rallies, or just socializing. The amphitheatre is especially spectacular because it descends from the center of the Great Court, which constitutes the common roof of 6 lecture buildings. Here are open elevated walkways from which students may enter the other major buildings of the campus at the second-story level or go down to the lower-level walkways through the amphitheatre. These 2-level granite walkways give Circle Campus a character far removed from the green lawns of traditional college campuses. And so does the design of the campus buildings outside the Great Court—the Student Union, library, and engineering buildings with their strong concrete skeletons and skins of brick and glass.

The campus is almost entirely completed. Graduate and undergraduate facilities have been added south of Taylor Street including sciences and engineering buildings. The behavioral sciences building, directly west of University Hall, was completed in 1969. The campus will be totally completed in 1975. Fully developed, the University of Illinois' $200 million Chicago branch will enroll 25,000 to 30,000 students on its 125-acre campus.

Presiding over the Great Court with its forum and the surrounding group of buildings, garden courts, and lecture centers is University Hall, a 28-story administration and faculty office

University Hall.

158

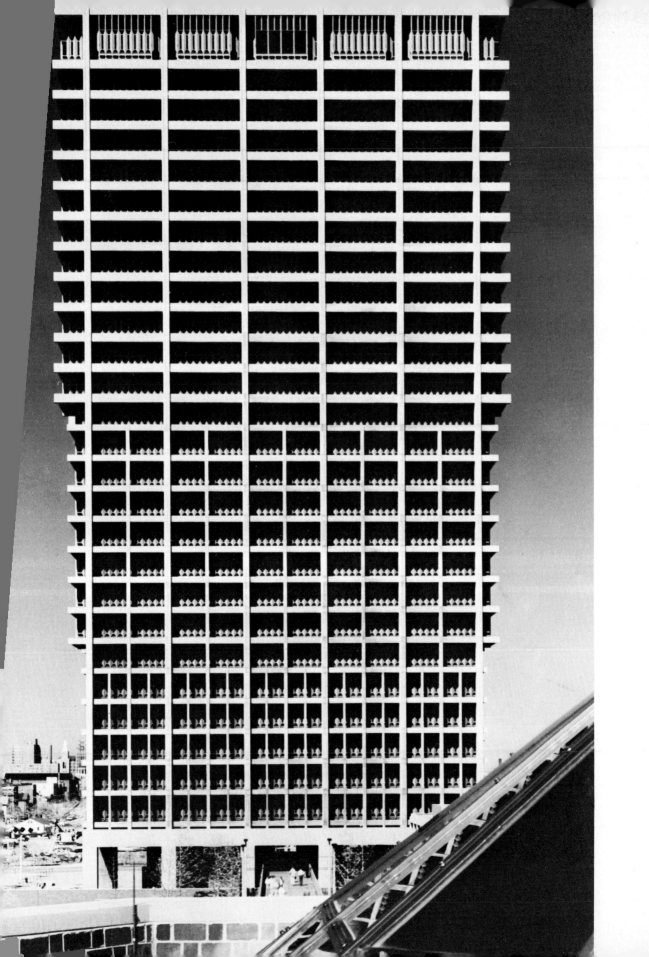

building. This high-rise structure spreads in width as it stretches skyward—it is 20 feet wider at the top than at the base—so that the upper floors provide more space. Narrow, almost Gothic windows squeeze between concrete channels to limit distracting outside views and unnecessary exterior light.

The Circle Campus, developed on a former slum that was Chicago's "Port of Entry" for thousands of immigrants, retains an important link to the past—the 2 buildings of the original Hull House, now a National Historic Landmark, resting quietly and with dignity near the main campus entrance on Halsted Street. These buildings perpetuate the saga of Jane Addams and her dedicated aides in helping the forefathers of many of today's students adjust to their new urban environment.

The University of Illinois has rehabilitated and restored the original 2 structures. Jane Addams' furniture and fixtures are in their proper places, so that here you have a delightful example of the architecture and furnishings of a late 19th-century Chicago residence, reflecting the individual qualities of the extraordinary, indomitable woman who once lived and worked there. As a

Above, Hull House.

160

museum, they now make a fitting memorial to Jane Addams.

In some ways it is unfortunate that this beautiful restoration stands on its original site, for it is now dwarfed by the massive contemporary structures around it. But in the controversy about the siting of the University's new campus (which necessitated taking over a whole block of the Hull House complex) sentiment for keeping the original Hull House at its original location was so great that respecting this wish of the area's residents became a necessary part of the pragmatic compromise.

Although the University of Illinois now occupies the site once used by the world-renowned Hull House, Jane Addams' work goes on in other parts of the city. The programs of Hull House continue at various locations—including a Spanish Outpost at 3352 North Halsted, a community house at 500 East 67th Street, and several theater groups.

You can tour Circle Campus by yourself at any time. Or you may arrange for guided tour service (preferably on one week's advance notice) by calling 663-8686 or by writing the Campus Information and Tour Center, Box 4348, Chicago 60680. Parking lots with

161

coin-operated gates, on the east, south, and west edges of the campus, are available to visitors.

Not only the architectural student will be fascinated with Circle Campus. Any adult—or child, for that matter—will be thrilled by the scale of this vast complex, reminiscent of the Mayan pyramids, temples, and courtyards, yet definitely modern in design and function.

In 1970, the campus was extended south of Roosevelt Road and north of Harrison Street and the total acreage was increased from 106 to 120. The current enrollment is 20,000 students, making it the largest commuter campus in the nation. Students are offered a choice of more than 2,000 courses for undergraduate credit and more than 1,400 for graduate credit. It should be noted that just one-half mile west are the University's Medical, Dental, and Pharmaceutical Colleges located on the West Side Medical Center Campus.

The southernmost building on campus is the Physical Education Building located on Roosevelt Road between Morgan and Newberry streets. Its primary feature is an Olympic-size swimming pool, complete with diving facilities and underwater windows for viewing swimming and diving. It is the largest indoor swimming pool in the Midwest. The basketball court will hold more than 3,000 persons on the movable bleachers.

The Education and Communication Building is located on Harrison Street between Morgan and Congress Parkway. This structure houses the College of Education, departments of speech, theatre, and music. The Jane Addams Graduate School of Social Work is also housed here. One feature is a small theatre that can be converted for any type of show use— proscenium, theatre-in-the-round, or motion picture.

In contrast with these contemporary buildings is the Maxwell Street Market, only 2 blocks south of the south end of the campus. There is an Old-World atmosphere about this outdoor marketplace, where almost anything can be purchased, especially on Sunday.

Another contrast is at the north end of the campus, just across the Eisenhower Expressway. A small section of shops clustered

Architectural and Art Laboratories.

together and known as "Greek Town" has restaurants that feature belly dancers as well as those that provide other kinds of atmosphere in addition to the good food.

Chicago Fire Academy—
558 West DeKoven Street (1100 S).
Architects: Loebl, Schlossman, and Bennett (1960)

Walk 2 blocks north to Roosevelt Road where you may board a bus going east one mile to Canal Street, where you then walk 2 blocks to DeKoven and the Fire Academy. In front of the red brick Academy stands a large bronze sculptured flame, by the Chicagoan Egon Weiner, expressing the fury of the Fire of 1871, which supposedly started on this very spot. The Fire Academy was built on the site of the old house and barn of the O'Leary family, whose famous cow is alleged to have kicked over a lantern and thus set off the whole catastrophe.

A 30-minute introduction to how our present-day fire fighters are trained for service in the Chicago Fire Department is available in a tour of the Academy—an experience that always has a fascination for everyone, especially young people whether fire buffs or not. Tours by appointment: 9:00 A.M. to 3:00 P.M. Telephone: 744-4000.

While you are at the Academy, don't miss the exhibit of photographs in the main lobby or the ancient (1835) hand-pumper fire engine.

Great Court with Science and Engineering Offices in background.

164

Walk-14

Meigs Field
Terminal looking
toward Soldier Field
across Burnham
Harbor.

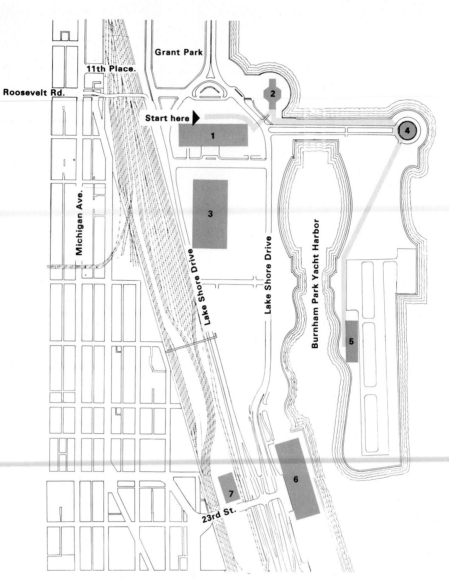

Grant Park

11th Place.

Roosevelt Rd.

Michigan Ave.

Start here ▶

1

2

3

4

Lake Shore Drive

Lake Shore Drive

Burnham Park Yacht Harbor

5

6

7

23rd St.

1. Field Museum of Natural History
   Lake Shore Dr. at Roosevelt Rd.

2. John G. Shedd Aquarium
   1200 S. Lake Shore Dr.

3. Soldier Field
   425 E. 14th St.

4. Adler Planetarium and Astronomical Museum
   900 E. Ashsah Bond Dr.

5. Merrill C. Meigs Field Passenger
   Terminal
   Outer Dr. at 14th St.

6. McCormick Place On-The-Lake
   East 23rd St. & the Lakefront

7. McCormick Inn
   Lake Shore Dr. at 23rd St.

Walk · 14

BURNHAM PARK : MUSEUMS

WALKING TIME: 1 hour or less for outside viewing. (For inside visits each museum rates a separate trip. You will want to spend anywhere from one hour, say, at the Shedd Aquarium to whole days at the Field Museum. Hours when the museums are open vary somewhat and sometimes change from summer to winter. Between the hours 10:00 A.M. and 4:00 P.M. you will find them all open (except on holidays). It is wise, however, to consult each museum separately just before making your visit.   HOW TO GET THERE: You can reach the Burnham Park area over the foot bridges from Michigan Avenue at 11th Street, or through Grant Park along Columbus Drive and the adjacent formal gardens. Or you can take a southbound CTA ''shuttle'' bus, No. 149 (Michigan-State-Wacker), on State Street, which will take you directly to the Field Museum at the north end of Burnham Park. If you drive, you will find the best parking near Adler Planetarium or Soldier Field.

On Chicago's lakefront just south of Grant Park is a great concentration of museums and other public facilities. Still just a portion of Lake Michigan in 1910, it was filled with land and developed in accordance with the Burnham Plan of 1909. Construction of the Field Museum was started in 1911, Soldier Field in 1924, Shedd Aquarium in 1929, and Adler Planetarium in 1931. In 1933-34 this stretch of land reclaimed from the lake was the site of Chicago's Century of Progress exposition and a few years later of its Railroad Fair. Here too are Meigs Field airstrip and McCormick Place, the nation's busiest convention center, now rebuilt after destruction by fire.

On the west bank of Burnham Harbor (east of the Drive, opposite Soldier Field) is a single marble column of the Roman composite style. It commemorates the 1933 flight of several Italian amphibious airplanes flown here to honor Chicago's Century of Progress exposition. They brought the monument with them— in sections—as a gift from the Italian government. Leader of the group was Marshall Italo Balbo, for whom Balbo Drive was named.

Field Museum of Natural History—
Lake Shore Drive at Roosevelt Road.
Architects: Graham, Burnham, and Company;
Graham, Anderson, Probst, and White (1911-1919);
architects for the new Stanley Field Hall (interior):
Harry M. Weese and Associates (1968)

Start at the Field Museum, pausing on the long flight of steps for a glorious view of Chicago's downtown skyline. Field Museum was built—and partly maintained—with funds donated by Marshall Field I, the founder of Marshall Field and Company, then by other members of his family and other Chicago families interested in its program. The huge structure is a variation of the Fine Arts Building in Jackson Park (now the Museum of Science and Industry—See Walk No. 19), which was built in 1893 for the Columbian Exposition and used as the Field Museum from then until 1920, when the Field collections were moved to their present quarters.

Part of the celebration of the Field Museum's 75th anniversary, in 1968, has been a redesigning of Stanley Field Hall—the

Field Museum of Natural History.

tremendous entrance space on the first floor, named for a
nephew of Marshall Field closely identified with the
museum's development.

The Field Museum is a distinguished showcase for prehistoric
and recent cultures, with a staff of scholars behind the scenes
who are constantly extending knowledge as the result of their
investigations in the fields of anthropology, botany, geology, and
zoology. Though they are classified according to these four areas
of knowledge, the exhibits seem endless in variety—from the
enormous stuffed African elephants and dinosaur skeletons in
Stanley Field Hall, and corridor after corridor of dioramas
showing hundreds of stuffed animals in their native habitats, to
the life-sized figures of prehistoric man in *his* environment;
from one of the world's finest collections of Oceanic art and of
American Indian art and artifacts, to displays of meteorites,
rare gems, and flowers. The Museum is in fact filled with
priceless specimens.

Adults $1.00; children 6-17, students, and senior citizens, 35¢;
families $2.50; admission free on Friday.

John G. Shedd Aquarium—
1200 South Lake Shore Drive.
Architects: Graham, Anderson, Probst, and White (1929)

Directly east of the Field Museum, reached by a pedestrian tunnel under the Outer Drive, is the Shedd Aquarium, built with funds donated by John G. Shedd, former chairman of the board of Marshall Field and Company. Far smaller than the Field Museum, this is nevertheless the world's largest building devoted exclusively to living specimens of aquatic life. A white marble structure with bronze doors, it has a simple Doric design, another example of the neo-classical tendency that inspired the style of so many public buildings of the time.

In more than 130 tanks of water the Shedd Aquarium displays some 7,500 living specimens, representing 350 different species of marine and fresh-water creatures.

Adults $1.00; children 6-17, students, and senior citizens, 35¢; families $2.50; admission free on Friday.

Opposite top, John G. Shedd Aquarium. *Bottom,* Adler Planetarium. *Below,* one of 12 zodiac ornaments on the planetarium.

Soldier Field—425 East 14th Street.
Architects: Holabird and Root (1924).

The stadium, Soldier Field, with a seating capacity of about 106,000, was constructed as a war memorial. It is the site of the annual All-Star football game, special fireworks each Fourth of July, political rallies, and various other activities. The 100-foot Doric columns that surround Soldier Field harmonize its architecture well with that of the Field Museum, just to the north. In 1950 the north end of the stadium was closed by the Administration Building of the Chicago Park District.

In 1971, the stadium was remodeled to accommodate the Chicago Bears, professional football team. The remodeling consisted primarily in improving the seating and placing additional seating at the north end of the football field. In other words, temporary stands have been placed at the north end in order to give fans a closer view of the games. The original length of the field was almost twice the distance of a football field. A synthetic turf was also placed on the field.

170

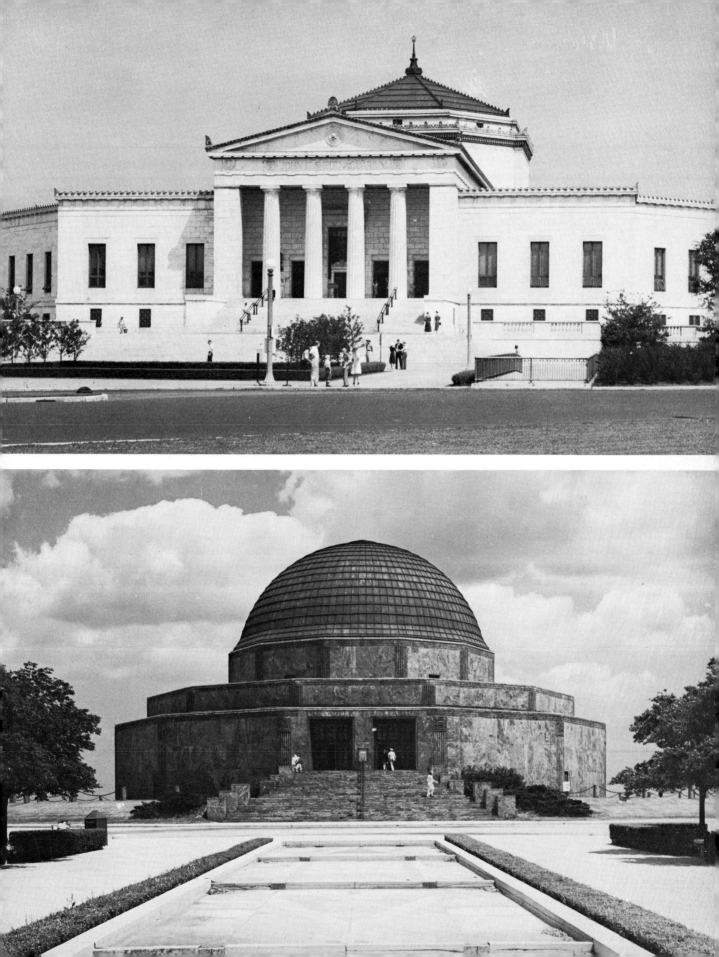

Adler Planetarium and Astronomical Museum—
900 East Achsah Bond Drive (about 1300 South).
Architect: Ernest A. Grunsfeld, Jr. (1931)

Directly east, about 2 city blocks away, is the Adler Planetarium, named for its donor, Max Adler, a former vice-president of Sears Roebuck and Company. Located on the lakefront at the end of a series of reflecting pools, this small granite structure with its planetarium dome is handsome and strong, devoid of all architectural superlatives.

The Astronomical Museum section contains one of the finest collections in the world of antique astronomical and mathematical instruments (second only to the collection in Oxford, England) as well as some of the most modern. Frequent 15-minute demonstrations of how some of these instruments work are given daily.

For anyone interested in stars and planets—and who of any age isn't?—the chief attraction of the Planetarium lies in its daily sky show inside the domed chamber in which the Zeiss projection instrument, also called a "planetarium," reproduces the natural night sky at any time or any place selected for fascinating explanations about what is going on up there. The lectures that accompany these projections of the sky make faraway scientific information simple and clear for anyone. For this sky show, which varies from month to month, a small fee is charged. Admission to the Planetarium itself and the other demonstrations is free.

McCormick Place On-the-Lake.

172

Merrill C. Meigs Field Passenger Terminal—
Outer Drive at 14th Street.
Architects: Consder and Townsend (1963)

The architects produced a delicate, well-planned building to
serve as the passenger terminal for Meigs Field. This lakefront
airstrip for light planes and helicopters is the largest downtown
space of its kind in the country.

McCormick Place On-The-Lake—
East 23rd Street and the Lakefront.
Architects: C. F. Murphy Associates (1971)

A new McCormick Place has been built on the site of the
previous building which was destroyed by fire in 1969. This new
structure has already demonstrated that it will outstrip its
predecessor as the world's busiest convention center. Gene
Summers was the architect in charge for C. F. Murphy
Associates. He had previously been an associate of Mies Van
der Rohe and the design clearly shows the Mies influence.

The basic requirements submitted to the architects were: 1) to
reconstruct the severely fire-damaged building with expediency;
2) to enlarge the prime exhibition area to 600,000 square feet;
and 3) to maximize the residual value of the existing structure.
The increase in building area had to be accomplished without
unduly removing valuable lakefront area. Special considerations
consisted of a complete fire-protection system that included
water reservoir, fire pumps, standpipe, sprinkler, and detection

173

systems. The design concept was to contain the two dominant functions of exhibit and theatre under a single unifying roof resting on a platform sheathed in masonry. A 75-foot cantilever of the roof affords protection to the pedestrian and vehicular passageways around the theatre unit and the truck dock area around the exhibit area.

Overall, the project contains approximately 600,000 square feet of exhibition area, a 4,300 seat theatre, 100,000 square feet of meeting rooms, a dignitary suite, and 42,000 square feet of restaurant and cafeteria facilities. A below-grade parking facility is located immediately south of the building for 2,000 cars.

Building materials consist chiefly of exposed face brick, painted concrete block, painted structural steel, terrazzo, and exposed concrete floors, plaster, and metal pan ceilings. The exterior curtain wall is made of painted steel framing with 7-by-8-foot gray, polished plate glass.

The building, or rather project, is a stunning and powerful statement that is a credit to the distinguished firm of architects as well as the many city officials who were involved.

McCormick Inn—Lake Shore Drive at 23rd Street. Architects: A. Epstein and Sons, Inc. (1973)

If you are exhausted from walking by this time, a good idea might be to cross over the bridge to the west and visit this new inn. This hotel is 25 stories, has 700 rooms and parking facilities for 500 cars. The tower is sheathed in bronze-tinted glass and has a brick base that houses the parking facilities.

Policeman's statue
commemorating the
tragic Haymarket
Riot.

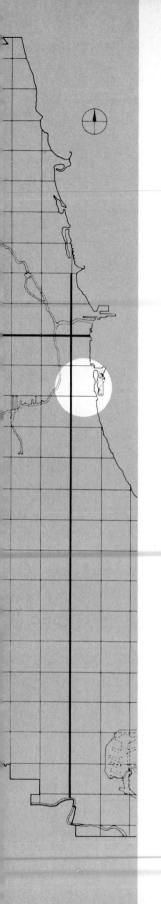

1. 630 South Wabash Ave.
   Formerly Wirt Dexter Bldg.

2. Chicago Police Department
   Headquarters
   1121 S. State St.

3. The Coliseum
   1513 S. Wabash Ave.

4. Glessner House
   1800 S. Prairie Ave.

5. Kimball House
   1801 S. Prairie Ave.

6. Keith House
   1803 S. Prairie Ave.

7. 1900 South Prairie Ave.

8. 2013 South Prairie Ave.

9. Second Presbyterian Church
   1936 S. Michigan Ave.

10. 2110 South Prairie Ave.

11. Raymond Hilliard Center
    2030 S. State St.

12. Chicago Housing Authority
    55 W. Cermak Rd.

Walk · 15

THE NEAR SOUTH SIDE :
South Wabash and Prairie Avenue

WALKING TIME: About 2 hours.   HOW TO GET THERE: Take a southbound CTA bus No. 4
(Cottage Grove) on Wabash Avenue, and get off at Harrison (600 S).

Just as the railroads were responsible for the original growth of
the near south side and again involved in its near demise, so will
the railroads play a significant role in its redevelopment.

Chicago was once the transfer point for all transcontinental
railroads. Anyone going from New York to California, for
instance, or Massachusetts to Oregon had to change trains here.
The 5 rail terminals in this part of the city provided millions of
transients each year, all eager to go shopping and sightseeing
between trains. It was thus that the section prospered for many
years. With the curtailment of railroad passenger service, this
enormous outside source of patronage dropped drastically, with
inevitable deterioration of the area.

The three railway passenger terminals formerly located here
have been consolidated with the Illinois Central, Union, and
Northwestern stations. There are about 400 acres of land
available for revitalizing this area. The city has plans for
developing a new-town-in-town here. This would include the
construction of apartment buildings, office buildings, and
light industrial plants.

◘ 630 South Wabash (formerly Wirt Dexter Building)
Architects: Adler and Sullivan (1887)

Once known as the Wirt Dexter Building, 630 South Wabash
is one of the simplest of Sullivan's famous structures, with none
of the elaborate ornamentation that he lavished, for instance,
on the Carson Pirie Scott building some 12 years later. The
narrow mullions in the central bay, with the slight moldings
crowning them, give a touch of distinction to the
otherwise unadorned facade.

177

Chicago Police Department Headquarters—1121 South State Street. City Architect Paul Gerhardt (1963)

Still farther south and one block west, on State Street, you come to the headquarters of the Chicago Police Department. This complex of buildings contains the world's most modern police communications system and a new police data processing system, installed in 1967. Here too are the crime detection laboratory, the central lockup, women's and children's courts, and administration office. Open to the public 24 hours a day. A self-tour sheet, supplemented by a taped message prepared for visitors by Superintendent of Police James Conlisk, are provided. For guided group tours—daily from 9:00 A.M. to 4:00 P.M.—reservations must be made, preferably by letter well in advance.

Before going upstairs, note the policeman's statue that commemorates the tragic incident that occurred on May 4, 1886, at Haymarket Square, near Halsted and Desplaines. The single policeman stands with his hand lifted, and carved in the stone below him are the words: "In the name of the people of Illinois, I command peace." These are supposedly the words spoken to a group of workingmen by the police captain who came to Haymarket Square with about 175 policemen to face some 2,000 workers who had come to protest police treatment the previous day at the McCormick works where a strike was in progress. In response to the police captain's words, the leader who was haranguing the group declared, "We are peaceable." But at that very moment someone from the crowd threw a bomb, killing several policemen and injuring many more.

Somehow this monument seems a sadly inadequate reminder of the tragic incident in Chicago's history and the equally tragic aftermath of panic in which four "anarchists" among the workers were tried, found guilty of murder, and executed, and three more were sentenced to life imprisonment. These three were later pardoned by Governor John Peter Altgeld.

The Coliseum—1513 South Wabash.
Architects: Frost and Granger;
engineers: E. C. and R. M. Shankland (1900)

Return to Wabash and continue south to the Coliseum, at 1513. The Coliseum has a colorful history as the location of many political conventions, horse shows, circuses, and roller skating derbies. The architectural design is unique—to say the least! The strange fortress-like sections on the Wabash Avenue side are a grim memorial to the Civil War—remains of a wall of Libby Prison, built in 1889 in Richmond, Virginia, and re-erected here. Of considerably greater architectural significance is the fact that 12 large, 3-hinged trusses cover the immense interior without supports. The use of iron and steel for these trusses was part of the development of the structural use of these metals here in Chicago.

◘ Glessner House—1800 South Prairie Avenue. Architect: Henry Hobbs Richardson (1886)

Continue south to 16th Street, walk east to Indiana, south on Indiana to 18th Street, and then one block east to Prairie Avenue. This street was once so far superior to its present run-down condition that it claimed some of the city's wealthiest families as residents—including such names as the Philip Armours, Clarence and Kate Buckingham, the Marshall Fields (both I and II), the W. W. Kimballs (of piano fame), the George Pullmans, and the M. M. Rothschilds.

According to the Chicago School of Architecture Foundation, which makes its home in the Glessner House, J. J. Glessner, a founder of the International Harvester Company, in 1885, commissioned the great architect Henry Hobbs Richardson to design a fitting house for him on Prairie Avenue, referring to the street as the finest residential street in Chicago.

It is appropriate that an architectural foundation should be housed in the only remaining example in Chicago of a design by one of the earliest and greatest of American architects. The Foundation has an architectural museum, library, and information center in the building. (For information call 326-1393.) Although this 35-room, fortress-like granite house seems a far cry from the delicate atrium houses of the architect Wong in Kenwood (see Walk No. 17), they have one feature in common: window placings of both are designed for privacy and quiet. All main rooms of the Glessner house face on a private courtyard, instead of on the street.

The citation from the Architectural Landmarks Commission reads:

> In recognition of the fine planning for an urban site, which

opens the family rooms to the quiet serenity of an inner yard;
the effective ornament and decoration; and the impressive
Romanesque masonry, expressing dignity and power.

In 1971, the Chicago Chapter of The American Institute of
Architects moved its offices to the Glessner House. This
appropriate move assures the Chicago School of Architecture
Foundation—the title holder—of a permanent tenant. The
Foundation also holds exhibits and conducts seminars and
walking tours in the downtown area. The time and starting place
of these tours can be determined by telephoning the Foundation
office at 362-1393.

Kimball House—1801 South Prairie.
Architect: Solon S. Beman (1890)

Across the street, at 1801 South Prairie, is the Kimball House,
designed like a Parisian mansion of the late 19th century. It is well
preserved and well maintained by its present occupant, Medalist
Publications, a division of Cahners Publishing Company.

Keith House—1803 South Prairie. Next door is the Keith
House, also built about 1890 but unfortunately *not*
well preserved or maintained.

1900 South Prairie—Farther south, a fine old mid-Victorian
3-story mansion, with mansard roof and classic columns
at the 2nd-floor porch.

2013 South Prairie—A 3-story house with a classic facade of
brick and stone trim. Note the Palladian motif at the 3rd-floor
window and the Ionic columns at the porch level.

2110 South Prairie—A 3-story limestone facade in Romanesque
style, with a large pediment at the roof, a design that
suggests the influence of Richardson.

This is all that remains of the once great wealth-laden avenue
of fine houses and mansions. In 1890 one of the grandest mansions
on this same Prairie Avenue was that of Marshall Field, built
for the multimillionaire merchant by Richard Morris Hunt, the
famous architect who had also designed the luxurious dwellings
of such New York millionaires as William H. Vanderbilt
and John Jacob Astor.

180

Nearly all the property in the area has been acquired by the Lakeside Press of R. R. Donnelley and Sons Company, who have constructed an enormous complex of buildings to print— among other things— *Time* magazine and many telephone directories.

Walk one block west to Michigan.

Second Presbyterian Church—
1936 South Michigan Avenue.

This fine old semi-Gothic South Side landmark church is a vestige of nineteenth century Chicago. Rebuilt in 1872 after being destroyed by the Chicago Fire in 1871, in what was then the city's finest neighborhood.

Glessner House.

The congregation was a wealthy and powerful one. Robert Todd Lincoln was on the Board of Trustees. Many of the wealthy packinghouse millionaires, such as the Swifts and Armours, and undoubtedly some of the nearby residents such as the Glessners, Pullmans and Marshall Fields attended here. Today the church, after being deserted by the membership, is slowly regaining congregants from the surrounding new high-rise apartments.

Note the stained glass windows of green pastoral scenes, lavender irises or fields of thick glass lillies. Eight of the windows were designed by the Tiffany Studios and two were done by British artist-designer Sir Edward Burne-Jones.

Before returning to Prairie, note the high-rise apartment buildings that house moderate-income families. These concrete towers were designed by Dubin, Dubin, Black and Moutoussamy and completed in 1971. They are the initial portion of a future Renaissance of the Near South of the Loop Area.

Raymond Hilliard Center—Chicago Housing Authority, 2030 South State Street (once the site of Chicago's infamous Levee). Architect: Bertrand Goldberg Associates (1967)

Continue south to Cermak Road (2200 S), and turn west to Michigan Avenue, where—at the northeast corner—you pass the *Michigan Hotel*, once the headquarters of Al Capone, vice lord of Chicago in the 1920's.

Now continue west 2 blocks to State Street to see the Raymond Hilliard Center of the Chicago Housing Authority: two 15-story cylindrical towers, containing 350 apartments for the elderly; and two 22-story semicircular concrete structures with open galleries, containing 350 apartments for families with children. The development also includes a community building, open-air theater, landscaped gardens, play lots, and parking areas. Apartments in the towers for the elderly are petal-shaped, extending from a central core that contains all the service facilities. This represents a breakthrough in Chicago, away from the institutional appearance commonly seen in older public housing projects. Some comparison with the Marina City design by the same architects (see Walk No. 4, Dearborn Street) is

182

inevitable and justified. Architect Bertrand Goldberg, continuing his exploration of scalloped forms (which began with Marina City) has designed a 4-building group that defies convention yet stays within the government's development costs ceiling. In all 4 buildings, major rooms are enclosed in load-bearing concrete walls, their irregular spacing controlled by the needs of the Center's program rather than structural considerations.

The land on which the Raymond Hilliard Center is built was once part of Chicago's most famous red light district, known as the Levee. The center of the Levee was the 2100 block of South Dearborn one block farther west, where for more than 10 years the Everleigh Club was managed by 2 beautiful sisters from Kentucky. According to Herman Kogan, the Everleigh Club was "the most affluent, the most expensive, and the best known" of all the bordellos in the area, in fact of all the world.[5] The Everleigh sisters believed in conducting a high-class establishment, catering to the "cultured." They introduced patrons to prospective partners in library, music room, or art gallery! Reform mayor Carter Henry Harrison the Younger for years had tried to bring pressure on the entire Levee. Finally, in 1911, the Everleigh sisters caused their own downfall by publishing an illustrated booklet advertising the comforts of their "Club." The mayor became sufficiently indignant at such open defiance from the ladies that he overrode all objections and actually closed down the "Club." The Everleigh sisters, who moved to New York with more than a million dollars that they had accumulated, could hardly have been crushed by the eviction. More than their departure, however, was needed before vice could be cleaned out of the Levee. "Extending down Dearborn Street from Nos. 2131-33," says Kogan, "were such other establishments as Ed Weiss' Saratoga Club, Georgie Spencer's, French Emma Duval's, Maurice Van Bever's Sans Souci."[6]

Chicago Housing Authority—55 West Cermak Road. Before leaving the area, note the central office building of the Chicago Housing Authority, at 55 West Cermak Road. This is the nerve center for the management and operations of approximately 40,000 public housing dwelling units—and the number is constantly increasing.

Walk-16

Crown Hall, Illinois
Institute of
Technology.

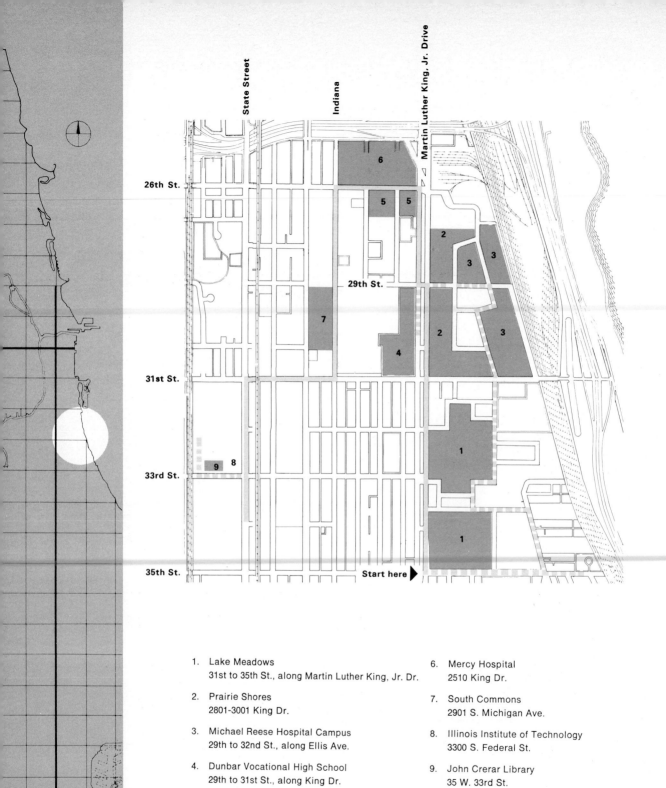

State Street

Indiana

Martin Luther King, Jr. Drive

26th St.

29th St.

31st St.

33rd St.

35th St.

6

5 5

2

3 3

7

2

3

4

1

9 8

1

Start here ▶

1. Lake Meadows
   31st to 35th St., along Martin Luther King, Jr. Dr.

2. Prairie Shores
   2801-3001 King Dr.

3. Michael Reese Hospital Campus
   29th to 32nd St., along Ellis Ave.

4. Dunbar Vocational High School
   29th to 31st St., along King Dr.

5. Prairie Courts
   26th St. & King Dr.

6. Mercy Hospital
   2510 King Dr.

7. South Commons
   2901 S. Michigan Ave.

8. Illinois Institute of Technology
   3300 S. Federal St.

9. John Crerar Library
   35 W. 33rd St.

▪▪▪▪ Alternate route

Walk · 16

THE NEW SOUTH SIDE :
Housing and Institutional Developments

WALKING TIME: About 2 hours.   HOW TO GET THERE: Take a southbound CTA bus No. 1 (Drexel-Hyde Park) or No. 2 (Hyde Park) on Michigan; or a No. 4 (Cottage Grove) on Wabash. Get off at 35th Street and Martin Luther King, Jr., Drive (formerly South Parkway). If driving, follow Lake Shore Drive south to 31st Street, then go west to King Drive and south to 35th Street.

Note the statue of a World War I black veteran at the intersection of King Drive and 35th Street.

Before setting out on the main part of this walk, go east on 35th Street to Cottage Grove (800 East) to note several items of historical interest:

1. *Stephen Douglas Monument and Tomb*, at 35th Street just east of Cottage Grove.
2. *St. Joseph's Carandelet Child Center*, across the street, which in 1864 was a soldiers' hospital for Civil War veterans.
3. *Groveland Park and Woodland Park*, just to the north, which *during* the Civil War was the site of a huge prison camp for captured Confederate soldiers. Around 1890, the peripheries of both these parks became settings for residential developments, which still are standing—some of the houses in good condition. Just to the north of the parks is a cluster of townhouses constructed in 1963, designed by the architects Pyskacek-Rosenwinkel. The land for this 1963 development was made available by the same urban renewal project that made Lake Meadows possible.

Lake Meadows—31st to 35th Street, along Martin Luther King., Jr., Drive. Architects: Skidmore, Owings, and Merrill (1956-60)

If you have taken the suggested walk to Cottage Grove, follow the broken line indicated on the map. The main walk starts with the Lake Meadows shopping center at 35th Street and Martin Luther King, Jr., Drive, from which you can continue north to the north boundary of Lake Meadows at 31st street.

187

Lake Meadows was planned especially to provide much-needed housing for middle-income families, and from its beginnings it has promoted interracial living. In addition to 10 sleek high-rise apartment buildings, with more than 2,000 living units, Lake Meadows has a shopping center, elementary school, medical center, and recreational space for both children and adults. Park space between the tall, glass-encased apartment buildings gives an effect of openness and freedom that is especially welcome here in the heart of a crowded city.

Lake Meadows replaced 100 acres of slums and started the revitalization of this badly deteriorated area, which early in the city's history had been considered Chicago's "Gold Coast." Though not a public housing project (Lake Meadows was financed by the New York Life Insurance Company), it can be called the first large urban renewal project in the country. Before federal urban renewal laws had been passed, Lake Meadows was developed under provisions of Illinois laws—the result of pressure from a coalition of organizations soon after World War II.

Prairie Shores—2801-3001 Martin Luther King, Jr., Drive. Architects: Loebl, Schlossman, and Bennett (1958-62)

Before the Lake Meadows undertaking was completed, a similar housing development called Prairie Shores was in progress just north of 31st along King Drive. Prairie Shores was developed by the board of trustees of Michael Reese Hospital, though it is now managed by a Chicago real estate firm. The primary purpose was to provide good nearby housing for the hospital's own medical staff and employees. It was hoped that rents could be kept low enough to permit families of moderate income to live side by side with faculty, students, and medical staff of various institutions in the area, so that the population of Prairie Shores would be mixed sociologically as well as racially.

About half the total plan is represented by 5 stunning apartment buildings, with some 1,700 living units. These high-rise, glass-encased structures with park space between are comparable in style to the Lake Meadows apartments. The buildings are set parallel to each other but at an angle to the Drive.

Michael Reese Hospital Campus—
29th to 32nd Street, along Ellis Avenue.
Architects: Schmidt, Garden, and Erikson (1897);
Loebl, Schlossman, and Bennett (since 1952)

The buildings of Michael Reese Hospital stretch along the east side of Ellis Avenue, to the east of Prairie Shores. The original building, more than 70 years old, remains the center of the huge complex. An entire campus of new buildings, devoted to special uses and connected by an underground pedestrian tunnel, has been constructed since 1952. The campus plan was developed by a planning staff directed by Reginald Isaacs, now professor of regional planning at Harvard University. Consultant for the plan was Walter Gropius, one of the founders of the Bauhaus in Germany and former dean of Harvard University's Graduate School of Design.

With about 1,000 beds, Michael Reese is the city's largest privately operated hospital. In addition to its clinical services, it carries on distinguished research in medical fields.

When the trustees of Michael Reese Hospital decided on developing Prairie Shores, they indicated in this way that they had also decided to remain in the present location as an anchor for the renewal area. The already successful—though incomplete—Lake Meadows development may have been a factor in both decisions.

Above, Prairie Shores.

189

Dunbar Vocational High School—
29th to 31st Street, along King Drive.
Architects: Holabird and Root (1960)

At the northern end of Lake Meadows, directly across King
Drive, is the Dunbar Vocational High School, a single building
stretching from 31st Street to 29th. This will probably serve
as the model for other vocational schools, for it is a well-planned
institutional building that seems to function with efficiency.

Prairie Courts—26th Street and King Drive.
Architects: George Fred and William Keck (1954)

Farther north on King Drive, spreading to 26th Street, is a public
housing project called Prairie Courts, which plays an important
role in the economic mixture of families in the area.

Mercy Hospital—2510 King Drive.
Architects: C. F. Murphy Associates;
Interior Designers: Mary Louise Schum
and Eileen Reilly Siemans (1968)

Just north of 26th Street, the new Mercy Hospital complex has
been developed. Mercy was the first hospital in Illinois, having
been granted its charter in 1851. Early patients included cholera
victims and Chicagoans injured in the Great Fire of 1871. It
now has a new 355-bed hospital in a high-rise building. This
handsome 14-story structure of white concrete and bronzed
glass has a unique design that is hard to describe, culminating
in an unexpected change of style at the top floor—the convent for
the hospital's sisters—which gives the impression of a very
wide cornice. The building carries almost a suggestion
of another culture; it might be a great Mayan temple
if the shape were different!

The interior design, however, has repeated reminders of the
religion that has inspired its services from the beginning.
These decorations too are unique, the work of a Spanish artist,
Nacio Bayarri, discovered by the interior designers (who
were assigned their responsibility as soon as construction of the
new hospital was started). On each floor, as you get off the
elevator, you will see a strikingly modern piece of sculpture or

Opposite, Mercy Hospital.

190

another kind of contemporary decoration. In the chapel one wall is made up entirely of a colorful mosaic mural, and another is a window wall decorated the whole length with lacy, welded-iron patterns representing—in a most unusual fashion— scenes in the life of Christ.

Mercy Hospital and Michael Reese together, dominating the "new South Side" (south of the Adlai E. Stevenson Expressway), constitute a large medical center for the area.

South Commons—2901 South Michigan. Architects: Gordon and Levin and Associates (1968)

Walking west to Michigan Avenue and back south to 29th, you come to South Commons, another renewal project. It has already introduced 1,800 housing units, planned not only for racial integration but for economic integration as well, and for families and persons of all ages. It expects eventually to provide space for some 35,000 people with middle incomes—both lower-middle and upper-middle. High- and low-rise apartment buildings and townhouses are combined with open spaces and a community center. The excellent site plan gives a feeling of spaciousness in spite of the fairly high population density. The green spaces and malls make this a delightful urban setting.

Illinois Institute of Technology—3300 South Federal Street. Architects: Ludwig Mies van der Rohe and Ludwig Hilberseimer; Friedman, Alschuler, and Sincere; PACE Associates (Planners, Architects, Consulting Engineers) (1942-58); Skidmore, Owings, and Merrill (1963)

Michigan and 30th Street mark the beginning of the Illinois Institute of Technology, which—like Michael Reese to the east and Mercy Hospital to the north—has become an anchor important to the successful renewal of the area. IIT itself has grown with the community; it now consists of technical colleges; departments of architecture and of city and regional planning; the Institute of Design, which was established in 1937 by Laszlo Moholy-Nagy as the successor to Germany's famous Bauhaus; a graduate school; and an evening division at which students can earn degrees in engineering. It now includes also the John Crerar Library, referred to separately below.

The 100-acre campus of IIT replaces what at the end of World War II was one of the city's worst slums, cleared through the machinery of urban renewal. The campus plan was prepared by Ludwig Mies van der Rohe and Ludwig Hilberseimer, both of whom had left the Bauhaus in Nazi Germany to come to this country in 1938. Mies, serving as dean of IIT's School of Architecture, designed many of the educational, administrative, and residential buildings, all of them low structures of severely simple design. Crown Hall is an exceptionally fine example of his work. The steel girders above the roof eliminate the need for interior columns, thus allowing uninterrupted space inside, which has flexibility of use. The proportions of the building are classic in symmetry and scale. If you can imagine Doric columns in front, you can "see" a Greek temple! The many designs by Mies on this campus—in the Administration Building, classroom buildings, chapel, Commons Building, and residence halls—all attest to his philosophy, "Less Is More."

It seems appropriate to the purpose of this engineering institute that several architects have been involved in its construction. Skidmore, Owings, and Merrill—who planned recent additions such as the handsome Crerar Library, gymnasium, and the Student Union Building—have followed the general design and spirit of Mies van der Rohe.

John Crerar Library—35 West 33rd Street.
Architects: Skidmore, Owings, and Merrill (1963)

After functioning for more than 40 years in a building at the northwest corner of Randolph and Michigan (architects: Holabird and Roche, 1920) and several years before that in the upper floors of Marshall Field's store, this famous library of science, technology, and medicine moved its incredible number of books and journals to its new building on IIT's campus, which will doubtless be its permanent home. Crerar is a "public" library established by a bequest of $2 million from its namesake. Though none of the books or journals may leave the building, they are always available to the public for use within the library itself.

Interestingly, this last move of the Crerar Library fulfills a request in John Crerar's will that it be "located in the South Division of the city inasmuch as Newberry Library will be located in the North Division."[7]

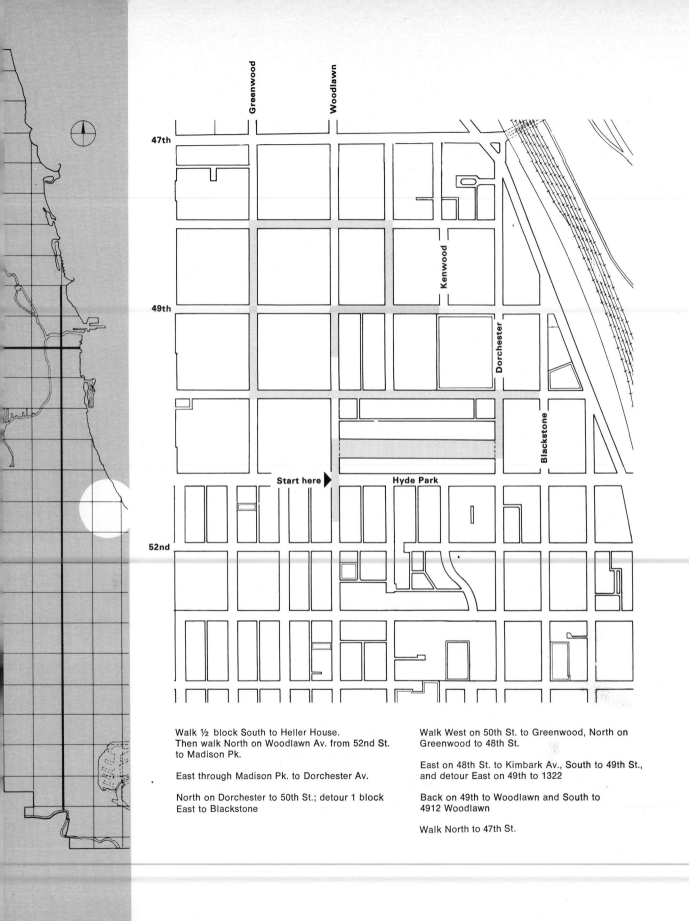

Greenwood

Woodlawn

47th

49th

Kenwood

Dorchester

Blackstone

Start here ▶

Hyde Park

52nd

Walk ½ block South to Heller House.
Then walk North on Woodlawn Av. from 52nd St.
to Madison Pk.

East through Madison Pk. to Dorchester Av.

North on Dorchester to 50th St.; detour 1 block
East to Blackstone

Walk West on 50th St. to Greenwood, North on
Greenwood to 48th St.

East on 48th St. to Kimbark Av., South to 49th St.,
and detour East on 49th to 1322

Back on 49th to Woodlawn and South to
4912 Woodlawn

Walk North to 47th St.

Walk · 17

KENWOOD-MADISON PARK

WALKING TIME: At least 2 hours.   HOW TO GET THERE: Take a southbound CTA bus
No. 1 (Drexel-Hyde Park) on Michigan Avenue. Get off at Hyde Park Boulevard (5100 S) and
Woodlawn Avenue (1200 E).

You are now at the south end of Kenwood, which lies just north
of the Hyde Park area. Here are some of the finest old mansions,
wooded gardens, and boulevards in the city. Among the houses
called to your attention here are a number that are famous because
of the architects who built them; these of course will be
identified. On the whole, however, houses have been selected for
their individual architectural quality, whether or not a
name-architect designed them.

At the turn of the century, Kenwood was actually a suburb
of Chicago, where many of the wealthiest families built
their estates. Residents have carried some of Chicago's most
noted—and notorious—names: Julius Rosenwald, Max Adler, Ben
Heineman, Harold Swift, and the tragically doomed families of
Leopold and Loeb. As the depression of the 30's struck some
of the owners and later, when the return of prosperity only
increased the costs of domestic help, as well as the difficulty of
securing it, the expenses of maintaining such mansions often
became too exorbitant to meet. Between much absentee
ownership and neglect of property by some who still lived there,
Kenwood was rapidly deteriorating. Houses were being sold
indiscriminately, and the usual flight of white residents at the
appearance of a few black families was threatening.

Citizens of Kenwood are to be thanked—and congratulated—
for saving the neighborhood. An interracial committee
of home-owners took the situation in hand. Dedicated to the
conviction that character and ability to maintain property, not
color of skin, determine whether or not a prospective purchaser
will be a desirable neighbor, they worked with real estate
dealers to establish a stable, well-integrated community. Naturally,

195

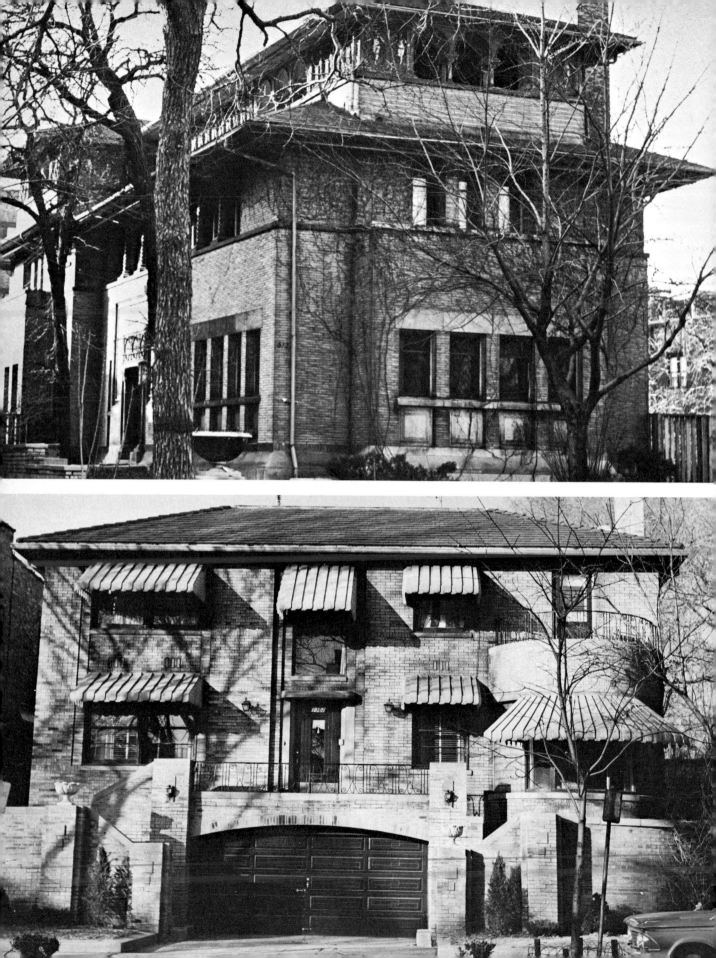

because of the kind of houses available, most Kenwood home-owners of both races have upper-middle or high incomes. For many years a local committee sponsored a "Kenwood Open House" weekend each spring, when outsiders were invited to call at a specified number of homes and witness the success of this undertaking.

In Kenwood, too, as in Hyde Park, urban renewal has been responsible for some effective rehabilitation and redevelopment. Two citizens organizations that cooperated actively with the city government in recent changes are the Hyde Park - Kenwood Community Conference and the South East Chicago Commission. Other groups interested in Kenwood's redevelopment are the Amalgamated Clothing Workers Union and the Lake Village Development Corporation, which are planning hundreds of new townhouses and apartments for middle-income, racially integrated tenants.

At Lake Park Avenue and Hyde Park Boulevard, the city has constructed a new *Kenwood High School* for the community, replacing the old inadequate building, which used a cluster of mobile vans for the additional classrooms needed. The new structure was completed in 1969. *(Architects: Schmidt, Garden, and Erikson)*

◘ Heller House—5132 South Woodlawn Avenue. Architect: Frank Lloyd Wright (1897)

This 3-story brick house is an early example of Wright's work. It seems at first quite unlike the "Prairie House" that he designed 12 years later, for the compact upright lines of the first 2 stories contrast markedly with the widespreading horizontal lines of the Robie House (see Walk No. 18, Hyde Park - University of Chicago). Yet the widely projecting eaves and the openness of the third story suggest some of the later design.

Note the molded plaster frieze at the top of the building— by the sculptor Richard Bock.

Madison Park—Between Hyde Park Boulevard and 50th Street, running from Woodlawn to Dorchester.

Cross Woodlawn at Hyde Park Boulevard (51st Street), and walk north about half a block to the entrance of Madison Park.

Opposite, top, Heller House. Bottom, 1302 East Madison Park.

197

Madison Park is not a park in the usual sense of the word. It is, instead, a small residential section of Kenwood that seems to belong completely to itself. As you pass through the large iron gate that tells you the name and the fact that it is private, you see a long stretch of green, with trees and mounds, bordered on each side by a street with a continuing line of houses, occasionally an apartment building, in varying styles, most of them built probably 2 generations ago. The minute you are inside the gate, you are overwhelmed by the almost rural quiet of the place. Madison Park stretches from east to west 3 blocks with no north-south streets coming through, and east-west traffic from outside is minimal. The strip of park down the center is used only by the residents—usually a few children playing happily and perhaps an adult lounging on the grass reading. Despite the city-like rows of houses close together on each side, Madison Park does indeed have much of the small-village atmosphere about it. It is populated by families of many races and ethnic origins, who have cooperated to maintain the beauty and serenity of this delightful area.

1239-41-43 East Madison Park—Architect: Y. C. Wong (1967)
At the west end of Madison Park, on the south side of the street, stop at 1239-41-43 and see 3 handsome new townhouses constructed in 1967, designed by Y. C. Wong. These are among the very few newly constructed buildings in the Park, but they seem to blend very well with their neighbors. A yellow brick wall shields lovely private gardens from the view of passersby. The horizontal lines of the stucco upper wall and glass windows give the north facade an appearance of strength. The south facade, which faces Hyde Park Boulevard, has garages conveniently located just below the living room terraces.

1302 East Madison Park (about 1925)—Across the street, at 1302, is a charmingly unconventional yellow brick apartment building. The pitched roof and garage below the main entrance suggest the style of many buildings in San Francisco. Other features that give this building individuality are stairs to the first-floor apartments on each side of the garage and attractive metal grillwork across the balcony of the main entrance.

1366-80 East Madison Park—Architect: Y. C. Wong (1961)
Farther down on the same side, at 1366-80, you come to 8

stunning townhouses well known in the Chicago area—the architect Wong's "Atrium Houses." The exterior walls have no windows whatever, the outside light for all the rooms coming from an interior open court, or atrium. The complete privacy and quiet provided by this arrangement are considered a decided advantage in urban living. If you are fortunate, one of the owners may show you around his home.

Farmer's Field—50th to 49th Street and Dorchester to Kenwood Avenue. With the Atrium Houses you have reached the east end of Madison Park, which is Dorchester Avenue. Walk north on Dorchester to 50th Street. At the northeast corner, to your right, stands the Church of St. Paul and the Redeemer, 2 Episcopal churches recently merged, in a relatively new building constructed after the old St. Paul's was damaged by fire. To your left, at the northwest corner of Dorchester and 50th Street, you will see the sign "KENWOOD PARK." This stretch of plain green "pasture" covering an entire block has long been known to Chicagoans as "Farmer's Field." Although the history of Farmer's Field seems somewhat hazy, a house-owner on 50th Street says that a resident of days gone by told him a cow used to graze there every day as recently as the 1920's. A downtown bank is credited with having bought the property with the commendable intent of keeping it unchanged.

1351-1203 East 50th Street—Now walk on 50th Street and note the row of townhouses extending from *1351 to 1319*. All are well-maintained houses about 75 years old. Farther on, at *1243 East 50th*, is an older house, built about 1875, a charming gray house with white trim, set in a garden. At *1220*, across the street, is an enormous red brick Georgian house with white door, shutters, and trim. The windows and entrance are in good scale. At *1229*, back on the south side of the street, is a gray frame house with very high ceilings, which has an appearance of great dignity and serenity. At *1207 and 1203* are 2 red brick, 2-story townhouses constructed as recently as 1965—designed by Grunsfeld and Associates. Set well back from the street, they blend perfectly with their older neighbors.

4940-4929 South Greenwood Avenue—Continue west to Greenwood and enjoy the beauty of the many old trees, fine shrubbery, and delightful front yards. These provide much of the charm of the area, and Kenwood home-owners are determined to keep it that way. The majority of the houses along Greenwood were built between 1910 and 1925.

Walk north on Greenwood and stop at *4940,* on the west side of the street. This is a 3-story, red brick mansion of collegiate Gothic design. Unusual Gothic ornamentation surrounds the front windows and doors. At the rear are a tremendously large yard and garden, and a garage with living quarters above.

Be sure to note the mansion across the street at *4939 Greenwood*—an enormous red brick house with quoins at the corners and high-pitched roof. Doric pilasters adorn the entrance porch. This was the home built by Max Adler, of Adler Planetarium fame (see Walk No. 14, Burnham Park: Museums).

And a bit farther north, at *4935,* is a heavy, 3-story building with semicircular facade extending the entire height. Note the stone columns at the entrance porch and the ornament on the pediment at the roof line. At *4935½ South Greenwood*, to the rear, is a 2-story coach house of similar design and material as 4935. Remodeled in 1963, it contains new kitchen, fireplace, and paneled study. It is typical of many of the old coach houses in the area.

At *4929 South Greenwood* is a well-proportioned red brick house of Georgian design. The white wood trim is in good scale with the rest of the facade.

◨ **Magerstadt House**—4930 South Greenwood. Architects: George W. Maher (1906); Arthur Myhrum (1968)   The Magerstadt House, on the west side of the street, was designed by a former assistant of Frank Lloyd Wright and quite naturally reflects to some extent Wright's style—the long plan and side entrance, for instance, and the wide overhang. On the other hand, Wright would surely not have used the two unnecessary pillars that pretend to support the porch roof. And the building as a whole is more massive than most of Wright's. The present occupants of the house completed its rehabilitation in 1968. The interior lighting, bathrooms, and kitchen have been completely remodeled; the woodwork has been restored and repainted. In general, the interior has a new glow, making this a truly delightful home.

Opposite, top left, 4935 Green-wood.*Top right,* Stained glass poppy detail in door of the Magerstadt House. *Bottom,* 4857 Greenwood.

200

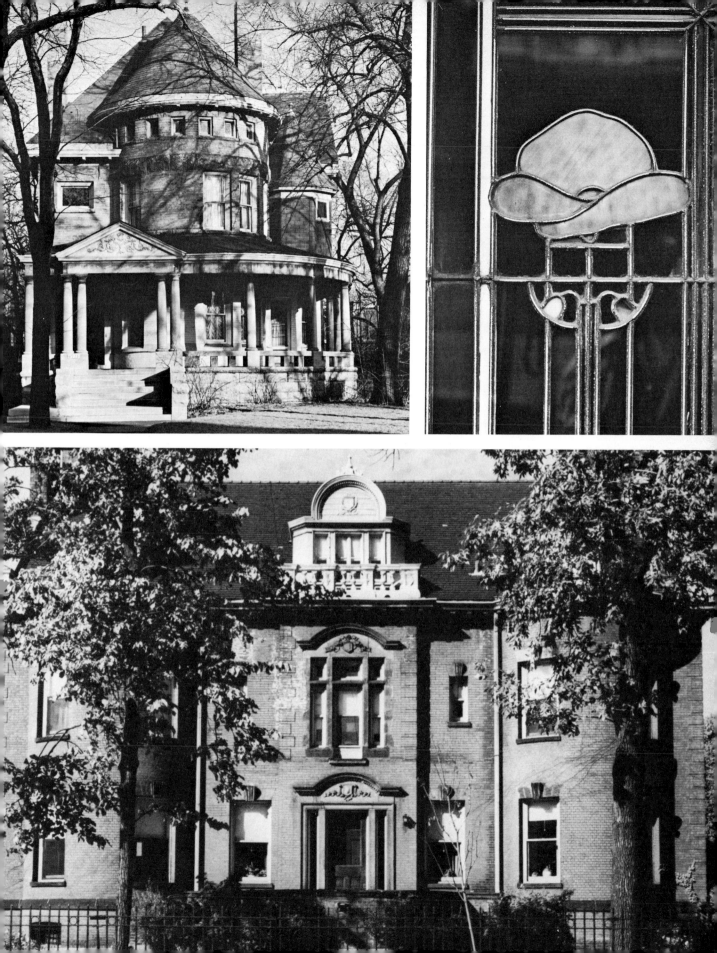

4920 and 4906 South Greenwood—The 3-story limestone, English Tudor house at *4920 Greenwood* is worth viewing. Take particular note of the enormous grounds and gardens, and of the iron picket fence.

At *4906 Greenwood* you will see a red brick symmetrical facade with a design similar to early Louis Sullivan.

1222 East 49th Street—Architects for remodeling: Crombie Taylor and Edward Noonan (1946)   Walk 2 blocks east—for a short detour—to a very charming former coach house built originally in 1906 and remodeled 40 years later. Although the exterior remodeling is at a minimum, concentrated primarily in the west wall and the entrance, it is characteristic of the quality and style exhibited in the interior remodeling. The stunning, all-glass west wall of the living room was formerly the coach entrance.

4900 South Greenwood Avenue—Back in the mainstream of the walk, on Greenwood Avenue, you come to a 3-story neoclassic red brick mansion at 4900. The enormous, light gray limestone Doric columns give this structure an appearance of a large apartment building rather than a private residence. Constructed about 1900, it still dominates the corner of 49th and Greenwood.

4850 South Greenwood Avenue—Architects: George Fred and William Keck (1967)   Here is a cluster of 3-story, red brick, freestanding townhouses, all with pitched roofs (one of them a mansard roof). They make a handsome addition to this section of Kenwood.

4819 South Greenwood Avenue—This stately Georgian mansion has red brick walls with quoins of the same material at the corners. The grand scale of the windows and the ceiling heights give the house an appearance of enormous dignity. The immense, well-landscaped grounds include a tennis court at the rear.

1126 East 48th Street—Architects for remodeling: James Eppenstein (1941); Arthur Myhrum (1963)   Walk north on Greenwood and then east on 48th Street until you come to 1126, a large gray brick house. Originally constructed in 1888, it has been remodeled twice, the major part taking place in 1963.

By removing the original front staircase the architect was free to design a stunning 3-story entrance hall on the side of the building, facing a landscaped patio to the east. He set a library adjacent to the entrance hall, with a wall of grillwork between, and placed a large living room at the front of the building, facing 48th Street. Other alterations have provided this house with modernized kitchen, spacious rooms on the 2nd floor—including a spendid master bedroom, with "His" and "Her" separate dressing rooms, bathrooms, and studies—and guest rooms on both 2nd and 3rd floors.

1125 East 48th Street—Architect for remodeling: Ernest A. Grunsfeld (1938) Across the street, at 1125, is a 2-story gray frame house, originally constructed about 1895 and remodeled more than 40 years later. The main house has an elegant entrance hall, dining room, and kitchen on the 1st floor, 4 bedrooms and 2 baths on the 2nd. The living room is in a 1-story east wing, with windows to the south, facing a large landscaped garden and play area.

1144-1158 East 48th Street—Architect: Y. C. Wong (1965) Farther east on 48th Street you come to a row of 8 townhouses that have been cited for architectural excellence—designed by the same architect who planned the famous atrium houses in Madison Park. The 9-foot walls that encompass the gardens around these homes are characteristic of this architect's emphasis on privacy for the home-owner.

Lake Village—47th Street—Ellis to Lake Park Avenue. Architects: Harry Weese and Associates; Ezra Gordon and Jack Levin (1971)

At this point, it is suggested that you walk north to 47th Street and note the charming red-brick townhouses, walk-up apartments, and high-rise buildings—all part of land cleared through urban renewal. A number of these structures have won architectural awards during 1971. The completed program will have approximately 500 dwelling units comprising a mix of social, ethnic, racial, and economic groups.

Just to the south and east of Lake Village are two striking high-rise buildings and parking garage of the Amalgamated Clothing Workers Union development consisting of

approximately 600 dwelling units. The architects were George
Fred Keck and William Keck. The majority of the units
are co-operative.

1322 East 49th Street—Architect for the 1-story wing, Frank
Lloyd Wright (1895)   Now walk east on 48th Street to Kimbark
Avenue (1300 E), then south to 49th Street, and east again
on 49th until you reach 1322. Here you will see a 2-story garage
house with a 1-story wing designed by Frank Lloyd Wright in his
earlier days. The yellow Roman brick and wide overhang of
the roof indicate that Wright was already experimenting
at this early stage of his career—with quite handsome results.

4858 South Kenwood—Sometimes attributed to Frank Lloyd
Wright or Louis Sullivan (1890)   The yellow frame, neoclassic
house to the east, at the corner of 49th and Kenwood, has
no hint of either Frank Lloyd Wright or Louis Sullivan, though
both have been given credit for designing it.

4915 and 4912 South Woodlawn Avenue—Now walk west
on 49th Street to Woodlawn, and then turn south for the last 2
stops on this walk. At 4915 Woodlawn is another red brick
Georgian house, with an excellent formal facade. Two circular
bays extend from grade to roof. The white wood trim is in good
scale, and so are the slender white Ionic pilasters at the entrance.

Across the street, at 4912, is a modern house in the heart of
this middle-aged group of homes—well set back from the sidewalk
and shielded by trees and shrubbery. (Architect: John Johansen,
of New York, 1950) Although constructed nearly 20 years ago,
the house looks surprisingly contemporary. The base is of
random-cut limestone and the overhanging balcony of wood.
Painted sections of the base—large rectangles in yellow, blue, and
green—give a splendid, light feeling to the house. The all-glass
stairwell contributes a special quality to this excellent design.

Although the proposed walk ends here, there are many more
homes in Kenwood that are beautiful and noteworthy, as those
who continue exploring will discover.

Walk-18

Henry Moore
Sculpture, "Nuclear
Energy."

HYDE PARK - UNIVERSITY OF CHICAGO

Hyde Park and the University of Chicago are practically inseparable. Faculty, university staff, married students, graduate and undergraduate students, alumni, and friends of the University are clustered about the campus in new and old houses, townhouses, and apartments. And a large percentage of the non-university residents of this interracial community are business and professional people.

Hyde Park families are civic-minded to a high degree and guard with real concern their parks, lakefront, and trees. They have sometimes been very much concerned about individual houses that were razed by recent urban renewal projects. At the same time, they recognize too that urban renewal has made many desirable changes in the neighborhood—removing some badly deteriorated apartment buildings, restoring many fine old homes, and constructing new buildings where land was cleared.

Because of the close relation between Hyde Park and the University of Chicago, no attempt has been made in this walk to separate arbitrarily University buildings from others in the area (though of course each University building is identified as such). For anyone interested in making a more thorough tour of the University campus by itself, free 2-hour tours are conducted by the U. of C. each Saturday, starting at 10:00 A.M. from Ida Noyes Hall, 1212 East 59th Street. (For any further information on these official tours call MI 3-0800, extension 4425 or 4429.)

It has seemed desirable, however, to divide this area into two walks, 18 and 19. These 2 walks must *not* be interpreted as a division between "town and gown." They are suggested only as a possible *geographical* division of an area that has no *logical* division, in the hope that each walk will be more pleasurable and less tiring than both together would be.

Since a purely arbitrary separation was necessary, it has been made at the most obvious geographical dividing line—the Midway Plaisance. Walk 18 will take you to Hyde Park - University of Chicago buildings that lie definitely north of the Midway; Walk 19 will take you to the Midway and the buildings along both north and south sides of it.

Opposite, Harper Court.

207

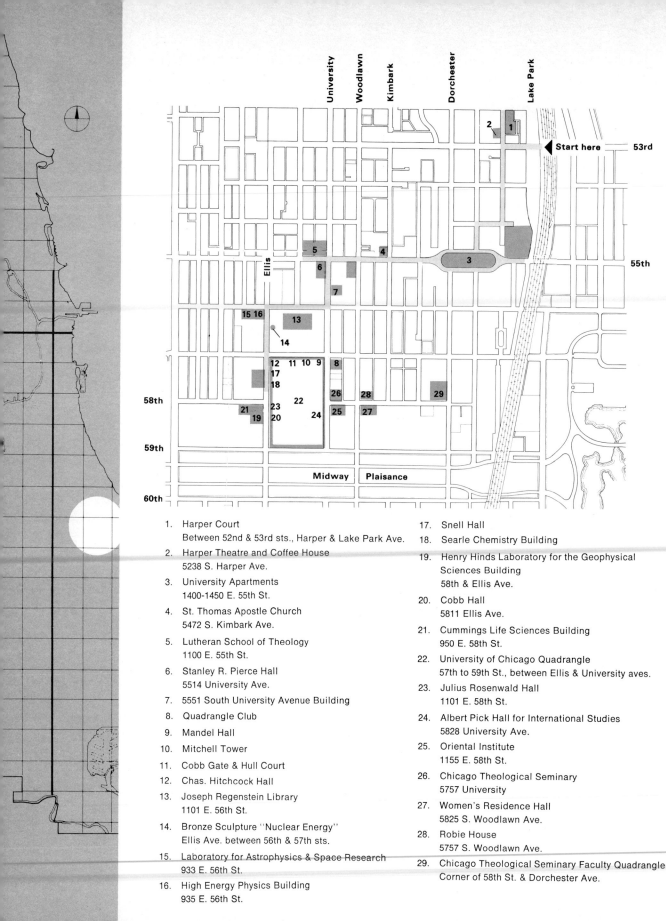

1. Harper Court
   Between 52nd & 53rd sts., Harper & Lake Park Ave.
2. Harper Theatre and Coffee House
   5238 S. Harper Ave.
3. University Apartments
   1400-1450 E. 55th St.
4. St. Thomas Apostle Church
   5472 S. Kimbark Ave.
5. Lutheran School of Theology
   1100 E. 55th St.
6. Stanley R. Pierce Hall
   5514 University Ave.
7. 5551 South University Avenue Building
8. Quadrangle Club
9. Mandel Hall
10. Mitchell Tower
11. Cobb Gate & Hull Court
12. Chas. Hitchcock Hall
13. Joseph Regenstein Library
    1101 E. 56th St.
14. Bronze Sculpture "Nuclear Energy"
    Ellis Ave. between 56th & 57th sts.
15. Laboratory for Astrophysics & Space Research
    933 E. 56th St.
16. High Energy Physics Building
    935 E. 56th St.

17. Snell Hall
18. Searle Chemistry Building
19. Henry Hinds Laboratory for the Geophysical
    Sciences Building
    58th & Ellis Ave.
20. Cobb Hall
    5811 Ellis Ave.
21. Cummings Life Sciences Building
    950 E. 58th St.
22. University of Chicago Quadrangle
    57th to 59th St., between Ellis & University aves.
23. Julius Rosenwald Hall
    1101 E. 58th St.
24. Albert Pick Hall for International Studies
    5828 University Ave.
25. Oriental Institute
    1155 E. 58th St.
26. Chicago Theological Seminary
    5757 University
27. Women's Residence Hall
    5825 S. Woodlawn Ave.
28. Robie House
    5757 S. Woodlawn Ave.
29. Chicago Theological Seminary Faculty Quadrangle
    Corner of 58th St. & Dorchester Ave.

Walk · 18

North of the Midway

WALKING TIME: 2 hours.   HOW TO GET THERE: Take an Illinois Central (I. C.)
suburban train at its Randolph and Michigan underground station, and get off at 53rd Street.
(All express trains and many of those marked "Special" stop at 53rd. Check before boarding
the train.) Or, if you go by car, take the Outer Drive south to 47th Street, turn west under
the I.C. railroad's viaduct, and then south on Lake Park Avenue (1400 E). Continue on
Lake Park to 53rd Street, where this walk begins.

Harper Court—Between 52nd and 53rd Streets, Harper and Lake Park Avenues, 2 blocks west of the Illinois Central's 53rd Street station.

The first stop on this walk is Harper Court. Originally designed
to provide space for Hyde Park artisans displaced by urban
renewal, Harper Court shows what can be done when city
government, university, and community organizations cooperate
in the clearance and rebuilding of a blighted area. The sunken
court has become the focal point of a group of art galleries, shops,
and restaurants that have added sparkle and zest to the
neighborhood. Shops selling dresses, fabrics, books, candles,
picture frames, and Scandinavian furniture have become
popular meeting places for Hyde Parkers.

Harper Theatre and Coffee House—5238 South Harper, across the street from Harper Court.

The Harper Theatre is the anchor of Harper Court. Remodeled
in 1963 from an ordinary movie theatre—which in turn had
replaced an old-time vaudeville house—it is now an intimate
movie house. Its unused coffee shop is furnished and
decorated with the tables, chairs, and classic pharmacist's
materials once adorning Finnegan's drugstore, which stood at
the corner of 55th and Woodlawn before redevelopment of the
area. Pieces of wrought-iron grillwork that decorate the Harper
Theatre lobby came from the balconies of the unusually
distinguished fire escapes of Theodore Starrett's Hyde Park
Hotel, demolished just before the Harper Theatre renovation.

209

University Apartments—1400-1450 East 55th Street. Architects: I. M. Pei; Harry M. Weese and Associates; and Loewenberg and Loewenberg (1959-1962)

Three blocks south of Harper Court, a major part of the Hyde Park renewal is evident in two 10-story apartment buildings in the middle of 55th Street, which has been widely extended on each side to allow a continuing flow of east and west traffic. Known as the University Apartments, these buildings constitute one of the first large-scale urban renewal projects of its kind. Citizens committees and governmental agencies cooperated to bring about these first-rate results. The South East Chicago Commission and the Hyde Park-Kenwood Community Conference did outstanding work.

Built in an extremely simple form, these twin apartment towers have a forceful horizontal rhythm, resulting largely from the long stretches of closely positioned windows. Although the buildings are set in the midst of city traffic, the landscaping—with trees, flowers, pool, and fountain—softens the effect. The many townhouses that surround University Apartments, to the north and the south of 55th Street, were designed by the same architects.

55th Street Shopping Center—To the east and north of University Apartments.   The mall of the 55th Street Shopping Center is of special interest. Among the stores here the *Hyde Park Co-op Supermarket* is particularly significant as a neighborhood development. Starting as a small buying club in the early 1930's, it is now owned by more than 11,000 members and in 1967 reported an annual business of more than $6 million. It claims to be the largest cooperatively owned retail grocery store in the country. The building is light and airy, with many features that facilitate family shopping. Summer and winter the large entrance is wide open during store hours. Customers merely pass through a curtain of air that keeps the inside temperature cool in 90° weather and warm on the coldest winter days.
(Architects: George Fred and William Keck, 1959)

St. Thomas Apostle Church—5472 South Kimbark. Architect: Barry Byrne (1922)

The influence of Frank Lloyd Wright on his former apprentice can be noted in the design of St. Thomas Apostle Church, at the

Opposite, St. Thomas Apostle Church.

210

corner of 55th and Kimbark. The warmth of color in the building
material, the sculpture around the entrance, and the human scale
on which all seems to have been constructed give this church
an especially appealing effect. Inside, the fourteen Stations of the
Cross, carved in bas-relief by the Italian sculptor A. Faggi,
are justifiably famous for the sweep and rhythm of their design.

Lutheran School of Theology—1100 East 55th Street.
Architects: Perkins and Will Partnership (1968)

Two blocks west of St. Thomas, on the north side of a
boulevard-like reconstructed 55th Street, is the Lutheran School
of Theology, consisting of 3 stunning sections with transparent
enclosures of lightly tinted glass between sweeping curved
steel columns that rest on sturdy pins, much like
those in bridge construction.

Diagonally across 55th Street, at 5500 Woodlawn, is the new
Augustana Evangelical Lutheran Church of Hyde Park, in
low, spacious design—planned by Edward D. Dart, of Loebl,
Schlossman, Bennett, and Dart. Within the main entrance stands
an impressively unconventional bronze statue of Christ, the
work of Egon Weiner. The statue was cast in Norway.

Stanley R. Pierce Hall—
University of Chicago, 5514 University Avenue.
Architects: Harry M. Weese and Associates (1959-60)

On the south side of 55th Street, one block west of the Lutheran
church, is Pierce Hall, a University of Chicago residence for
undergraduate students. A high-rise tower, with an effective
2-story extension, this has become a distinguished addition to
the University campus. Tiers of bay windows—a feature restored
by this architect, after years of disuse—accentuate the vertical
lines of the structure. Actually the building houses 4 separate
residence halls—Henderson, Shorey, Thompson, and Tufts.

5551 South University Avenue Building—
Architects: George Fred and William Keck (1937)

Now walk south on University and note the brick building on
the east side of the Street at 5551—one of the earliest modern
buildings in the area with cooperative apartments. The 2
architects themselves live in 2 of the 3 apartments, each of
which extends over an entire floor. Across the front of the
building at ground level are 3 garages, and the entrance is
placed inconspicuously at the side, far back from the street.
Contrast in the brick facade on the University Avenue side is
provided by dark metal louvres, 2 at each floor level—for the
2 wide windows—with a stretch of contrasting brick between

Opposite, Stanley R. Pierce Hall.

213

them. At the time this building was erected its design was considered quite extreme, though today it blends well with other architecture in the area and seems to meet naturally the needs of the city dweller.

Quadrangle Club—1155 East 57th Street.
Architect: Howard Van Doren Shaw (1914)

Continue south on University Avenue past the old gymnasium to 57th Street where you will be standing on the northwest corner. Look across to the southeast corner where you will see the faculty club known as the Quadrangle Club. It contains a second-floor, cathedral-type dining hall with great wood trusses that span this spacious room. There are tennis courts south of the club. There are smaller dining and meeting rooms.

Mandel Hall—1131 East 57th Street.
Architects: Shepley, Rutan and Coolidge (1903)

The exterior was modeled after the great hall of Crosby Place in England, built around 1450 as the home of Sir John Crosby. The donor was Leon Mandel, a prominent Chicago merchant. The auditorium seats about 1000. There is a bronze tablet in the lobby by sculptor Lorado Taft that is a portrait of Senator Stephen A. Douglas.

This building, located at the northeast corner of the Quadrangle, is not only a university landmark but one for the entire Chicago area as well. Named for the donor retail merchant family, the structure has been the showplace for years for drama, dance, ballet, musicals, and symphony concerts.

The entire building has been carried out in English Gothic and harmonizes with the other early member structures of the Quadrangle. The great hall, lounges, dining halls, and theatre are well worth a visit. Just to the west of the hall is the outdoor summer theatre area known as Court Theatre.

Mitchell Tower—1131 East 57th Street.
Architects: Shepley, Rutan and Coolidge (1903)

Mandel Hall is actually part of Mitchell Tower and the Hutchenson Commons complex at the corner of 57th Street and University Avenue. The exterior is part of the English Gothic tradition in Indiana limestone and was copied from the tower of Magdalen College, Oxford University. The tower houses the Alice Truman Palmer Bells, University Theatre, (Mandel Hall) campus radio station (WHPK-FM). The tower is four stories plus the bell chamber.

Now, walk a few feet west to Cobb Gate.

Cobb Gate and Hull Court—
opposite the Regenstein Library.
Architect: Henry Ives Cobb (1897)

This great Gothic gate, in the spirit of those at Oxford and Cambridge universities, was constructed as a part of Hull Court of the Quadrangle. It consists of Anatomy, Botany (named Ida B. and Walter Erman Biology Center), Zoology buildings and Cullver Hall.

Charles Hitchcock Hall—1009 East 57th Street.
Architect: D. H. Perkins (1902)

This early residence hall was designed by Dwight Perkins, an early advocate of shedding old architectural trappings. This simplified Gothic style is representative of his feelings. The structure houses 105 students and contains a club room, infirmary and library. A "preacher's room" was furnished at one time.

Now, return to the north side of 57th to the new Joseph Regenstein Library which stands on the site of former Stagg Field.

Joseph Regenstein Library—1100 East 57th Street.
Architects: Skidmore, Owings and Merrill (1970)
Partner in Charge: Walter Netsch

The University's new Graduate Research Library is an exceptionally popular addition to the intellectual life of the campus. Of the same gray limestone as its Gothic neighbors, it has a modern design that is impressive in scale.

Actually, it has 7 service floors and some 577,000 square feet. With a total volume capacity of 3.5 million books, it now houses the University's 1.9 million collection in the social sciences and humanities, excluding law, art, and theology. It is a graduate research library, costing $21 million, and was built principally through the generosity of Chicago industrialist, Joseph Regenstein. The interior is highly functional. Each of the major service floors is divided into four areas; book stacks, offices, faculty studies, and reading areas. The architecture harmonizes well with the adjoining buildings. The vertical wall elements and narrow recessed bay windows relieve the structure's mass. Exterior walls are formed by deeply grooved, cut limestone slabs, which add nice texture to the surface.

This magnificent structure is a welcome addition to a campus of many distinguished buildings. Now walk west to Ellis.

Bronze Sculpture, "Nuclear Energy"—
Ellis Avenue between 56th and 57th streets.
Sculptor: Henry Moore (1967)

Between Regenstein Library and Ellis Avenue, halfway down the block, is a great bronze sculpture—12 feet high, weighing 3 tons, which stands on a base of black polished granite. Entitled "Nuclear Energy," this extremely simple but impressive work of art by the sculptor Henry Moore commemorates man's achievement in completing the first atomic chain reaction— as explained in one of the 4 plaques mounted on a slab of marble in the grass across the sidewalk. Under a Stagg Field bleacher near this same spot, on December 2, 1942, Enrico Fermi and 41 other distinguished scientists accomplished the great breakthrough that introduced the Atomic Age. Speaking of the sculpture himself, Moore has explained that it relates both to the mushroom cloud of a nuclear explosion and to the shape of a human skull, with reminiscences of church architecture in the lower part.

Now walk north to 56th and west to the

Laboratory for Astrophysics and Space Research—
933 East 56th Street.
Architects: Skidmore, Owings and Merrill (1964)

This two-story, cast concrete structure with recessed walls of glass windows is a part of the University's Institute for Nuclear Studies and carries out research in the space sciences. The building was partially financed by a grant from The National Aeronautical Space Administration.

High Energy Physics Building—935 East 56th Street.
Architects: Hausner and Macsal (1967)

This three-story and penthouse building is actually a reinforced concrete research laboratory for the physical sciences. The simple, sturdy design serves the purpose well.

Now walk south on Ellis, crossing 57th and note the vast number of structures that compose the University Quadrangle. Some are original structures and some of more recent construction such as the new Chemistry Building at the southeast corner of 57th and Ellis. This walk will take you through the Quadrangle, but first it is essential that you see some of the buildings just outside the Quadrangle. Walk south to Snell Hall.

Snell Hall—5709 South Ellis Avenue.
Architect: Henry Ives Cobb (1893)

This 55 student residence hall has an Indiana limestone facade styled in the English Gothic period. It is an integral part of the early Quadrangle and today stands with all its new neighbors as a part of an excellent tradition of developing and growing with the spirit of the times.

Searle Chemistry Building—5715 South Ellis Avenue.
Architects: Smith, Smith, Haines, Lundberg & Waehler, New York (1967)

This five-story structure is mainly a series of scientific laboratories and offices. It is sheathed in Indiana limestone to harmonize with its neighbors. However, the Gothic design has been simplified and creates no visual "cacaphony" whatever.

Now, walk over to the Hinds Laboratory Building.

**Henry Hinds Laboratory for the
Geophysical Sciences Building**—
University of Chicago, 58th and Ellis.
Architects: I. W. Colburn and Associates;
J. Lee Jones (associate architect) (1969)

One block farther south on Ellis, on the west side of the street, is a building of startlingly unique architecture, the University's Geophysical Sciences Building—the first in a science center that will eventually occupy the entire block. Cross to the east side of

Ellis for a better view. Much of the design was determined by the demands of present-day research and teaching in the geophysical sciences. It seems at first to have no relation whatever with the neo-Gothic buildings of the original Quadrangle directly across from it, but it has actually made concessions to the earlier style. The brick walls, for instance, which carry the load, are covered with a thin layer of Indiana limestone, the material used in the older buildings, and the brick itself allowed to show only here and there. And the numerous towers, though of highly individual form, supposedly bring the entire building into greater harmony with the Gothic-towered structures of the old campus. Note the metal bay windows that are not only colorful, but highly practical.

Cobb Hall—5811 Ellis Avenue.
Architects: Henry Ives Cobb (1892)
Architects for Remodeling: Burnham and Hammond (1967)

This structure is at the central west edge of the Quadrangle and is one of the original members. It is four stories with an Indiana limestone exterior that includes bay windows. The undergraduate classrooms and facilities include an auditorium, biology laboratory, and art gallery.

There is a marble bust by Lorado Taft on the south wall of the main entrance. It is of Silas B. Cobb, for whom the building is named.

Cummings Life Science Center—950 East 58th Street.
Architects: I. W. Colburn and Associates; Schmidt, Garden and Erickson; Harold H. Hellman, University Architect (1973)

This stunning high-rise research center is designed with vertical brick piers in relief against a background of a limestone facade. The rhythm of the varying pattern of the bases of the piers is delightful. The narrow windows clearly indicate the necessarily confined interior research laboratories.

Colburn has treated the facade with different materials and height than the Geophysical Building just around the corner. Nevertheless, there is a strong similarity in style and both

buildings come off as part of a great medieval fortress through which one enters across a symbolic moat. Both rely on their contemporary "flying buttresses" for their exciting vertical lines. In other words, both buildings achieve a rightful place on a campus that includes many outstanding architectural contributions.

The structure is ten stories high with two penthouses and is the tallest building on campus. The construction is reinforced

Geophysical Sciences building.

concrete. There are forty narrow towers located at the perimeter of the building. They contain exhaust ducts from laboratories. The towers are dark red, face brick and the main structure is clad in Indiana limestone.

Next cross Ellis to enter the Quadrangle.

University of Chicago Quadrangle—
57th to 59th, between Ellis and University.
Architects: Henry Ives Cobb; Shepley, Rutan and Coolidge; Charles Klauder; and others
(1890 to the present)

Across the street from the new Geophysical Scienes Building is the original campus of the University of Chicago, called "The Quadrangle." Before entering the Quadrangle, however, look back across Ellis to note the University Press, the University Bookstore, and then the enormous complex of buildings that accommodate the biological sciences. Here are the biological research laboratories and the University's hospitals and medical school in one perspective view.

Occupying 4 solid blocks, the Quadrangle as a whole follows the original plan prepared by Henry Ives Cobb in 1890—a large central quadrangle flanked by 3 small quadrangles to the south and 3 more to the north, all surrounded by buildings of Indiana limestone in the late English Gothic style. Cobb himself designed all the buildings that were constructed before 1900, and later architects used the neo-Gothic style exclusively through the 1940's. This mass of Gothic structures comprises the architectural heritage to which subsequent architects generally deferred.

The University's Administration Building sits on the main east-west axis at the western perimeter of the Quadrangle. It is a five-story modified Gothic exterior and contains the major administrative offices. As you step into the Quadrangle, you are struck by the planned arrangements of structures, walks, roads, landscaping—into a large intricate, orderly web of convenience for students and faculty. Buildings are laid out on the various axes and sub-axes—and do not meet the eye at first glance. It is a joyful experience to wander onto a small

Gothic chapel that is partly hidden behind a larger academic building and surrounded by trees. On the other hand, each building has been designed or renovated to form a complex of similar disciplines, conveniently located for students.

Julius Rosenwald Hall (Now part of Business School Complex)—1101 East 58th Street.
Architects: Holabird and Roche (1915)
Architect for Renovation: Samuel A. Lichtmann (1972)

This Indiana limestone, English Gothic has been successfully remodeled and is now a part of the complex of business school buildings. There is a completely modernized group of classrooms, offices, and library to replace the former geography disciplines.

Rosenwald, along with several other of the original Gothic structures in the Quadrangle, has been successfully renovated inside while retaining the original qualities of the exteriors. The University is to be commended for this.

The student newspaper, the *Maroon* quoted Eero Saarinen from the *Architectural Record* of November 1960,[8] during the time when he was consulting architect to the University of Chicago:

> Wandering in the University of Chicago today, one is amazed at the beauty achieved by spaces surrounded by buildings all in one discipline and made out of a uniform material; where each building is being considerate of the next, and each building —through its common material—is aging in the same way. It is significant that on a small court on the University of Chicago campus [referring to the one used by Court Theatre] built between 1894 and 1930, three different architects—Henry I. Cobb; Shepley, Rutan, and Coolidge; and Charles Klauder— built the four different sides of the court. All are in the Gothic style, and the court gives us today a beautiful, harmonious visual picture.

The cohesiveness of the old quadrangles does not rest entirely on the use of the Gothic style. In fact, the Administration Building, which encloses the main Quadrangle on the west, defies this tradition, conforming only in the material used. In large part the harmonious effect comes from the fact that these architects all envisioned their buildings as contributions to a larger unity.

Albert Pick Hall For International Studies—
5828 University Avenue.
Architects: Ralph Rapson & Associates, Inc.;
Burnham and Hammond, Inc. (1971)

Albert Pick Hall is at the extreme eastern edge of the Quadrangle. As you approach it, your eye catches the remarkable combination of planes and surfaces—all in gray limestone to match the color of its neighbors. It is like emerging from the twelfth to the twentieth century in one short walk. The Gothic spiral is there, not only in the limestone, but the great flying buttresses—some of which are corbeled and others supported on columns.

The entire effect of the great verticality that reaches for the sky is indeed a strong architectural statement.

The University Avenue entrance has an interesting use of glass and metal for a portion of the facade. Their horizontal lines seem to balance the aforementioned verticality.

There is a strong metal sculptural work near the entrance. The sculptor is Virgiinio Ferrari and the title is "Dialogo." The work rests on a 14-foot, square limestone base from which the four separate forms rise toward the center.

Oriental Institute—1155 East 58th Street.
Architects: Mayer, Murray, and Phillip (1931)

Across the street from the eastern edge of the Quadrangle, on the east side of University Avenue, is the internationally famous Oriental Institute. It contains one of the world's major collections of art, religious, and daily life objects from the Ancient Near East: Egypt, Palestine, Syria, Anatolia, Mesopotamia, and Iran. The time range covered is from about 5000 B.C. to about 1000 A.D. Open daily 10:00 A.M. to 5:00 P.M.; closed Mondays.

Chicago Theological Seminary—5757 University
Avenue. Architect: Herbert H. Riddle (1914)

This striking red brick structure with stone trim is a unique combination of English Georgian and Gothic design. The striking 162-foot tower can be seen from the Quadrangle or from the Quadrangle Club (the faculty club) one block away.

The interior contains a chapel that seats 200. The stained glass windows of the chapel were executed by the Willett Stained Glass Studios of Philadelphia. There are classrooms, administrative offices, and a library all conveniently located in the central or main building. The residential floors are located in the west wing and the President's House is in the east wing.

Women's Residence Hall—5825 Woodlawn.
Architect: Eero Saarinen (1958)

A residence hall for women students, on the south side of 58th Street, is first-rate architecture, although it is not up to the very high standards of design established by Saarinen in the Law School Quadrangle. (See Walk 19.)

◘ Robie House—now Adlai Stevenson Institute of International Affairs, 5757 Woodlawn.
Original Architect: Frank Lloyd Wright (1909)
Architects for restoration: Frank Lloyd Wright Office, Wesley Peters (in charge), William Barnard, Jr., Contractor (Son of original contractor) 1964; Skidmore, Owings, and Merrill (1967)

Declared a National Historic Landmark, 1964

On the east side of Woodlawn, at the corner of Woodlawn and 58th Street, is Frank Lloyd Wright's famous Robie House, which was recently renovated from public subscriptions after it had been donated to the University by William Zeckendorf. Built as a private home, this is probably the most well-known example of Wright's "Prairie House." The Citation by the Architectural Landmarks Commission reads:

> In recognition of the creation of the creation of the Prairie House—a home organized around a great hearth where interior space, under wide sweeping roofs, opens to the outdoors. The bold interplay of horizontal planes about the chimney mass, and the structurally expressive piers and windows, established a new form of domestic design.

In 1967, after being restored and refurnished in its original style, the Robie House became the Adlai Stevenson Institute of International Affairs.

Chicago Theological Seminary Faculty Quadrangle—
corner of 58th and Dorchester.
Architect: Edward D. Dart, of Loebl, Schlossman,
Bennett, and Dart (1963)

Robie House.

Now turn east on 58th Street, and stop at Dorchester to see a
surprisingly unconventional group of recently constructed
buildings—homes for Chicago Theological Seminary faculty.
No attempt was made here to harmonize the architecture of the
houses with that of the older buildings around them. On the
contrary, they defy previously accepted patterns with
refreshing individuality. Instead of following the lines of the
street, for instance, as the endless rows of houses in Chicago—

224

and most other cities—do, their sides face the street on a diagonal, as if set there deliberately somewhat askew. The roofs, instead of being flat or gabled, slope steeply from one side to the other with wide overhang. All 8 houses, harmonizing well with each other, are clustered around a central green that is elevated so that it can slope down to the sidewalk.

A plaque on the house at the corner reports an award for excellence in architecture.

This is the end of Walk 18. To return to the Loop, walk north to 57th Street and then east 3 blocks to the elevated station (55th, 56th, 57th) of the Illinois Central suburban line that brought you out to Hyde Park.

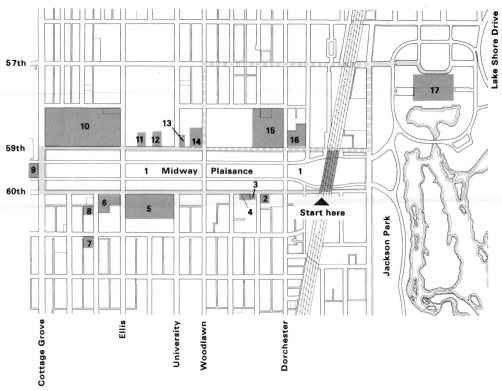

1. Midway Plaisance
    59th to 60th St., Jackson Park to Washington Park

2. Sonia Shankman Orthogenic School
    1365 E. 60th St.

3. Public Administration Center
    1313 E. 60th St.

4. Center for Continuing Education
    1307 E. 60th St.

5. Laird Bell Law Quadrangle
    1111 E. 60th St.

6. School of Social Services Administration Building
    969 E. 60th St.

7. Social Services Center
    921 E. 61st St.

8. Midway Studios
    6016 Ingleside Ave.

9. Fountain of Time
    West end of the Midway

10. Pritzker Medical Center
    950 E. 59th St.

11. William Rainey Harper Memorial Library
    1116 E. 59th St.

12. Social Science Research Building
    1126 E. 59th St.

13. University President's House
    5855 University Ave.

14. Rockefeller Memorial Chapel
    E. 59th St., corner of Woodlawn Ave.

15. The Laboratory Schools Complex

16. International House
    1414 E. 59th St.

17. Museum of Science and Industry
    E. 57th St. at S. Lake Shore Dr.

▭ ▭ ▭ ▭   Alternate route

Walk · 19

The Midway Plaisance and Its South and North Sides

WALKING TIME: 1½ hours.   HOW TO GET THERE: Instead of getting off the I.C. suburban train at 53rd Street—as you did for Walk 18—stay on until 59th Street, having made sure in advance that your train will stop there! Or, if you go by car, follow the instructions given for Walk 18, continuing on Lake Park until you reach 59th Street.

Midway Plaisance, stretching from Jackson Park on the east to Washington Park on the west, between 59th and 60th streets.

Before coming down from the I. C. elevated platform, look west for an overall view of the Midway Plaisance, a block wide and some dozen blocks long, stretching all the way from Jackson Park (just behind you) to Washington Park on the west— all green lawns, trees, and sidewalks, with two one-way drives and two local drives for east-west traffic.

This great green mall was constructed in 1890 as the formal entrance to the 1893 Columbian Exposition, to be held in what is now Jackson Park. The sunken parts of the Midway Plaisance are a reminder that these were filled with water back in 1893— impressive lagoons to be admired before you reached the exposition proper.

Other reminders of that famous world fair are the enormous gilded statue of the Republic, by Daniel Chester French, now placed farther on in Jackson Park, where it is passed daily by hundreds of commuters on their way to and from the Loop, and the Museum of Science and Industry, which is the last stop on this walk. (Though it stands 2 blocks north of the Midway, it seems an appropriate ending for a Midway walk.) Another legacy from the fair, the charming Japanese teahouse on an island in a Jackson Park lagoon, which was the delight of Hyde Parkers a generation ago, was first damaged by fire and then completely abandoned.

Called merely "The Midway" by neighborhood residents, this parkway is especially popular with University of Chicago students, who use its long stretch of sunken lawns for sunning

227

and studying in summer and for exercise in winter, when it is flooded for ice skating.

Statuary marks each end of the Midway. On the east stands a sturdy mail-clad warrior on horseback, a tribute from Chicago's Czechoslovakians to their first president, Masaryk. The figure is supposedly one of the Blanik knights, who—according to legend—slept in a mountainous cave in Czechoslovakia until the time should come to arise and rescue their country. On the west is Lorado Taft's "Fountain of Time," which will be included in this walk.

228

This walk starts on the south side of the Midway just west of the Illinois Central Railroad.

You are now on the South Campus of the University of Chicago. A considerable portion of this section was obtained through the city's urban renewal program. Through this method, the University was able to expand and achieve greater service to the community and its students and faculty.

Sonia Shankman Orthogenic School—
1365 East 60th Street.
Architects: I. W. Colburn & Associates (1966)
(For renovation of a former church plus addition of a three-story wing)

This rather strange combination of a renovated church and residential wing houses this famous school for emotionally disturbed children, founded by the equally famous Dr. Bruno Bettleheim.

Public Administration Center—1313 East 60th Street.
Architects: Zantizinger, Borie and Medary (1937)

The Gothic design of Indiana limestone and brick houses the offices for 23 city, state, national, and international organizations interested in government and public administration. The structure is four stories and contains an extensive library that services the in-house organizations as well as university scholars. The donor for the construction was the Spelman Fund of New York.

The main floor lounge contains portraits of Louis Brownlow and Charles Merriam, two of the center's founders.

Center for Continuing Education—
1307 East 60th Street.
Architect: Edward Stone (1963)

Next is the Center for Continuing Education, which is the University's conference and hotel center, made possible by funds from the W. K. Kellogg Foundation. Living quarters, conference

Opposite, Library building, Laird Bell Law Quadrangle.

229

rooms, restaurant, and cafeteria provide liberal facilities for out-of-town conferees. Restaurant and cafeteria are open to the public. (The structure is not considered one of Stone's best works.)

Laird Bell Law Quadrangle—The University of Chicago Law School, 1111 East 60th Street.
Architect: Eero Saarinen (1960)

Turning west, you pass the Industrial Relations Center at 1225, also affiliated with the University, and come to the University Law School. This elegant low quadrangle is far and away the most successful building on the campus of the University. It blends well with the Gothic dormitories to the west and the American Bar Center to the east.

At the east end is a completely closed auditorium, which contrasts markedly with the enormous library west of it, for the library uses all-glass walls set at effective angles with each other. Inside the building, the auditorium is connected by wide corridors with lecture rooms and lounges that extend to the west. Actually, there are two auditoriums—one set over the other. One is used as a court room for demonstrations and the other for lectures. The stunning sculpture in the pool outside, called "Construction in Space in Third and Fourth Dimensions," is the work of Antoine Pevsner, who created it specifically for the Law School.

School of Social Service Administration Building— 969 East 60th Street.
Architect: Ludwig Mies van der Rohe (1965)

The Social Service Administration Building of the University, the last building to be noted on this side of the Midway, is a Mies van der Rohe creation. Black steel and glass and an open plan give the structure an imposing appearance. It seems not at all out of place or off tempo and fits well with the other buildings on 60th Street. The policy of inviting distinguished 20th century architects to design new buildings has been most rewarding to the campuses of Harvard, Yale and the University of Chicago.

Social Services Center—921 East 61st Street.
Architects: Hausner & Macsai (1971)

The University has assumed an active role in servicing the
adjacent community through this Social Services Center.
Students are trained and nearby children and mothers are
helped. Through child care training, the mothers are made to feel
confident and better able to meet their responsibilities.

The structure is plain, and presents a facade of efficiency and
strength. The exterior material is Indiana limestone.

The cost of construction was shared by U.S. Department of
Housing and Urban Development and the U.S. Department
of Health, Education and Welfare's Children's Bureau.

Midway Studios—6016 Ingleside Avenue.
Originally constructed in 1929 and renovated in 1965
Architects for Second Renovation: Loebl, Schlossman,
Bennett & Dart (1972)

The University donated this building and land to Lorado Taft
where he successfully executed many sculptural commissions
throughout his career. Today it is the art center for the
University and contains major studio workshops. Painting is
taught in Taft's stone-cutting studio, sculpture is taught in the
former plaster casting workshop. Painting is also taught in a
former studio and lithography in still another. One former studio
now serves as a student center and Taft's private studio is used
by students for independent work. All in all, it represents a
fine tribute to a great sculptor of the late nineteenth and
early twentieth century.

Fountain of Time—west end of Midway Plaisance,
at entrance to Washington Park.
Sculptor: Lorado Taft (1922)

After an interval of neglect, Lorado Taft's haunting sculpture
called "The Fountain of Time" has fortunately been restored.
A hooded, "craglike" figure of Time (to use Taft's own
adjective in describing his mental image), with his back to the
Midway, gazes across a pool at a long procession of human
beings as they move through life. The Chicago sculptor said

that his inspiration came from these lines in a poem by
Austin Dobson:

> *Time goes, you say? Ah no!*
> *Alas, time stays; we go.*

Both the immobility of Time and the onward sweep of human
life are well expressed in this unusual sculpture.

Be sure to walk all around the Fountain of Time, to view it
from every angle. On what seems to be the back is another
procession of people, including a figure of the sculptor himself
and his Italian assistant.

Now return east but this time go to the north side of the Midway
where the first complex of buildings will be the Pritzker
Medical Center of the University.

Pritzker Medical Center Complex

Argonne Cancer Research Hospital
950 East 59th St.
Architects: Schmidt, Garden & Erikson (1953)

Philip D. Armour Clinical Research Hospital
950 East 59th St.
Architects: Schmidt, Garden & Erikson (1963)

Albert Merritt Billings Hospital
950 East 59th St.
Architects: Coolidge and Hodgdon (1927)

Bobs Roberts Memorial Hospital
920 East 59th St.
Architects: Coolidge and Hodgdon (1930)

A. J. Carlson Animal Research Facility
5820 Ellis Ave.
Architects: Schmidt, Garden & Erikson (1968)

Chicago Lying-In Hospital
5841 Maryland Ave.
Architects: Schmidt, Garden & Erikson (1931)

Nathan Goldblatt Memorial Hospital
950 East 59th St.
Architects: Schmidt, Garden & Erikson (1950)

Goldblatt Pavilion
950 East 59th St.
Architects: Schmidt, Garden & Erikson (1961)

Hicks-McElwee Memorial Hospital
950 East 59th St.
Architects: Coolidge and Hodgdon (1931)

Peck Pavilion
950 East 59th St.
Architects: Schmidt, Garden & Erikson (1961)

Charles Gilman Smith Hospital
950 East 59th St.
Architects: Schmidt, Garden & Erikson (1953)

Silvain and Arma Wyler Children's Hospital
950 East 59th St.
Architects: Schmidt, Garden & Erikson (1966)

The Pritzker School of Medicine is the prototype of the medical school in the total academic setting. Located on the Midway between Cottage Grove, Ellis, and 58th Street, it covers about 25 acres at the southwest corner of the campus.

The University of Chicago Medical Complex consists of several inter-connected hospitals and clinics with a total bed capacity of 722. The hospitals provide clinical teaching and research facilities for students and staff. Each year, more than 17,300 patients are admitted, 170,000 outpatient visits are made and some 57,000 persons receive emergency treatment.

In 1961, the University affiliated with the Michael Reese Hospital and Medical Center to provide mutual assistance and cooperation in areas of common concern for patient care, medical education, and research.

One of the latest in a never-ending series of new buildings and wings of buildings is the Silvain and Arma Wyler Children's Hospital located in the central courtyard that is an extension of Drexel Avenue. The continued practice of adding so many buildings and wings of buildings all interconnected has resulted in a great limestone, metal, and glass monolith. There is no evidence of an original plan. The result is an appearance of constant improvisation—which it undoubtedly is.

1. McElwee Memorial Hospital

2. Hicks Memorial Hospital

3. Goldblatt Memorial Hospital

4. Argonne Cancer Research Hospital

5. Armour Clinical Research Building

6. Billings Hospital

7. A. J. Carlson Animal Research Facility

8. Abbott Memorial Hall

9. Ben May Laboratory for Cancer Research

10. Bobs Roberts Memorial Hospital

11. Charles Gilman Smith Hospital

12. Peck Pavilion

13. Cummings Life Science Center

14. Chicago Lying-In Hospital

15. Wyler Children's Hospital

The multitude of buildings in the Pritzker Medical Center makes it difficult to identify each one except by use of the accompanying photograph and listing by number. If you decide to walk around to the Ingleside and 58th Street border, note the Cummings Life Sciences Center Building that is a part of Walk 18, with special emphasis on an exceptionally fine piece of sculpture named "Aileronde" and created by sculptor Antoine Poncet (1972).

This ten-foot high abstract marble is a welcome addition to this section of the University. The sculptor's statement seems to be "live for life."

Now return to the Midway and continue east.

William Rainey Harper Memorial Library—
1116 East 59th Street.
Architects: Shepley, Rutan and Coolidge (1912)
Architects for Renovation: Metz, Train, Olson and Youngren (1972)

This impressive English Gothic structure was for many years the main library of the University. Since the completion of the Graduate Regenstein Library, Harper now serves the undergraduate student body. As can be seen, it is a part of the original Quadrangle group. It has three stories and a high, handsome, commanding tower. The main reading room is reminiscent of a twelfth-century collegium with its high wooden trusses and equally high Gothic windows.

Social Science Research Building—1126 East 59th Street. Architects: Shepley, Rutan and Coolidge (1912)

This solid greystone Gothic structure serves as part of a great twelfth-century facade along the north side of the Midway.

The next stop is the President's House.

The President's House—5855 University Avenue.
Architect: Henry Ives Cobb (1895)
Architect for Renovation: Arthur Myhrum (1969)

This fairly large, three-story limestone and Roman brick, English Tudor Gothic house is set at the corner of University and the Midway. Directly to the east is the mammoth Gothic Rockefeller Chapel. Strangely, the house is not overpowered by the chapel, principally because of the equally strong open, green spaces that separate the two.

The house has been remodeled several times. The original entrance was on the Midway and is now on University Avenue. The delightful garden to the east is a part of the house that is used for receptions when weather permits. A great elm tree is its crowning glory. One must confess that although the house appears gloomy from the exterior, the garden and the great Midway upon which it faces more than compensates for any of its shortcomings.

Next, walk over to Rockefeller Chapel.

Rockefeller Memorial Chapel—
1156-80 East 59th Street.
Architect: Bertram G. Goodhue, whose associates— after his death—supervised the construction according to the plans he had drawn up (1928)

At 59th and Woodlawn stands Rockefeller Memorial Chapel, one of the most imposing buildings of the University's campus, donated by and named in honor of the University's founder. This is an excellent example of the late Gothic style by a prominent architect interested in the Gothic revival. The Carillon Tower bells (72 of them) are noteworthy for the excellence of the tones and the quality of the sound. They were given, a few years after the chapel was completed, by the same donor in memory of his mother, Laura Spelman Rockefeller.

The chapel is the scene of many University functions, such as concerts, pageantry, graduation ceremonies, and other convocations. And, to add a social note, the Rockefeller-Percy wedding was held here in 1968!

The colorful banners hanging inside Rockefeller Chapel come from a collection of 44 *liturgical* banners created by Norman Laliberte for the Vatican Pavilion at the World's Fair in New York that ended in 1965. The artist, a Canadian-American now living in Brewster, New York, is said to be a deeply religious man, who has been able to catch the simple appeal, even the

Opposite, Rockefeller Memorial Chapel.

236

humor, of medieval religious art work. Known officially as the Mary MacDonald Ludgin Collection, these banners were a gift to the University in 1966 from one of its trustees, Earle Ludgin, in memory of his wife.

As you stand outside Rockefeller Chapel on the corner of 59th and Woodlawn, look to the north for a glimpse of 2 other places of worship—the beautifully executed red brick tower of the U. of C. Theological Seminary's chapel one block north and one block east, at 58th and University, and the exquisite spire of the First Unitarian Church one block farther north, at 57th and Woodlawn.

To proceed to the Museum of Science and Industry, the last stop on this walk, continue down the north side of the Midway, passing other U. of C. buildings—Ida Noyes Hall, the laboratory school of the University, and International House—before turning north to 57th Street.

The Laboratory Schools Complex

Emmons Blaine Hall—1362 East 59th Street.
Architect: James Gamble Rogers (1903)

This building is part of the teacher training program of the

238

University. The Lab Schools serve grades kindergarten to 12th. The structures are linked with each other by passageways or walks. Besides Blaine Hall they consist of:

Henry Holmes Belfield Hall—5815 South Kimbark Avenue.
Architect: James Gamble Rogers (1904)

Blaine and Belfield Halls are French Gothic in Indiana limestone.

University High School—5834 South Kenwood Avenue.
Architects: Perkins and Will (1960)

This exterior is modern in every sense of the word and fits in well with its Gothic neighbors. The exterior of limestone, aluminum and tinted glass is pleasant and inviting. Besides classrooms, the building contains a library, cafeteria and student lounge.

Bernard E. Sunny Gymnasium—5731 South Kenwood.
Architects: Armstrong, Furst & Tilton (1930)

This Indiana Gothic limestone structure contains a two-story gymnasium and swimming pool. There are also exercise rooms, locker rooms and offices. The nearby athletic field is more than ample for the various athletic events and daily exercise routines.

Above, Museum of Science and Industry.

239

International House—1414 East 59th Street. Architects: Holabird and Root (1932)

This stately limestone, modified Gothic structure is one of four such centers founded by John D. Rockefeller, Jr. The other three centers are located in New York City, Berkeley, California, and Paris, France. Although these different houses share common origins and goals, each is a separate institution with no formal or legal ties to each other.

Although International House of Chicago was established in 1932 as a department of the University of Chicago, it is financially self-supporting and has its own Board of Governors which establishes general policy for the House and is responsible for its overall operation, subject to final review by the University's Board of Trustees.

International House serves as a social and cultural center for approximately one thousand foreign students, staff, and visitors associates with the University each year. The House has a capacity of 526 residents. The director of International House also serves as adviser to foreign visitors for the University of Chicago.

Now return to Dorchester Avenue and head north to 57th Street. On the way note the stunning new apartment building on your right followed by the elegant old Cloristers Apartments—both of which house many faculty families. At 57th turn east to Jackson Park and the Museum of Science and Industry.

Museum of Science and Industry— East 57th Street at South Lake Shore Drive. Architect: Charles B. Atwood, of D. H. Burnham and Company (1893). Architects for restoration: Graham, Anderson, Probst, and White for the exterior; Shaw, Naess, and Murphy for the interior (1929-40)

Before climbing the stairs at 57th Street and Lake Park (where you can get an Illinois Central suburban train back to the Loop as frequently as at 59th Street) walk one block east into Jackson Park for a good view of the Museum of Science and Industry. A visit inside, as with the museums around Burnham Park (see Walk No. 14), rates a separate trip. You could spend whole days here without completing the exhibits.

Just a view of this enormous building is an experience. Erected as the Palace of Fine Arts for the 1893 Columbian Exposition, it follows an elaborate Greek revivalist style—precisely duplicating various parts of temples on the Acropolis at Athens. Ionic columns, doorways, and the giant-sized caryatids (13 feet tall, weighing about 6 tons each) are copied from the Erectheum; the carving on the metope panels and frieze is reproduced from the Parthenon. Materials used, however, were not those of the Acropolis temples. For the original "temporary" building heavy brick walls were merely covered with plaster, and the Ionic columns were constructed of wood lattice frame, then covered with a plaster composition called staff.

Though widely admired as the showpiece of the Columbian Exposition, this building and others in the neoclassical style brought forth the bitter statement from the Chicago architect Louis Sullivan so often quoted: "The damage wrought by the World's Fair will last for half a century from its date." Whatever its influence on architecture, however, the "Palace of Fine Arts" has become a decidely modern museum with chief emphasis on technology, a popular place visited by millions of people each year.

The transformation was by no means simple or painless. The Palace of Fine Arts building was abandoned in 1920, when the Field Museum, which had been using space here, moved to its own building nearer the Loop. Not until several years later was it rescued from neglect. The extraordinary amount of money needed to restore both exterior and interior as a permanent building and to establish it as an industrial museum came largely from Julius Rosenwald, though his initial contribution of $3 million was apparently inspired by a bond issue of $5 million for this purpose passed by the voters of the South Park District. (Rosenwald's later contributions brought his total gift up to about $7.5 million dollars.)

In the current museum exhibits, you can see yourself on closed-circuit television, hear yourself on the phone, watch chickens being hatched, see how the human embryo develops from conception to birth, go down into a section of an actual coal mine, operate the extensive miniature railroad, or walk through the town of yesterday. The press of a button will put into motion principles of physics, electronics, or chemistry, dramatizing the basics of science and mathematics as nothing else ever did.

For this particular walk, however, just look at the building and ponder on the incongruity between the beautiful, Greek-temple exterior and the 20th century science and technology it houses!

Walk-20

Row of townhouses
by Louis Sullivan at
1826-34 Lincoln
Park West.

Walk · 20

OLD TOWN TRIANGLE

WALKING TIME: 1½ hours.   HOW TO GET THERE: Take a northbound CTA bus No. 10
(Lincoln-Larrabee) on Wells Street (4 blocks west of State). Get off at Wells and
Eugenie (1700 N).

Note two high-rise apartment buildings, one at Eugenie and
LaSalle designed by Dubin, Dubin, Black and Moutoussamy and
completed in 1972, and the second at Eugenie and Wells,
designed by Schiff and Friedes and completed in 1972. The
LaSalle Street tower has an adjacent shopping and
community center. It has an excellent food mart.

Now, walk one block north to 1751 Wells to a unique
development designed by Ezra Gordon and Jack Levin (1973).
It is named Kennelly Square for the former Werner-Kennelly
warehouse at 1750 Clark, which has been remodeled and
is part of this complex. The east building is called the warehouse.

The development includes a 25-story high-rise apartment
building on Wells; a 10-story apartment building on Clark;
a 54,000 square foot commercial space, swimming pool,
restaurant, and community facilities. The shopping gallery is
skylighted and is accessible by a bridge over an open sunken
arcade where the restaurant is located.

Next, walk one block to Lincoln Avenue and see another
interesting high-rise apartment building, Hemingway House, that
also caters to young adults by including shopping and other
amenities as a necessary ingredient.

By this time you have already noted the enormous amount of
new construction that has taken place recently in Old Town.
It is estimated that approximately 3,000 dwelling units in
high-rise apartment buildings have been constructed.

Hemingway House—1825 Lincoln Plaza.
Architects: Solomon, Cordwell, Buenz and
Associates (1971)

Hemingway House contains 260 apartments and 20,000 square
feet of shops and offices. All parking is below grade. The tower
on the north end of the site minimizes sun shading of adjacent
yards and structures. The height of the two-story commercial
structure was scaled to correspond to the predominant height of
the cornice line of existing structures on Lincoln Avenue,
thus preserving the vertical scale of the entire block.

Now return to Eugenie and Wells.

Start at Eugenie Avenue and walk west to *Crilly Court,* a famous
bit of Chicago. At the end of World War II, this section of the
city was overcrowded and rapidly deteriorating. The owner of
several large walk-up apartment buildings decided to deconvert
and rehabilitate his buildings, two of which were back to back,
separated by an alley. By replacing old wooden porches with
steel balconies and stairs, and transforming the yards into
gardens and delightful play areas, he changed the entire
character of the buildings. The city, taking cognizance of his
fine work, named the short connecting street to the west Crilly
Court after its innovator.

Crilly Court established the procedure for much fine conservation
and rehabilitation work that characterizes the Old Town
Triangle area. Many painters, sculptors, musicians, poets, authors,
and architects have now made this area their home.

There are so many late 19th-century townhouses and walk-up
apartment buildings here you may think that when you've seen
one you've seen them all. Not so; each is a pleasant surprise,
sometimes found tucked in between taller buildings or set back
far from the street. The rich texture of the fine brickwork and
stone ornament make an architectural "find" of many of
the buildings.

Continue west on Eugenie to the west side of Crilly Court, where
townhouses cover this entire side of the short thoroughfare.
Crilly Court itself is a private road with characteristics that
suggest a quiet side street in the west end of London about the
time of Sherlock Holmes!

246

Hemingway House.

Opposite, Piper's Alley.

225 Eugenie—Walk across the street for a better view of this recently remodeled 3-story frame house, with a new stucco wall and patio that make for privacy, and a charming entrance and facade.

235 Eugenie—Architects: Harry M. Weese and Associates (1958). A delightful contemporary structure of 7 maisonettes. These comprise 14 dwelling units of 2 stories each, the architect having placed 2 "layers" of 2-story townhouses in a row of 7.

1700 North Park Avenue—(300 W), New Orleans House. A modern structure in red brick and glass, 5 stories high, with the glass line slanted in from ceiling to floor. Parking is at grade, partially under the building. By adding high-density apartments to the area, this building detracts from the low-key atmosphere of the rest of the block.

1701, 1707, 1715, 1717 North Park Avenue (across the street)— Four-story walk-up apartments, well maintained; spacious, with high ceilings and fine-textured brickwork.

Old Town Players—1718 North Park. On the west side of the street again, you will see a charming old church building, tucked away behind trees, with a patterned brick walk. This structure has been remodeled into the home of the Old Town Players, a repertory theatre group—oldest of many small theatre groups in the city. The interior has been most successfully remodeled into a delightful arena for classical as well as modern drama. Performances weekends only. (For information phone 645-0145.)

Midwest Buddhist Church—1763 North Park.

At this point of the walk, stroll along *St. Paul (1732 N)*, to view the charming townhouses, trees, shrubbery, and vines there. Then return to North Park Avenue. Continue north past Willow (1746 N) and stop at the Midwest Buddhist Church, at 1763. Visitors are welcome.

This church, an important center for Buddhists in Chicago, sponsors two outdoor festivals each year—the brief Obon ceremony in July and the 3-day Ginza festival in August, at which classic Japanese dances and other Oriental activities are performed in lantern-decorated streets near the church.

Left top, Row of townhouses, Crilly Court. There are many attractive gardens in the rear. *Bottom,* Modern, double townhouses at 235 Eugenie.

A new Midwest Buddhist Church has been erected on the Ogden Mall at Lincoln and Menomonee. It is so magnificent that it enjoys the title of "Midwest Buddhist Temple." This older structure has been retained by the congregation and is used as a community center and judo school.

316 and 334 Menomonee (1800 N)—Turn west on Menomonee to see a successful rehabilitation of an old apartment building at 316; and at 334 another example of successful rehabilitation, set behind a lovely garden.

1838 and 1835 Orleans Street (340 W)—At Orleans Street, walk north to 1838 and enjoy the ornate, red brick, high-ceilinged, mid-Victorian structure there. An excellent rehabilitation job. Note too, across the street at 1835, the charming old vine-covered townhouse and patio—well maintained.

1817 and 1801 Orleans—Now come back south on Orleans. Note the rehabilitated house at 1817, a 3-story, red brick, pre-Civil War structure. The Orleans apartment building, at 1801, is a rather poor facsimile of a New Orleans facade.

235 Menomonee—Farther east on Menomonee stands a daring rehabilitation of an apartment building: the 3rd story has been removed in order to give the 2nd-floor living room a ceiling 2 stories high. Excellent!

1802 Lincoln Park West (300 W)—Walk west again on Menomonee and turn north on Lincoln Park West. Stop at 1802—a charming, well-maintained mid-Victorian house, built about 1880. The brick wall and fine old trees make a delightful pattern.

1814 and 1816 Lincoln Park West—Farther north in the same block you come to 2 red brick, high-ceilinged houses in fine condition—surely the result of *tender, loving care!*

1826-34 Lincoln Park West—A row of 2-story, red brick townhouses set back from the building line. Designed by Louis Sullivan, these homes have a special charm, due partly to the terra-cotta ornamentation and good landscaping.

1836-38 Lincoln Park West—The showpiece in this group is the brick-and-frame Swiss-type house at 1838, which has unusually heavy wood ornament above the first floor. In a garden at the rear are 2 more brick houses, the one at 1836 having once been the home of Charles Wacker, first chairman of the Chicago Plan Commission—for whom Wacker Drive was named (see Walks No. 11 and No. 12). The 2-story frame house with a garden to the north is another example of how a well-maintained house can be kept livable and delightful.

1830-38 Lincoln Avenue—Turn to your right at Lincoln Avenue and walk southeast to see the 5 houses from 1830 to 1838. A walk in the alley to the rear is most rewarding, for they all have delightful rear patios. At the time of the Old Town Art Fair, held the second week in June each year, these patios are opened to the public.

1848 Lincoln Park West—Now return to Lincoln Park West, and continue north to 1848, to see another example of remarkable rehabilitation. The vertical brickwork at the center of the bay window carries all the way from grade to roof for a stunning effect.

1915 and 1917 Lincoln Park West—Still farther north, 2 fascinating rehabilitated townhouses. Although they were remodeled about 10 years ago, the work seems still fresh.

Ogden Mall—Named Ogden Mall as part of the Department of Urban Renewal's exciting new plan for the closing of Ogden Avenue, this new pedestrian mall is only partially completed. It is a diagonal thoroughfare, for which the portion to be closed extends from Clark Street on the east to North Avenue, about a mile to the southwest. When completed, it will be the major axis of a green belt connecting Lincoln Park to the residential community to the west.

Lincoln Park Tower—1960 Lincoln Park West. Architects: Dubin, Dubin, Black and Moutoussamy (1967)

This apartment building has a first-rate design. It includes swimming pool and restaurant at the lobby level. It is well sited with respect to Lincoln Park and Ogden Mall.

The four torches and the mall appear as a symbol of a renewed community. Across the street on the north side of Armitage is another high-rise, reinforced concrete apartment building

Lincoln Park Tower.

251

named Lincoln Park Terrace also designed by the same architects, Dubin, Dubin, Black and Moutoussamy (1972). The circular balconies give it an individual appearance that does not in any way echo the Lincoln Park Tower design.

Midwest Buddhist Temple—435 West Menomonee. Architect: Hideaki Arad (1972)

Follow the alignment of the former Ogden Avenue—now Mall—and continue in a southwesterly direction. First, pass two small studio apartment buildings with shops at grade level. The urban renewal plans call for a combination of residential, commercial, and institutional development along the Mall. At this writing, much of the area has yet to be built upon. However, one can already see the preliminary results of the exciting concept of this new pedestrian mall.

The patient persistence of Lewis W. Hill, Commissioner of Urban Renewal and Development and Planning, is largely responsible for the apparent success in implementing the plan.

At first glance, from a distance of two or three blocks, the temple seems to be set on a high plateau. As one gets closer, it is apparent that although it is on flat ground, the illusion persists until one is almost next to it. The reason for this is the unusual method the architect used in setting the chapel up high above the main portion of the structure.

The chapel has a shingled, modified gable roof which at a distance gives the appearance of a pagoda. The base of the temple is made up of a concrete wall that is striated by a rough, bush hammer technique. The first floor wall continues up above the first floor ceiling line to become the parapet wall for a deck that surrounds the chapel.

The temple congregation owns property to the east and west and intends to build a parsonage and Japanese garden. Hopefully, this will be done in the near future.

Also known as the Temple of Enlightenment, the rectangular floor plan places a large social room directly beneath the high chapel. The social room is set a few feet below grade with an open corridor at grade level on the two long sides. The corridor gives access to classrooms and offices.

Opposite, top, Midwest Buddhist Temple. *Bottom*, St. Michael's Square.

The high chapel can be reached from the social room as well as from outside. The main entrance consists of an impressive concrete stairway where one passes through heavy iron gates with the bush hammered concrete wall on either side. One first reaches the deck before entering the chapel. The deck is actually the roof over the corridors described earlier. It provides the means to hold ceremonial processions as well as a place to accommodate large crowds waiting to enter the chapel.

The exterior walls of the chapel are stucco finished with windows of translucent glass.

Upon entering the chapel, one is aware of its simple character with white walls and ceiling and heavy timber trusses. There is an altar at the south end that consists of a gold-leaf sanctuary and shrine that contains a small gold, standing buddha. The altar has two large brass candelabras and vases with lovely floral arrangements.

The exterior remains the boldest part of the temple. It has the strength and vitality of the ancient Japanese shrines along with the simple straight lines of contemporary architecture.

St. Michael's Church—Eugenie at Cleveland.

Continue southwest two blocks to this enormous church, convent, rectory, elementary school, and community center. The brick and stone church was originally built in 1869 and partially destroyed by The Great Fire of 1871. It was restored in 1872 and expanded over the intervening years to its present size.

Originally, St. Michael's was a large German-speaking parish. Today, one mass on Sunday is given in Spanish; the other is in English. This reflects the changing character of the neighborhood. The large number of new townhouses and apartment buildings recently completed on all sides of the church indicate that there will soon be a resurgence of attendance.

The semi-Gothic-Romanesque-German Baroque character of the exterior and interior of the church comes as a pleasant surprise, if one is not an absolute architectural purist. The interior has an enormously high ceiling with Gothic-type vaulting supported by slender columns with semi-classic capitals.

The great monumental altar is carved wood with many sculptured figures capped by a figure of St. Michael with a great sword and a great jeweled crown overhead, over which stands a jeweled cross. There are murals on either side of the altar. All in all, it is a fascinating Baroque setting.

The urban renewal program has made St. Michael's a part of the Ogden Mall with a large pedestrian masonry court at the entrance facade.

Larrabee Street

Now walk two blocks west to Larrabee and see the enormous amount of new construction on land recently cleared by urban renewal. Fascinating new townhouses, apartment buildings, and a new fire station all add up to a scene of dynamic revitalization for the area.

Walpole Point

Both sides of Larrabee as well as Lincoln Avenue starting at Dickens to Grant Place.
Architect: Seymour Goldstein (1973)

Here, in the heart of the mid-north Lincoln Park conservation area, a new kind of neighborhood has been redeveloped. On a rather "tight site," the architect has successfully managed to plan a series of play yards, gardens, green areas, tot lots, and patios in between structures and open parking areas. There are many inviting open terraces, sunken courtyards, and walks that together make Walpole Point a pleasing experience.

There are two types of dwelling units—townhouses and apartments. Eighty of the townhouses are initially ownership for moderate income families. The remaining 76 townhouses will be retained by the developer for renting. The 96 apartment units will be rented also. The developer intends to eventually sell all the remaining townhouses to middle-income families. Thus, the development has a diversity of economic, social, and cultural families that already gives the area a look of stability.

Combinations of the red brick, peaked, and cantilevered roofs with angled double windows and arched openings give the effect of variety and distinctive character.

The Farm-in-the-Zoo
on Lincoln Park's
South Pond.

1. Chicago Historical Society
2. Lincoln Park Zoo
3. Chicago Academy of Sciences
4. Viking Ship, Children's Zoo and Main Zoo
5. Lincoln Park Conservatory
6. Francis W. Parker School
7. Lincoln Park Casting Pond

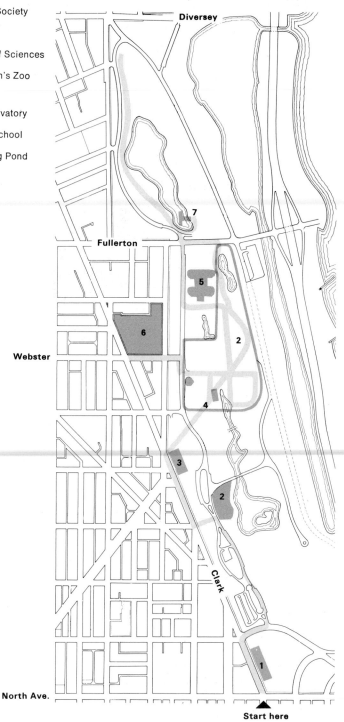

Diversey

7

Fullerton

5

6

2

Webster

4

3

2

Clark

1

North Ave.

Start here

Walk · 21

LINCOLN PARK : Museums, Zoos, Conservatory

WALKING TIME: 1½-2 hours (more if you want to enter the museums).　　HOW TO GET THERE:　Take a northbound CTA bus No. 36 (Broadway) on Dearborn Street (1 block west of State Street), and get off at North Avenue (1600 N) and Clark Street.

Lincoln Park, like New York's Central Park, was designed by the landscape architect Frederick Law Olmsted. It is Chicago's largest park, covering some 1,000 acres of land just off the lake all the way from North Avenue (1600 N) to Hollywood (5700 N). This walk, however, will take you only through the southern part, no farther than Diversey Avenue (2800 N). In this section you are in the old Lincoln Park, as it was before the various northern extensions—on land redeemed from the lake—were added. And here you will find practically all of the park's special attractions.

At the southernmost border, where Dearborn Street ends at Lincoln Park, a rugged bronze figure of Abraham Lincoln stands to greet you, ignoring the very adequate bench behind him— despite its distinguished designer, Stanford White. This Lincoln statue, by Augustus St. Gaudens, is only one of nearly 30 large, miscellaneous statues in Lincoln Park—of such disparate personages as Garibaldi, Hans Christian Andersen, Beethoven, Shakespeare, John Peter Altgeld, and Emanuel Swedenborg. Perhaps the 2 most unexpected in this locale are the large nude figure of Goethe and the conventional equestrian statue of Ulysses S. Grant, though he appears not at all in *Grant* Park, where St. Gaudens' *seated Lincoln* is the main attraction (See Walk No. 1, Michigan Avenue: South).

The statue of Benjamin Franklin was recently moved from the enlarged zoo area to a commanding site just north of the pedestrian underpass and the Chicago Historical Society.

Chicago Historical Society—
North Avenue and Clark Street.
Architects: Graham, Anderson, Probst and White (1925)
Architects for New Wing: Alfred Shaw and Associates (1972)

Only a few steps away from the Lincoln statue is—appropriately —the Chicago Historical Society, especially famous for its Lincoln and Civil War materials. It has occupied this building— a 2-story brick structure with a well-proportioned Georgian facade—less than 40 years, but the Society was organized well over a hundred years ago, in 1856.

An imposing gray limestone west wing was completed in 1972. The architect was Alfred Shaw and Associates. This wing makes it possible for the Society to exhibit many important items that heretofore had to be stored in the basement.

In referring to the building addition, Andrew McNally III, president of the Society, told the trustees:

> The planned addition to our building will provide space for our collections, space for new exhibits, space for handling school children, and space for us to conduct lively and exciting programs.

To anyone interested in this country's history, a visit to the museum is already a "lively and exciting" experience. The past comes vividly to life through dramatic displays, period rooms, costumes of famous Americans, and a collection of early autos and horsedrawn vehicles, as well as through the exhibits of manuscripts, paintings, prints, and maps. Seasonal contributions by the museum are an old-fashioned Christmas tree and an old-fashioned Fourth-of-July celebration with a reading of the Declaration of Independence, speech and band and fireworks.

Opposite, Interior of the Chicago Historical Society's new wing.

260

Old Hollywood films are sometimes shown Sunday afternoons.

Open daily 9:30 A.M. to 4:30 P.M.; Sundays and holidays 12:30 to 5:30 P.M. Family $1.00; adults 50¢; children 6-17 and senior citizens 25¢. Monday free (Tuesday if Monday is a holiday).

Just north of the Chicago Historical Society, with its records of the city by the lake and of the people who made the records, is the tomb of one of those historic people—Ira Couch. Ironically, the rather small Couch Mausoleum is often overlooked, though its presence is proof that the Couch family won a lawsuit against the city to keep it here when the city cemetery was discontinued and the graves moved to private cemeteries. Ira Couch, originally a small tailor, became in 1836 one of Chicago's pioneer hotel owners—the proprietor of the Tremont House, then located at the northwest corner of Lake and Dearborn streets. The only other reminder of the park's earlier function is a boulder farther north, placed by the Sons and Daughters of the American Revolution over the grave of David Kennison, the last participant in the Boston Tea Party to die—in 1852, when he was 115 years old!

Lincoln Park Zoo, favorite haunt of thousands of Chicago's children, is actually 3 zoos—the Farm-in-the-Zoo and the Children's Zoo, as well as the century-old main zoo of the traditional kind. Children will be delighted to find the *Farm-in-the-Zoo* just a short walk from the Lincoln statue, through the underpass to the north. Although originated as a way of familiarizing city children with the farm animals they never see, it has proved equally fascinating to children coming in from the country. You will find here not only the smaller animals of farm life—chickens, ducks, and geese; pigs and sheep—but horses and cows as well. In the dairy barn are cows for milking and in another are beef cattle. In still a 3rd barn, recently added along with the beef cattle barn, horses are on display. The milking parlor in the dairy barn with all its modern equipment may not seem natural to a generation old enough to remember watching the "hired hand" squirt the milk from the cow into a big open pail (now considered unsanitary), occasionally aiming a stream into the mouth of a waiting cat beside him. But the present generation of course finds the farm machinery—milking machines

262

and tractors and all the rest—more natural and more interesting.

In the main barn are many exhibits and demonstrations. There you can see samples of what is actually produced on a farm and learn how many ways they are used. You can also watch the process of manufacturing a number of things that are made from farm products or especially needed on the farm—fertilizer, leather, or soap, for instance. Eventually, the Lincoln Park Zoological Society hopes, the Farm-in-the-Zoo will have 6 buildings.

Open daily 9:45 A.M. to 5:00 P.M. Free.

Across the road from the Farm-In-The-Zoo is the *David Kennison Boulder* (already referred to), which marks the grave of the last survivor of the Boston Tea Party group, who—unexpectedly—died in Chicago.

The Lincoln Park Zoo and the Children's Zoo were consolidated in an ambitious expansion and remodeling program which was completed in 1971. Harry Weese and Associates were the chief planners and architects. They worked with the staff of the Chicago Park District and Board of Commissioners. Robert Black, chief engineer for the district, was in charge of construction. The Chicago Zoological Society, a private nonprofit citizens organization, also assisted.

The remodeled zoo now has rock and boulders with moats that give the animals a more natural setting. Spectators are given seating space to watch sea lions and other animals play in the pond. Many other improvements have restored the zoo to its former position of eminence.

Chicago Academy of Sciences—2001 North Clark.

The 2nd museum in Lincoln Park is the Chicago Academy of Sciences, a small natural history museum, which stands just one block north of the David Kennison Boulder, west of the farm. Founded in 1857, only one year after the founding of the Chicago Historical Society, this is the city's oldest museum, in fact the oldest *scientific* museum in the west. Here too Chicago's past is brought vividly to life—a past, however, long antedating anything you may have seen in the Chicago Historical Society's exhibits. For here you may walk through a section that reproduces

Chicago of 350 million years ago—when it was only part of a coal forest! And a series called "Chicago Environs" presents dioramas showing animals and plants that flourished here when the area was still open prairie.

Officially the Matthew Laflin Memorial, this building is a real tribute to one of Chicago's early businessmen. Matthew Laflin came to Chicago in the 1830's, having sold out his business in the east to a man by the name of du Pont! He started one of the first stock yards in Chicago, near enough the hotel he had built to synchronize the 2 businesses. Another of his business ventures in Chicago was a bus line—which he later sold to somebody by the name of Parmelee! This restless innovator shared an ambition with many other early Chicago leaders—to rest at last in the city's cemetery with an imposing monument above him. Like many others he was distressed when the graves and monuments there were moved and Lincoln Park substituted. Unlike the others, however, he found a magnificent solution. Though he couldn't be *buried* where he had hoped to be, he *could* have an impressive monument there. That monument is the building of the Chicago Academy of Sciences, for which he provided $75,000—the Chicago Park District supplementing this with $25,000 from its own budget. The interior is currently being remodeled, but the Romanesque exterior still stands as a worthy memorial indeed for one of Chicago's earliest successful businessmen.

Viking Ship, Children's Zoo and Main Zoo.

Farther on, just west of South Pond's northern end is the *Viking Ship*, one of the historic carry-overs from the 1893 Columbian Exposition. This is the very boat—a copy of a 10th-century Viking ship—that was built by Norway at that time and sailed across the Atlantic with a crew of 12 men who brought official greetings from their country to the citizens of Chicago.

Toward the north end of South Pond during the summer months is the *Children's Zoo*, exhibiting all the baby animals that were born at the Zoo during the previous winter and spring. If you arrive at feeding time, you may see baby cubs drinking from bottles and perhaps some chimpanzees in high chairs eating with spoons!

Opposite, Chicago Academy of Sciences.

265

Open daily 10:00 A.M. to 5:00 P.M.

The main *Lincoln Park Zoo* is the park's biggest exhibit. Now
nearly a century old, it occupies 25 acres of the park's total
acreage and is maintained by the Chicago Park District. The Zoo
is said to have more than 2600 different kinds of animals, birds,
and reptiles, representing a good cross-section of animal life.
The schedule of feeding hours suggests some of the variety:
starting at the monkey house at 1:00 P.M., or 11:00 A.M. in summer,
it moves to the sea lions, then to the bird houses; on to the
bears, wolves, and foxes; then to the small mammal house, and
finally ends up at the lion house at 4:00 P.M., except Mondays.
(The animal feeders can probably tell you when the reptiles are
fed and why the lions are neglected on Mondays!)

In the *Zoorookery,* a specialty at the Lincoln Park Zoo, land
and water birds make their home in a large attractive rock garden,
and are free to come and go as they like.

Zoo hours: daily 9:00 A.M. to 5:00 P.M.; Saturdays, Sundays,
and holidays 10:00 A.M. to 6:00 P.M.

Lincoln Park Conservatory—Just beyond the outdoor cages
of the Zoo lies the Lincoln Park Conservatory, covering 3 acres
of land. Its glass walls and roof protect a seemingly infinite
collection of plants. The show houses, some of which date back to
1891, display a large collection of potted palms, a fernery, and
a bit of real tropics where tropical fruit trees are propagated.
(The Conservatory has 18 propagating houses, which may
sometimes be seen by a visitor.) A Japanese garden comforts the
old-timer—somewhat—for the loss of the outdoor Japanese
garden that for years decorated a small island in Jackson
Park, one of the reminders of the 1893 Columbian Exposition.

Four annual exhibits have become traditional: a show of azaleas
in February and March, of lilies and spring plants in April,
chrysanthemums of course in November, and poinsettias and
Star of Bethlehem in December and January.

This is considered one of the finest conservatories in the
country. Incidentally, most of the flowers that appear in Chicago's
numerous parks are started in the greenhouses connected
with this conservatory.

266

Open daily 9:00 A.M. to 5:00 P.M. Free.

Don't overlook the park's outdoor gardens near the conservatory—Grandmother's Garden, water-lily ponds, fountains, and formal gardens.

And did you remember to toss a coin—for luck—into one of the Conservatory's pools or little waterfalls?

Francis W. Parker School—330 Webster Avenue (2200 North). Architects: Holabird and Root (1962)

Before continuing in the park, cross Lincoln Park West at Webster Avenue (2200 N) to see the Francis W. Parker School. This U-shaped, 3-story, hard-burned red brick structure replaced an ancient 4-story half-timber Tudor Gothic building constructed in the early 1900's.

Note the sculptured figures of children at the main entrance facing Clark Street. They were produced by sculptor Abbott Pattison, an alumnus.

An outstanding independent private school (prekindergarten through 12th grade) this was one of the first progressive schools in the country, following the creative teaching concepts of John Dewey and Francis Parker. This is the school that brought a cow to graze in the front yard, so that city children could have some touch of experience with the country. (This was in the days before the Farm-in-the-Zoo at Lincoln Park across the street.) Visitors sometimes question the wisdom of the overall architectural plan—placing the building on the Clark Street side of the property and leaving the side facing the park, which is some of the most valuable land in Chicago, for a play field. The school's board of trustees, however, who are as progressive as its policies, agreed to allow the green belt from the park to continue to Clark Street as its contribution to the community.

In a delightful courtyard facing south you will see a reflection pool, flower garden, and stainless steel sculpture by John Kearny. This charming setting is often the background for school functions, such as plays, receptions, and other ceremonies. The brick wall separating the courtyard from the play field contains some original terra-cotta plaques from the razed Garrick Theatre

Building designed by Louis Sullivan—first known as the Schiller Building, which stood at 64 West Randolph until its demolition in 1961. (The Second City theatre group also used stones from this building. See Walk Number 10.)

Lincoln Park's Casting Pond—Statues of Linné, Jefferson, and Altgeld.   Before you cross Fullerton Avenue, be sure to note the heroic-scale limestone statue of a male figure with 4 female figures at the 4 corners of the pedestal. The male figure is the 18th-century Swedish botanist Carl von Linné.

Farther north, along Stockton Drive just beyond Fullerton, lies Lincoln Park's North Pond, the *casting* pond for the use of anyone interested in developing that particular fisherman's skill. And just beyond the casting pond and ball-playing areas stands a golden statue of Alexander Hamilton, erected in 1952, designed by the architect Samuel Marx. (See also Walk No. 24.) This is the northernmost point in your walk. If you go over to the statue and up onto the plaza on which it is mounted, you will have a rewarding view—the Elks Memorial to the west (see Walk No. 24); To the north, the direction that Hamilton himself is facing, and slightly east, is a bronze figure of John Peter Altgeld, governor of Illinois not long after the Haymarket Riots (see Walk No. 15), who lost his political career but gained eternal fame for his courageous integrity in freeing the men he was convinced were unjustly charged with the bomb throwing on that dark day. To the east you will see the Diversey Yacht Club, and to the south (if you are willing to turn your back on the great gentleman!) a panoramic view of Chicago's always impressive skyline.

Pickwick Village
Apartments.

269

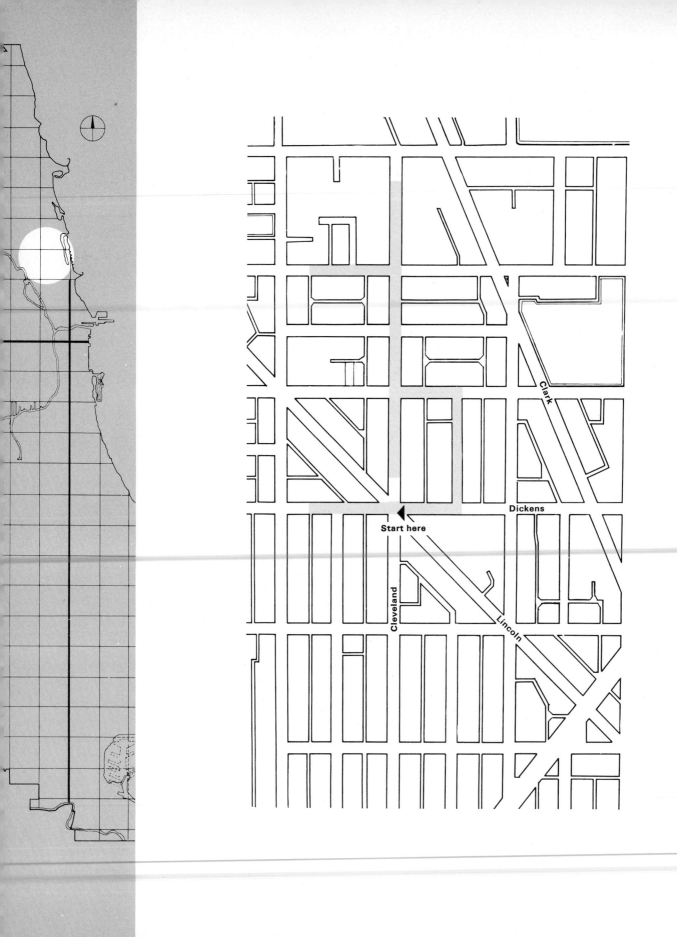

Clark

Dickens

Start here

Cleveland

Lincoln

Walk · 22

LINCOLN PARK CONSERVATION AREA :
Dickens, Hudson, Cleveland, and Belden Avenues

WALKING TIME: 1½ hours.   HOW TO GET THERE: Take a northbound CTA bus No. 10
(Lincoln-Larrabee) on Wells Street (4 blocks west of State). Get off at Dickens (2100 N)
and walk west on the south side of the street.

You are now in the heart of the Lincoln Park Conservation
area, where many improvements have been made and are still
taking place. The city through urban renewal *and* the citizens
through active participation in planning and cooperation with the
city have produced an outstanding program for the rehabilitation
of the entire 3-square-mile area. The little sign "LPCA" that
you see on windows or doors stands for Lincoln Park
Conservation Association and—being interpreted—means:
"We believe in the future of our area and are willing to work and
fight for it if necessary." (One of the ways the LPCA works for
the future of the area is by raising funds at a Puppetry Fair, held
annually the first weekend in October at the Francis W. Parker
School, 330 West Webster.)

Note first the new brick parkways and recently planted
trees, especially if you recall this area as it used to be—muddy
or dusty, where grass never grew.

The walk will take you around a number of streets in the area
where you can see interesting results of the conservation efforts.
Dickens, Hudson, Cleveland, and Belden avenues have been
selected, because along these streets—in close walking distance
of each other—are outstanding examples of architectural
rehabilitation. So many houses have been remodeled successfully
here that comment cannot possibly be made on each. What is
chiefly significant is that so much good remodeling *has been
done* and in the process has upgraded a whole area to the
point of enormous charm, grace, and vitality.

Pickwick Village—515-29 Dickens. Architect: Stanley Tigerman
(1965)   Stop first at a new structure called Pickwick Village on
the corner of Mohawk at 515-29 Dickens—a complex of eight

3-story townhouses on an open court with shrubbery and a piece of abstract sculpture. Each house has a rear patio screened off from neighbors and passersby. An off-street parking area is provided. This is a well-planned housing group, which blends with its older neighbors but still has the advantage of newer facilities.

Dickens Square—550-54 Dickens.   On the north side of the street, farther west, is an example of fine rehabilitation, not only of individual buildings but of a whole development. Six old structures, which had been in deplorable condition for years, were successfully restored to the original appearance of their exteriors and rehabilitated inside. *At 550* the center of the first 2 stories is effectively treated with glass from floor to ceiling. Gardens, patios, and open courts have been grouped around the buildings. The entire development is enclosed by a red brick wall with a series of arches, providing rhythm—as well as privacy—to this enclosure of 19th-century gentility.

540 Dickens—Architect: Arthur Carrarra (1959)   Now come back east to 540 Dickens. The exterior of this house (painted white) has been remodeled, with its entrance placed at grade instead of at the former 2nd-floor location. The style of General Grant's period has been retained outside, while the interior has been made contemporary with new lighting, new fixtures, and new central fireplace. Charming gardens can be viewed from the street over the old iron picket fence.

2100 Hudson (432 W)—Architects: Booth and Nagle (1968)   Now walk east to Lincoln Avenue at Cleveland, continue one block to Hudson, and head north. This is a quiet short block of charming, old, well-maintained houses owned by professional writers, painters, and sculptors. The contemporary character of one *new* group of 6 townhouses, at 2100, is shown by the trim, clean lines.

Policeman Bellinger's Cottage—2121 Hudson. Architect: William W. Boyington (before 1871)   On the east side of the street, a plaque on the building at 2121 states: "This is Policeman Bellinger's Cottage, saved by heroic effort from Chicago Fire of October 1871." It is clear that even heroic efforts could not save many houses, for the majority in this area were built after 1871. Note how well maintained the houses are at *2115-17* and at *2116-18* across the street. At *2127 and 2131* are examples of charming and successful rehabilitation.

2134-38 Hudson—On the west side of the street are some restored and remodeled townhouses, grouped around a well-landscaped courtyard, very well maintained.
Now return to Cleveland Avenue.

2111-21 Cleveland (500 W)—Walk west to Cleveland, then turn south to see the group of 4-story red brick former townhouses at 2111-21, now successfully converted into apartment buildings. The below-grade patio at 2111-15, with marble floors and stone walls, adds charm to the exterior. The original entrance doors and roof cornices have been refinished. New glass panels at the below-grade apartment give the structure an air of modernity.

2114 and 2116 Cleveland—On the west side of the street, at 2114 and 2116, are 2 red brick townhouses constructed about 1880. Wooden bay, turret windows, and a mansard roof make this remodeled apartment building very attractive.

2125 Cleveland—On the east side again, excellent rehabilitation work in the facade at 2125—yellow brick at the first floor and stained pinewood at the second floor, with a balcony and glass panel doors that reach from floor to ceiling.

2124 Cleveland—Across the street, at 2124, is a red brick, mid-Victorian house built about 1880, with delightfully slender white Doric columns at the entrance and balcony overhead, and a mansard roof, with fascinating iron picket work at the roof peak. This building has been remodeled into apartments with no loss of the original charm.

2129-31 Cleveland—Architect: Richard Barringer (1958)   Two townhouses of red brick with bay windows and entrances at grade, instead of at the second floor as they were before remodeling. The exterior facades retain most of the original dour appearance, but the interiors have been done over successfully.

2137-39-41 Cleveland—Still another series of old townhouses successfully remodeled into apartments—3 ivy-covered houses of brick and stone. Here too, new entrances at grade replace the former 2nd-floor entrances; yet the charm and general character of the old facades have been retained.

2234-36 Cleveland.

455 Grant Place (2232 N)—At the corner of Cleveland and Grant Place is a newly constructed 3-story apartment building of hard-burned brick, built around an open court. The court entrances are below grade in a patio facing Grant. This is a well-planned complex that blends with the surrounding, older structures.

2215 Cleveland—Architect: Bruce Graham (1969) Here is a stunning example of a well-designed urban townhouse—two-story, monolithic concrete, including a walled-in garden that completely encloses the site. There are travertine marble walks, and a black steel bar gate.

2234-36 Cleveland—A 3-story frame duplex townhouse. The brick face on the grade level and wood siding at 2nd- and 3rd-floor levels are painted gray. Black and white trim around windows and white Corinthian columns at entrance complete this charming, very old structure, built around 1874.

515 Belden (2300 N)—At Belden turn west to 515, where there is a complex of about twenty 2-story townhouses built around an open court. Although fairly well designed, the density is much too high and can only result in noise, traffic, and neghborhood congestion in general.

534 Belden—On the other side of the street, farther west, are some red brick townhouses remodeled into apartments. From the white limestone and glass entrances to the new balcony at the former entrance, this is a most successful enterprise.

538-544 Belden—A marvelous old sandstone apartment building. The remodeling includes metal grillwork on the balcony, black trim around doors and windows, and a black cornice on the ornate roof—for a most attractive effect.

2325 Cleveland—Back on Cleveland Avenue, at 2325, you will see a 3-story house painted gray, set back from the street, with an iron picket fence. A square bay window and roof turret give this 1880 house a definite stamp of individuality.

Contemporary Art Workshop—542 West Grant.

Walk west on Grant Place to 542. On the way note the many fine old townhouses that have been remodeled and restored to make an incredible handsome row after row. Also, note the

274

rebuilding process under way at the Grant Hospital whereby the old and mediocre structure has given way to a pleasant contemporary design that somehow fits with its neighbors.

The Contemporary Art Workshop, directly across the street from Grant Hospital, is an artists' workshop as well as school teaching painting, sculpture, jewelry, print making, and weaving. John Kearney, a well-known Chicago sculptor, heads the workshop. A tour can be arranged by calling 525-9624.

Now turn back south to Grant and walk east, passing new apartment buildings and townhouses on your right and professional office buildings at your left. At Clark note how Grant Place has been closed to through traffic. Also, note the delightful square at Belden with benches, landscaping, and a piece of limestone sculpture attributed to Lorado Taft. This is a good spot to end the walk and rest before returning to your place of origin. Before leaving, read the following reasons why this area has achieved a successful rehabilitation.

In considering that changes that have been made in this area, it is well to note that certain basic ingredients are essential to the success of extensive rehabilitation in any given area:

1. The area involved should be near schools, transportation, and recreational facilities.
2. The physical work required for rehabilitation must be feasible and then done well.
3. There must be a market that will pay the inevitably higher rents.

The Lincoln Park Conservation area meets all 3 of these requirements. Both this fact and the determination and dedication of its residents have contributed to its conspicuous success. Added to these is the fact that the City's Urban Renewal Program has given the area a tremendous assist.

Walk-23

Arthur J. Schmitt
Academic Center,
DePaul University.

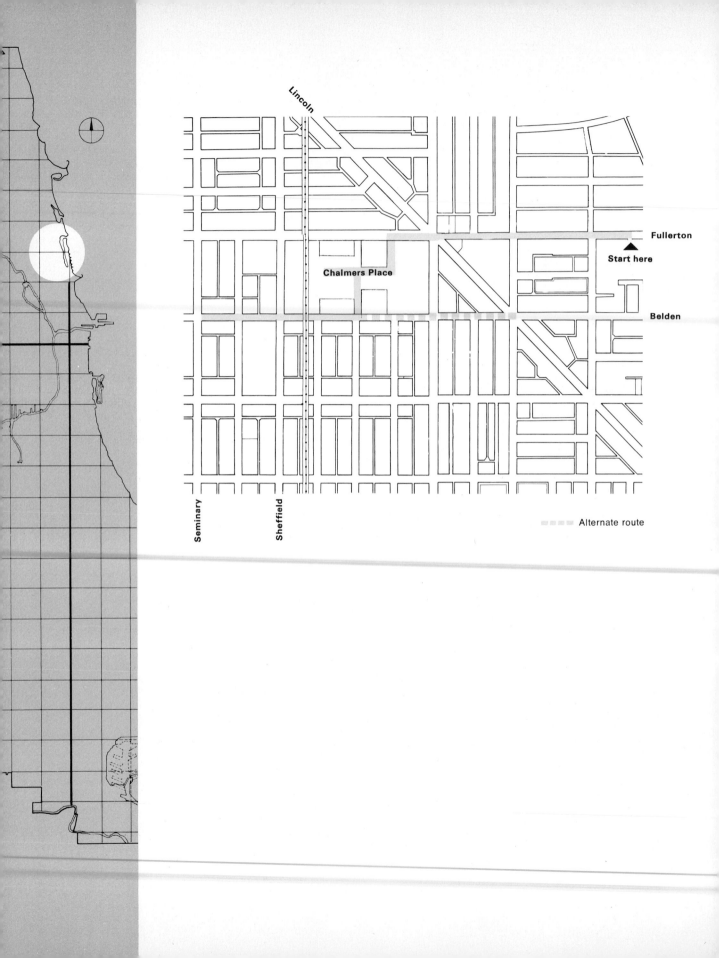

Lincoln

Fullerton

Start here

Chalmers Place

Belden

Seminary

Sheffield

Alternate route

Walk · 23

FULLERTON AVENUE, McCORMICK SEMINARY, DePAUL UNIVERSITY

WALKING TIME: About 1½ hours.   HOW TO GET THERE: Take a northbound CTA bus No. 22 (Clark Street) on Dearborn Street (1 block west of State). Get off at Fullerton Avenue (2400 N). Walk west to Cleveland Avenue (500 W), where this walk starts.

The community you will enter now is most fortunate in having several exceptionally fine institutions in its midst. A walk through the area will quickly demonstrate the pride with which these institutions and the people regard their community—a factor essential to success in almost any community conservation effort.

This walk will take you primarily to institutions of learning or healing, and through their campuses, but you will also come to pleasant walking areas with many interesting old townhouses en route.

Cenacle Retreat House—513 West Fullerton.

After the first 2 blocks on Fullerton, going west from Clark Street (which are not the most exhilarating part of the walk), you will come to a number of points of interest. You will pass a large convent, the Cenacle Retreat House, constructed in 1965 of hard-burned brick; it is an imposing, well-maintained addition to the community.

St. Paul's Church and Parish House—
Of the Evangelical and Reformed Church (United Church of Christ), 655 Fullerton.

The buildings at 655 Fullerton were erected in 1950, after a large fire had destroyed the earlier church and parish house of St. Paul's. The design is modified Spanish Romanesque, with red brick and stone trim. The tall, well-proportioned spire, which is well located, gives the church the proper, much-needed height. The buildings relate well to each other, for the site planning is good.

279

Children's Memorial Hospital—2300 Children's Plaza. Architects: Schmidt, Garden, and Erikson (1961)

At 700 Fullerton is the nationally known Children's Memorial Hospital—official address, 2300 Children's Plaza. This is one of the various hospitals served by Northwestern University's Medical School. (See Walk No. 9, Lake Shore Drive) The design of the hospital building, which was developed at various stages by the same architects, is strong but not too severe.

McCormick Theological Seminary— 800 West Belden. Architects for recent additions: Holabird and Root (1965, 1968)

Cross Halsted and continue west to the McCormick Theological Seminary, on a completely enclosed 20-acre campus stretching from Fullerton back south to Belden, and from Halsted on west to Sheffield. This Presbyterian seminary has been educating students for the ministry since 1859. Just walk west on Fullerton to the first entrance gate with an opening for pedestrians, and take a little time to enjoy this beautiful campus. Note especially the new classroom building (1965) and the McGow Memorial Library (1968), both designed by Holabird and Root. The architecture of the McClure Memorial Chapel (1961), which is Georgian, is in contrast of course with the contemporary design of the 2 buildings just named, though it was also designed by Holabird and Root. There is no jarring effect, however, because the site planning is first-rate and the space is adequate.

Chalmers Place (900 W)—part of McCormick Theological Seminary campus.

Now turn west and stroll around Chalmers Place, a private square. In this pleasant green area, comparable to Louisburg Square in Boston, are 3-story 19th-century townhouses facing on the north and south sides of the Place. To the west is the limestone Commons building of the Seminary, in collegiate Gothic, with dining halls and conference rooms. And to the west of the Commons is a second green space and square, with a student dormitory, an apartment building for married students, and a gymnasium. (To the east are the school buildings, already described.)

DePaul University—Lincoln Park Campus, 2323 North Seminary.

Now return to the McCormick Seminary chapel; walk south to Belden, then west under the L tracks to DePaul University's Lincoln Park Campus—official address 2323 North Seminary (1100 W). (DePaul University also operates a downtown branch, at 25 East Jackson.)

The first building of interest here is *Alumni Hall, 1011 West Belden,* a huge limestone building with granite base, which houses the University's athletic center.

An outstanding structure on the University's newly expanded campus (DePaul is undergoing tremendous growth and expansion of facilities) is the *Arthur J. Schmitt Academic Center, at Belden and Seminary avenues (architects: C. F. Murphy and Associates, 1967).* This is an imposing concrete building with 6 floors of classrooms, offices, and seminar rooms. By raising the entrance level well above the street, the architects have given this structure an imposing approach and the effect of great height. The cantilevering of the upper level will remind you of the 222 North Dearborn Building, also designed by C. F. Murphy Associates. (See Walk No. 4, Dearborn Street.)

De Paul University Center—2324 Seminary Avenue. Architects: C. F. Murphy and Associates (1971)

Directly across the street from the imposing and overwhelming Arthur J. Schmitt Academic Center is the De Paul University Center designed by the same architects in the same theme of great masses of concrete planes and surfaces. Although not nearly as overpowering a structure, it does manage to maintain its own individuality. This is probably due to the fact that only a portion is higher than one story and thus presents a strong horizontal mass that extends from a three-story windowless section that gives the appearance of a modern Mayan Temple.

The interior holds a pleasant surprise by the placing of the reception hall, cafeteria, lounge, and snack room in a series of facilities that wrap around a large green, grass atrium. The three-story section contains a chapel and offices for faculty and advisers.

Residence Hall—2319 Clifton.
Architects: Freidstein & Fitch (1971)

The Center extends all the way west from Seminary to Clifton and there on the opposite side is a pleasant and spacious-looking student residence hall. Again, concrete forms vertically and horizontally frame the large windows of the individual rooms. Although De Paul is primarily a commuter university, there is a demand for housing by a substantial number of students. The quiet and warm lounge sets the tone for the entire structure—scholarly dedication.

Before returning east on Belden, it is suggested that if you are interested in seeing the church for which the university is named, you might walk east to Sheffield and then one block south to Webster.

Church of St. Vincent De Paul—Webster at Sheffield.

This very large edifice is constructed with a grey limestone skin in a French Romanesque style. The nave has a high, barrel-vaulted ceiling supported by the ribs that are extended from the free-standing columns. At the transept, there are two large arches that are sprung from opposite corners to form an X in the ceiling.

The semi-circular apse contains a white marble sculptured altar with two small altars on either side. As you turn to leave, note the great, circles-within-circles, stained-glass windows. The blues, reds, and vermillions are quite lovely when the sun is shining.

Now, return north to Belden and east to Lincoln. There are several fascinating restaurants, bars, and theatres in the vicinity. John Barleycorn, Memorial Pub, Body Politic, The Bakery, Deli-Restaurant, and Kingston Mines are some of the best known.

North Side of
Fullerton Avenue.

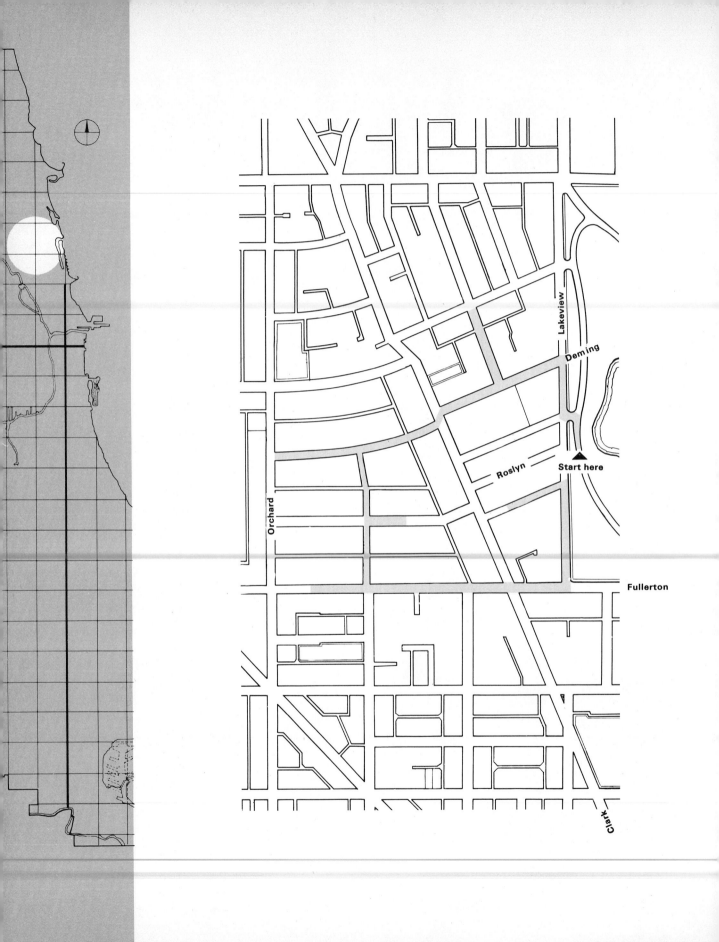

Walk · 24

DEMING PLACE AND NEARBY STREETS

WALKING TIME: 1 hour.   HOW TO GET THERE: Take a northbound CTA bus No. 153 (Wilson-Michigan) on State. Get off at Roslyn Place (2500 N) at the edge of Lincoln Park, and walk 2 blocks north to Deming Place (2534 N). If you are driving, you will find parking space available during the day.

Deming Place at Lakeview Avenue consists primarily of high-rise buildings. Later on in this walk, you will enjoy the pleasant surprise of seeing charming residential nineteenth and early twentieth century townhouses. You will also have the pleasure of following streets with houses set back of spacious lawns with great and handsome old trees. Some of the streets will curve and thus add to the element of surprise. Walking here is a delight.

The first stop is at the corner of Deming Place and Lakeview Avenue.

Columbus Hospital (North Wing).
Architects: DeSina & Pellegrino (1973)
Consulting Architects: Albert Schunkewitz and S. Chan Sit

This 10-story wing is formidable in comparison with the main hospital building. The precast stone panels against the tinted glass windows with their anodized aluminum trim give a strong emphasis to the vertical lines of both facades. The entrance and portico on the corner has additional strong vertical lines in the striated bronze columns.

The power plant and parking garage just to the west has equally strong vertical lines. This time it is in the striated and brush-hammered reinforced concrete facade.

Directly across the street is the genteel Marlborough Apartments, making quite a contrast to the Columbus neighbor. The Indiana limestone facing on the two lower floors along with the brick work and bay windows of the 12 floors, makes this charming building a pleasant sight.

285

Swedish Engineers Society of Chicago—
503 Wrightwood, formerly the Francis J. Dewes House.
Architect: Cudell Herez (1964)

Now, walk west on Deming to Hampden, then 1 block north to
Wrightwood (2600 N). There on the corner, at 503 Wrightwood,
is the headquarters of the Swedish Engineers Society of Chicago
—a limestone structure in baroque style, with enormous male
and female figures supporting the upper balcony of wrought iron,
a departure from the exclusively female caryatids of ancient
Greek sculpture! Heavy ornament surrounds the entrance and
upper window. A Mansard roof tops off the building. The annual
celebration December 13 for the crowning of Santa Lucia
features superior smorgasbord and special Swedish
entertainment.

Townhouses, Apartment Buildings, and Churches

Although many of the comments that follow may sound
repetitious, you may be sure that the buildings referred to will
not *look* repetitious, for all have a most welcome individuality.

Deming Place

Walk back south to Deming, passing a contemporary 6-story red
brick building with Cor-Ten steel balustrades on the balconies.
Cor-Ten steel was used on the Civic Center Building and
Chicago's Picasso (see Walk No. 3 Dearborn Street).

Next, walk west on Deming.

466 and 468 Deming—These twin townhouses with their
ivy-covered red brick facades are a joy to behold. The huge bay
windows with their black painted wood trim; the playful
dormer windows and brickwork at the third floor, are crowned
with a pair of delightfully curved and graduated brick wall.
It is a reminder of nineteenth century Boston or Philadelphia.
Chalmers Place on Walk 23 has some similar houses.

470 to 480 Deming—These are 5 townhouses with red brick
facades and individual bay windows.

Columbus Hospital has expanded to the extent that it now
covers almost the entire south side of Deming from Lakeview to

Opposite, Swedish Engineer's Society.

Clark. Architecturally, the hospital unfortunately lacks unity and reflects the fact that each phase was a separate design function.

Now walk west to Clark Street and note that you are at the southern end of a two-mile strip of ethnic restaurants, art galleries, taverns, boutiques, and health food stores. This is a recent phenomenon and is the result of several former Old Town merchants moving here and attracting new merchants. It is known as New Town.

St. Clement's Roman Catholic Church—642 Deming.

Cross Clark Street (which runs NW in this part of the city) and continue west on Deming. Here the street starts to curve and the buildings are set back farther from the street. The lawns seem actually greener and the trees bigger and shadier! Continue west to Orchard Street (700 W). At the corner of Deming and Orchard stands St. Clement's Roman Catholic Church, just beyond St. Clement's Convent, at 622. French Romanesque, with limestone facade and a rose window over the entrance, this church has a pleasant surprise awaiting visitors who go inside. Above the spot where the apse and transept meet is a dome with mosaic tile figures that give the viewer a feeling of being in the 11th or 12th century.

Opposite, St. Clement's Church. *Left,* Window detail, 2438 Orchard Street.

289

Geneva Terrace (600 W)—Retrace your steps back east to Geneva Terrace, and turn south. Here, unexpectedly, are again some 19th-century townhouses with gardens and trees. *At 2461 Geneva* note the small house at the rear of the garden—built in pre-Civil War style.

Arlington Place (2440 N)—When you reach Arlington Place, walk east to 525. Note the pristine red-brick and stone facade with white wooden Ionic columns, all in good scale. This also reflects the style of the period before the Civil War.

Fullerton Avenue (2400 N)

Return to Geneva Terrace and continue south to Fullerton Avenue. West on Fullerton is an entire block of 19th-century townhouses. As you walk back east, note in particular these examples, all on the north side of the street:

646   A 3-story brick house.
638   A typically 19th-century house with bay window.
618   A 3-story house competely covered with ivy.

At the corner of this block you come to the *Lincoln Park Presbyterian Church,* a limestone structure in Romanesque style, old and well maintained. In the next block east on Fullerton are several more 19th-century townhouses, set back about 25 feet, with well-kept lawns and trees. At *530 Fullerton* is the *Episcopal Church of Our Savior,* a charming structure of the late 19th century, in English Romanesque design.

Park West Tower Apartments—444 Fullerton Parkway. Architects: Dubin, Dubin, Black and Moutoussamy (1972)

Situated at the corner of Fullerton Parkway and Clark Street, this 20-story building has been expertly placed on the site so as to command excellent sight lines for most of the apartments. There is a lower level plaza on Fullerton with restaurant facilities.

The building contains 200 apartments and was financed by the Illinois Housing and Development Authority. The exterior is a poured, reinforced concrete with a simple and efficient pattern of columns and spandrels.

345 Fullerton Parkway.
Architects: Harry Weese and Associates (1973)

These striking concrete twin towers have a particularly
powerful base and entrance.

Lake View Avenue (400 W)

2400 Lake View Avenue Building
Architect: Ludwig Mies van der Rohe (1963)

As you cross Clark Street again, returning east, you come to
the most famous building on this walk—at least the building
planned by the most famous architect, Ludwig Mies van der Rohe.
This is the apartment building at 2400 Lake View Avenue—
a handsome structure sheathed in aluminum, with columns
exposed at the base and the vertical lines carried by mullions.

The luxurious character of the apartments is indicated by
the exterior plate glass and the marble walls of the lobby, to say
nothing of the swimming pool adjoining the lobby.

Wrigley Mansion—2466 Lake View.

At the corner of Lake View and Arlington avenues, one block
north, is the high-ceilinged Wrigley Mansion, a fine old building,
well maintained. The exterior has limestone base and brick
facade, with brick quoins at the 4 corners and abundant
ornamentation at the 3rd-floor level.

Arlington Place

426 Arlington—Walk a few steps west on Arlington, to see
another 19th-century townhouse, also well preserved. Observe
the brick-and-limestone facade, with arches over the
wooden bay windows.

431 Arlington—On the other side of the street, at 431, is a 3-story
house with limestone facade and charming wooden bay windows.

438 Arlington—Back on the north side of the street is another
19th-century house, a 3-story Gothic revival in stone.

418 Arlington—And a little farther east, the last stop of this
walk, a pleasant old brownstone, well maintained.

Broadway

Lakeview

Diversey

Pine Grove

▲
Start here

▦▦▦ Alternate route

Walk · 25

LAKEVIEW, DIVERSEY, SURF, NEW TOWN

WALKING TIME: 1 hour.   HOW TO GET THERE: Take a northbound CTA bus No. 153
(Wilson-Ravenswood) on State or Michigan and get off at Wrightwood Avenue (2600 N).

2650 Lakeview Avenue.
Architects: Loebl, Schlossman, Bennett and Dart (1973)

This handsome 40-story apartment building and its Y-shaped
neighbor, 2626 Lakeview Avenue—also a 40-story apartment
building—are excellent examples of where two owners and their
architects cooperated in the planning so that nearly every
apartment in each building enjoys excellent site lines. The
2626 building was designed by architects Loewenberg
and Loewenberg (1970).

The tinted glass and anodized aluminum window frames against
the striated vertical lines of the concrete give the 2650 building
a delicate and slim line. The bay windows are well placed and
go toward creating a domestic appearance, in spite of the
great height of the structure.

Now walk north on Lakeview.

2700 Lake View—*Architect: David Adler (1920)*   The handsome
structure on the west side of Lake View, at 2700, is the
former *Ryerson Family Mansion.* (The Ryersons also owned
homes on Astor Street. See Walk No. 10, Gold Coast.) The house
here on Lake View is said to be a replica of an 18th-century
London townhouse. It is now occupied by a
community organization.

2704-2708-2710 Lake View—North of the Ryerson Mansion are
3 townhouses, all in the same style and tied together with a
common roof and party walls—a characteristic seen in so many
of our modern rows of townhouses. A stone base, dark red
brick facade, wooden columns painted white, and slightly
different ornamentation and details at each entrance give these

houses an effect of special charm and grace. Note the delicate transom tracery over the doorways.

Elks National Memorial Building, 2750 Lake View—*Architects: for the main building, Egerton Swartout (1926); for the Magazine Building, Holabird and Root (1967).* Next, on the same side of the street, is the monumental Elks National Memorial, originally constructed in memory of Elks who had died in World War I. The Memorial building consists of a great central rotunda—75 feet in diameter, 100 feet high—and 2 main wings. The base and columns support the huge dome, which is made up inside of pieces of marble from all over the world. The entrance is—of course!—adorned by 2 bronze elks. The Magazine Building is a recent addition, to provide a place for the many documents of the society. Indiana limestone is used throughout. The Elks Memorial main building is open to visitors daily from 10:00 A.M. to 5:00 P.M.

Diversey (2800 N)

Apartment Buildings—Diversey and Sheridan Road. Architect: Ludwig Mies van der Rohe (1957)

At the northeast corner of Diversey and Sheridan Road, diagonally across from the Elks Memorial, are 2 aluminum-sheathed tower apartment buildings, designed by Mies van der Rohe and developed by the late Herbert Greenwald. The 2 towers are expertly sited so as to give each apartment a spectacular view. The columns are exposed at the ground level; mullions divide the windows and carry the vertical sweep upwards. The 2 structures have a sculptured, almost poetic quality.

2800 North Lake Shore Drive.
Architects: Solomon, Cordwell & Buenz (1970)

As you approach this imposing apartment structure, note the buff color of the reinforced concrete exterior. The rugged columns and spandrels spaced in a rhythmic pattern give the block-long exterior an interesting facade.

If at this point you are feeling palpitations, go directly north

Opposite, Elks' Memorial building.

294

behind the 2800 building and there you will find
St. Joseph Hospital.

St. Joseph Hospital—2850 North Lake Shore Drive.
Architects: Belli and Belli (1963)

This complex of buildings contains the main three-winged,
12-story structure, parking decks, and nurses building. The
hospital serves the entire north side with its modern facilities.
The design, unfortunately, is eclectic and does not achieve what
the designers set out to accomplish.

Before returning to Sheridan Road, you will be rewarded by
looking south into Lincoln Park to see three important
pieces of sculpture.

Sculpture in Lincoln Park at Diversey

First is a standing figure in bronze of John Peter Altgeld,
Governor of Illinois during the Haymarket Square riot and
bombing of 1893. His courage and liberalism in pardoning three
of the men convicted of murder is described in Walk No. 15,
the Near South Side, at the Police Monument in the Central
Police Department lobby at 1121 South State.

Next is an allegorical bronze of Johann Wolfgang von Goethe—
a male figure of heroic scale, dedicated in 1913 to this great
poet and author by the German people of Chicago.

About 100 yards south of the Goethe statue is a sculptured
memorial to Alexander Hamilton, the first Secretary of
the Treasury of the United States. The figure of Hamilton,
standing erect, though made of bronze is appropriately painted
gold; it is mounted on a huge black granite structure, which
makes a dramatic contrast. This monument was erected in 1952
from funds supplied in memory of Kate Sturgis Buckingham—the
person who herself had left funds for the Buckingham Fountain
in Grant Park in memory of her brother. (See Walk No. 1,
Michigan Avenue: South.) The memorial was designed by
Samuel Marx.

Next, is the Meat Cutters Building at the northwest corner of
Diversey and Sheridan Road.

Amalgamated Meat Cutters and Butchers Union Building—
2800 North Sheridan. Architects: E. F. Quinn and
Roy T. Christiansen (1951); (1950-64)

In a 3-story light gray limestone structure is the central office
of a large and important trade union, the Amalgamated
Meat Cutters and Butcher Workmen of North America. Two
sculptured groupings are located on either side of the main
entrance. The concept, suggested by the Union's executive
director and carried out by the Chicago sculptor Egon Weiner, is
made clear by the title—"Brotherhood in Bronze." Each group
consists of 4 kneeling figures, representing the 4 races of
mankind (often identified as African, American Indian, Asian,
and European), all of whom are kneeling as a symbol of
man's dependence on a higher power.

Now, walk west on Diversey one block.

Goethe statue opposite Mies van
der Rohe apartments, Diversey and
Sheridan.

297

Brewster Apartments—2800 North Pine Grove.
Architect: R. H. Turnock (1893)
Architect for Remodeling: Mieki Hayano (1972)

The remodeling work and design have been handled with
sensitivity and good taste. Indeed, the architect for the
remodeling deserves the kudos of a grateful city. He has even
added a fine touch of drama by constructing the metal
ornament that is set in the parkway just in front of
the main entrance.

The red polished marble appears at the entrance moldings and
window columns of the first floor. By all means obtain permission
to enter. Once inside, you will see the delightful open grillwork
and cage of the elevator, the light court, skylight and metal
grillwork of the stairways. It seems strange that the original
architect, who once worked with William Lebaron Jenney, should
have produced so remarkable a building only once in his lifetime.

The apartments have been tastefully remodeled and now have
modern wiring and plumbing. Nevertheless, this 9-story structure
with its high ceilings and bay windows—rugged, rough-faced
with dark gray granite—seems out of place—something like
a sleeping giant—right on Diversey with all its noise
and movement.

Surf Street (2900 N)

Britton I. Budd Apartments and Green Senior Center—500 Surf.

On Pine Grove, walk north to Surf. The Britton I. Budd
Apartments and Green Senior Center, though no great
architectural masterpiece, are worth noting because of their
function. This remodeled structure, operated by the Chicago
Housing Authority, is a mecca for many of the older
citizens of the area.

Greenbriar Apartments—550 Surf, and
Commodore Apartments—559 Surf.

Walk west along Surf Street to the corner of Surf and Broadway.
Here, on opposite sides of the street, stand 2 huge apartment
buildings, which were constructed about 1890—the Greenbriar,

at 550, and the Commodore, at 559. These dignified brick structures have open courts, high ceilings, and smooth brick walls. The design of each facade is modified Georgian. Entrances are from Broadway as well as from the courtyards facing Surf. When the sun is in the west, it shines through the lobbies into the courtyards. Both buildings are well maintained, affording tenants excellent living quarters.

This walk has shown you, among other things, quite a variety of apartment buildings—examples of modern architecture, from Mies van der Rohe's to the Chicago Housing Authority's, and 3 buildings dating back to the 1890's: the Brewster, Greenbriar, and Commodore.

You are at Surf and Broadway in the center of a strip of interesting boutiques, restaurants, taverns and art galleries. It is called New Town. You crossed a portion of it in the previous walk. Stroll a couple of blocks north and enjoy some of the fascinating sights and rhythm of this section.

Whenever you wish to return to the Loop, you can take a CTA bus on Broadway or return to Sheridan Road where you will find the convenient 153 or 151 going south.

Walk-26

3824-3826 Alta Vista.

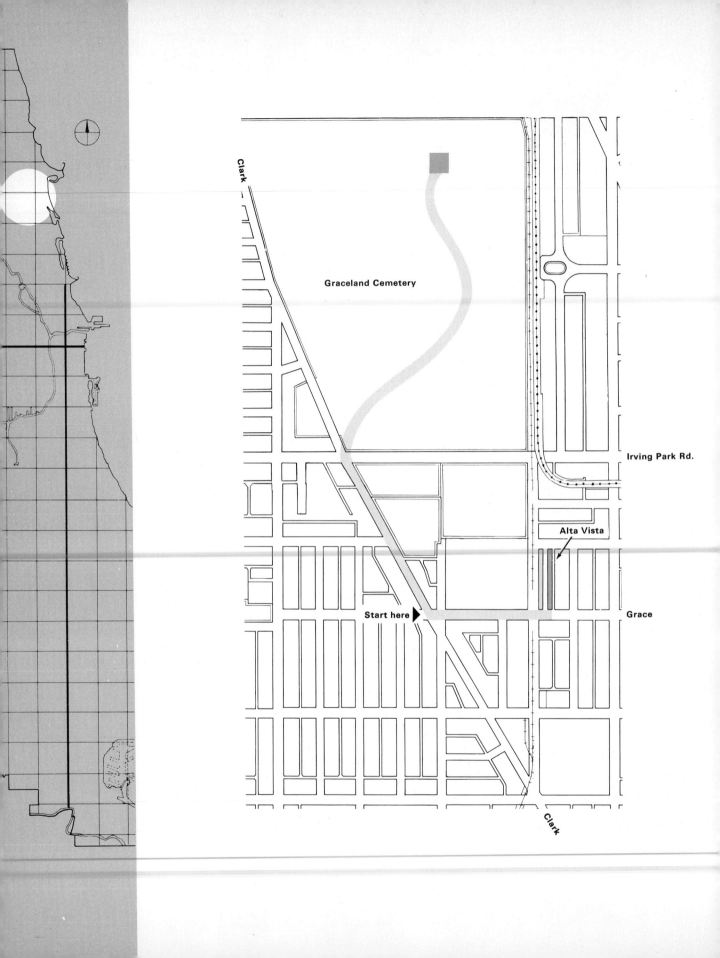

Clark

Graceland Cemetery

Irving Park Rd.

Alta Vista

Start here ▶

Grace

Clark

Walk · 26

ALTA VISTA - GETTY TOMB

WALKING TIME: 1 hour or less.   HOW TO GET THERE: Take a northbound CTA bus No. 22 (Clark Street) on Dearborn Street. Get off at Grace Street (3800 N). Walk 2 blocks east, past the House of Good Shepherd Convent, to Alta Vista (1054 W).

This short block has townhouses on both sides of a narrow street, which might be in Boston or Philadelphia or London. It seems to belong to a past century; it is definitely not a street of today. The well-maintained old houses—constructed at one time by one builder, who gave each house an individuality in design—are like an oasis in the surrounding desert of run-down housing. Most of the residents here are friendly and proud of their homes. Some are willing to show them to visitors.

Alta Vista was designated in 1972 as an Architectural Landmark District. This designation was made by the Chicago Historical and Architectural Landmarks Commission with the consent and approval of the Chicago City Council. This action will prevent encroachment or destruction of the district. The owners volunteered this action and enthusiastically participated in all the public hearings.

3801—In this house, on the east side of the street, limestone columns surround a wooden entrance in a pleasant eclectic design.

3805—An attempt at classic detail in the facade makes this another eclectic design. Note the stained-glass transom.

3802—On the other side of the street, a classic Georgian facade. The large wooden cornice at the roof line and over the entrance relate well with the bay window of the living room. Good scale.

3812—Another stained-glass transom over the entrance doorway.

303

3814—A Greek revival facade, with Doric pilasters of wood at the entrance and windows. A wooden cornice at the roof level gives the facade a sense of good scale.

3819—On the east side again, still another stained-glass transom—clearly one of this architect's favorite features. Ionic wood columns at entrance and 2nd-floor windows. A bay window at the first-floor level.

3824—Back on the west side of the street, a limestone facade and bay window. A doorway in natural finish completes this interesting townhouse.

3826—An English half-timber facade gives variety to the facades here at the northern end of the street.

3830—An old brick facade of good scale and workmanship.

3845—On the east side again, the last house on this walk, with wooden cornice and red brick trim.

On your return to Grace Street, walk behind the houses on the west side of Alta Vista. You may catch a glimpse here and there of some attractive patios and gardens.

◨ **Getty Tomb**—Graceland Cemetery, 4001 North Clark. Architect: Louis H. Sullivan (1890)

Now return to Clark along Grace and either walk or ride to Graceland Cemetery about four blocks north.

After entering the gate, proceed in a northerly and easterly direction until you reach a small lake at the northeast corner of the cemetery. By walking around the lake you will see some of the most incredible monuments ever assembled. They are of every size, shape and style, yet within certain areas, there is a flow of continuity. Where else but at a museum would one find an assemblage of such eclectic forms—the ancient pyramid, the obelisk, the classic columns and Gothic turrets?

The names on the various tombstones and sculpture read like a Who's Who of early Chicago. Such names as Ryerson, Field, Armour, Pullman, Palmer, Wacker, Glessner and Rockefeller-McCormick serve to remind us of the stability of that era. Along with Mayors Harrison and Busse, the

Opposite, Some of the various doorway treatments on Alta Vista.

305

distinguished architects, Louis Sullivan, Daniel Burnham and Mies Van der Rohe are included.

You will find the Getty Tomb in the northeast section of the cemetery, on the northwest side of the lake. The lower half of this is plain, unadorned stone. The ornamentation of the upper half and of the bronze doors is exquisite, with two designs well harmonized. This was proclaimed an Architectural Landmark:

> In recognition of the design which here brings new beauty to an age-old form: the tomb. Stone and bronze stand transformed in rich yet delicate ornament, a requiem for the dead, an inspiration to the living.

After leaving Graceland Cemetery, you will undoubtedly agree that the Getty Tomb transcends in beauty all other monuments there.

Louis Sullivan's Getty Tomb.

Arcaded
townhouses,
Pullman.

307

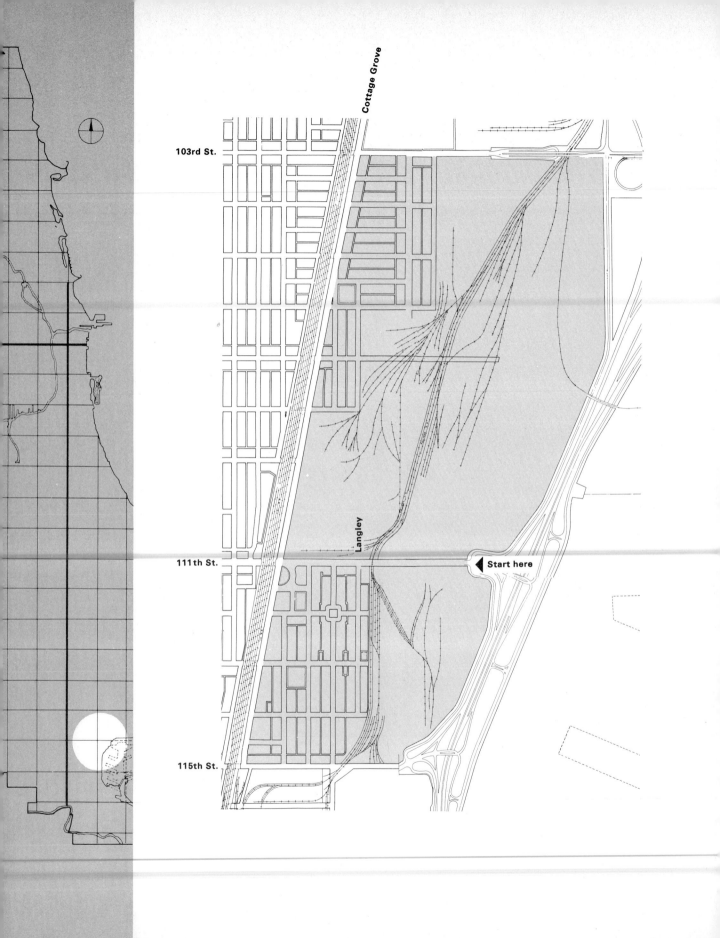

Cottage Grove

103rd St.

Langley

111th St.

Start here

115th St.

Walk · 27

PULLMAN

WALKING TIME: 1 hour.   HOW TO GET THERE: Take an Illinois Central (I. C.) suburban
train at Randolph and Michigan (underground station) to Pullman. (Inquire about which train
you should take.) Time—about 30 minutes. If you drive, take the Dan Ryan Expressway-East
to 112th Street, Pullman.

The community of Pullman, near Lake Calumet on Chicago's
Far South Side, was built as a model industrial town by George M.
Pullman, an early Chicago engineer. The town and all its
buildings, one of the first developments in this part of Chicago,
were designed by the architect Solon S. Beman and the landscape
engineer Nathan F. Barrett. In the late 1870's Pullman selected
this site for his Pullman Palace Car Company, which
manufactured his recently devised Pullman railroad cars. (The
first sleeping car was built in 1858, and the Pullman Palace
Car Company, a partnership of George Pullman and Andrew
Carnegie, was formed in 1867.)

For his model company town Pullman bought a long, narrow
triangular tract of land bordering the western shore of
Lake Calumet. Boundaries of the land were 103rd and 115th
streets north and south, Langley and Cottage Grove east and west
—4500 acres of what was then undeveloped prairie in the Village
of Hyde Park (not yet a part of the City of Chicago). The land
was purchased by the Pullman Land Association and the
Pullman Palace Car Company.

The town, which would be served by the Illinois Central
Railroad, was to have all the community facilities near the IC
depot—a hotel, a church, a school, and an arcade building with
stores, offices, library, theatre, and bank—everything owned
of course by the Pullman company. Work began on the Pullman
plants and 1,750 housing units in 1880. Early the next year
the first residents began moving into the 2-story row houses and
the cheaper apartment buildings planned for lower-income
workers. The factories were located north of 111th Street, along
with related enterprises, such as the Pullman Car-Wheel

works, the Allen Paper Car-Wheel works, the Pullman Iron and Steel Company, and the Union Foundry.

A walk through Pullman today gives you the sense of visiting an unreal town, though the houses, hotel, and village square are much the same as they looked at the turn of the century—an excellent showcase of town planning principles of the late 19th century. This is not a deserted ghost town (though the Pullman ownership and domination have vanished), but it does seem more like a movie set than an actual part of Chicago. In viewing the Florence Hotel, for example, an elaborate 4-story building with many gables and turrets, you may wonder whether it seemed real even to the Pullman residents of that day and just how much Pullman's workers ever used it. Mr. Pullman himself doubtless entertained there many guests to whom he showed his village with pride.

In this "model town" project Pullman was doubtless motivated partly by philanthropy as understood in his day and partly by enlightened self-interest (though he wouldn't have called it that). He believed that his employees would be happier if they could live near their work, in houses or apartments more attractive than the usual workers' homes, surrounded by all the facilities needed for daily living.

But Pullman's model town failed to bring happiness to his workers. Unrest hit the community—in those days made up mostly of German, Irish, Scandinavian, Scotch, and English descent—because they couldn't own their own homes and they felt that rents and prices in the company-owned store were too high. By 1889, when petitions were filed for the annexation of Hyde Park to Chicago, feeling was so high among the Pullman workers that they voted for annexation over Mr. Pullman's opposition. Still the community remained very much an independent town within the city and for a while it prospered. As orders and production increased in the Pullman plants, more workers settled there, until the population by 1892 included more than 20 nationalities. Additional housing built north of 103rd Street became known as North Pullman.

Real trouble lay ahead, however. The decline of the company town began with the depression of 1893-94, following the great boom Chicago had experienced with the Columbian Exposition of 1893. Unemployment rose and wages dropped, but rents and food prices remained pretty much the same. Mr. Pullman's refusal to restore his employees' wages to their previous figures and his prompt dismissal of several members of a committee that had called on him to discuss the matter precipitated a company-wide strike.

Since some of the workers belonged to the American Railway Union headed by Eugene V. Debs, the strike quickly became a nationwide issue, with an organization called the General Managers Association coming to the support of Pullman. After considerable violence and destruction of property, as well as the workers' refusal to run the trains, President Cleveland sent federal troops to take over—so that the mail could go through. Although at first the president's action caused even greater violence, it ultimately broke the strike. Eugene Debs was thrown in jail and his union weakened to the point of ruin. And Pullman's bitter, defeated workers returned to their jobs on his terms, not theirs. The only victory they won was a decision by the Illinois Supreme Court not long afterward that the Pullman Company's charter did *not* give it the right to own and manage a town. So ended Mr. Pullman's Utopian dream of a perfect village for his workers!

Yet the buildings remain. After 1900 a greater number of Polish, Italian, and Greek immigrants came to Pullman, and older residents began to move out. From 1920 to 1940 the Pullman area remained fairly stable, merely becoming an older community. Residential growth extended into North Pullman as the industry continued to expand, but south of 103rd Street it has been negligible since about 1930. A number of industrial plants have developed in the Pullman area, and the Dan Ryan Expressway now defines the old community's eastern boundary.

The Administration Building and Clock Tower

The Administration Building complex, constructed in the early 1880's, is located at the corner of East 111th Street and South Cottage Grove Avenue. Originally about 700 feet in length, this red face brick structure was made up of three parts; center section, flanking wings, and pavilions. The center section

311

Pullman Works.

313

contained three floors of corporate offices of the
Pullman car works.

In 1907, a large addition was attached to the southern wing.
This addition, approximately 60 feet in height, begins south of
the center section and continues south parallel to the old wing,
the facade of which was covered with the installation of the
new structure. Its architectural treatment is only vaguely
sympathetic to the original appearance, and because of differing
design characteristics (especially with respect to height and
property setbacks), the symmetrical qualities of the original
complex have disappeared completely.

The Florence Hotel

Named after George Pullman's favorite daughter and located at
the corner of East 111th Street and South Cottage Grove
Avenue, this structure was (and is) one of the first buildings to
greet the visitor to the town when stepping off the Illinois
Central train at the 111th Street Station. During the early history
of the town, many persons roomed here while either studying
the various aspects of the community or visiting on George
Pullman's personal invitation.

Although slight changes have been made to the facade, and a
large annex added to the northeast corner of the building after
1910, the hotel's fine overall appearance and pleasing
qualities are readily associated with the district.

The Greenstone Church

Located at the corner of East 112th Street and South
St. Lawrence Avenue, the Greenstone Church is perhaps the
most charming building in the entire district. Its name is derived
from the green color of its New England serpentine-stone
facade. The massiveness of the masonry coupled with the large
spire and arches suggests the influences of the Gothic Revival
and Romanesque styles utilized in the late 1800's. The influence
of architect H. H. Richardson is therefore suggested.

Since the Presbyterians had rented the church in 1885, the
Catholics and Swedish Lutherans asked Pullman's permission to
build their own structures. He resisted their pleas for years

but finally leased property to them so they could build. Swedish Elim Lutheran Church (1888), and Holy Rosary Roman Catholic Church (1890), both designed by Beman, were constructed on vacant land some blocks west of the town to satisfy the needs of these congregations.

Today, the Greenstone Church is in excellent condition. Both the interior and exterior have undergone extensive restoration, and it remains much the same as it did when George Pullman attended services there.

The Market Hall

This structure is located in the middle of the intersection of East 112th Street and South Champlain Avenue. By deliberate design, the building was placed at this location to break up the sometimes monotonous regularity of the streets' grid system.

The Pullman Stables

This structure is located at the corner of East 112th Street and South Cottage Grove Avenue. According to a town rule, all the horses of residents and visitors had to be kept here, apparently to prevent unnecessary clean-up tasks as well as to provide a profitable service. The volunteer fire company was also housed in this building for a number of years, and was known for its good service.

Around the turn of the century, a popular Sunday afternoon activity was to rent a carriage team, tour the countryside, and enjoy a family picnic. The company provided for this service at the stables, and individuals could rent a horse and buggy for $3 a day.

A service station, auto repair shop, and awning company now occupy the building, but interesting reminders of the past are still apparent, including two carved horses' heads located above the 112th Street entrance to the garage.

Pullman Housing

In an article on Pullman in the April-June 1970 issue of "Historic Preservation," a publication of the National Trust for

Historic Preservation, Norbert J. Pointner describes the
workers' housing as follows:

> No other element of the town deserves more attention than the
> quality of the workers' housing. A majority of the 6,000 persons
> employed by the Pullman Palace Car Company and its
> associated industries lived in the company-owned and
> maintained dwellings. The buildings were predominantly brick
> row houses containing from two to seven rooms. The company
> brick yard produced over 30 million bricks during each of
> several peak years to meet construction demands. Foundations
> and trim were made of stone and the roofs were slate. These
> row houses, produced in blocks of two or more, provided
> economy of construction and maintenance compared to
> individual free-standing units. The resulting residential densities
> are nearly three-quarters of the density of present-day Chicago,
> yet every home had direct access to a private fenced yard and
> a woodshed which opened onto a paved alley. The alley also
> served as access for vendors and trash collection, a company
> service included in the rent.
>
> A variety of dwelling unit types was to be found on and within
> each block throughout the town. These architectural differences
> were designed to meet the varying income, status, and family
> characteristics of the workers, and furnished a basis for
> meaningful variation in the street facades. Adding to the
> richness and identity of each street were structural and artistic
> variations in detailing, landscaping, roof line, lintels, chimney
> configuration, and brick coloring. Continuity was maintained by
> similarity of proportions, repetition of key details, brick-textured
> surfaces, setbacks, and the rhythmic lines of eaves and lintels.
>
> No dwelling was more than two rooms deep in order to secure
> cross ventilation and sunlight. Additional light was obtained
> on the top floors by the use of skylights and the usefulness of
> basements was increased by windows. A space of 100-110 feet
> was allowed between parallel rows of houses facing across
> the tree-lined streets. The quality of construction, concern for a
> healthful environment and variety of dwelling types help to
> account for the staying power of this historic community.
> During the 90 years of continuous use, families have been able to
> move from one home to another to meet changing family and
> financial conditions without leaving the community and
> established social and personal ties.

316

Unity Temple.

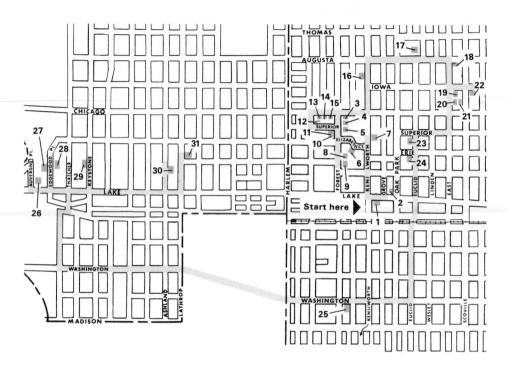

OAK PARK

1. Oak Park Unity Church
   and Parish House
   Lake St. and Kenilworth Av.

2. Memorial Fountain
   on Lake St. near Grove Av.

3. Frank Lloyd Wright House
   428 Forest Av.

4. Dr. W. H. Copeland House
   400 Forest Av.

5. Arthur Heurtley House
   318 Forest Av.

6. Mrs. Thomas H. Gale House
   6 Elizabeth Court

7. H. P. Young House
   334 N. Kenilworth

8. P. A. Beachy House
   238 Forest Av.

9. Frank Thomas House
   210 Forest Av.

10. E. R. Hills House
    313 Forest Av.

11. Nathan G. Moore
    House & Stable
    333 Forest Av.

12. Francis Wooley House
    1030 Superior St.

13. Walter Gale House
    1031 Chicago Av.

14. R. P. Parker House
    1027 Chicago Av.

15. Thomas H. Gale House
    1019 Chicago Av.

16. O. B. Balch House
    611 N. Kenilworth Av.

17. Harry S. Adams House
    170 Augusta Blvd.

18. W. E. Martin House
    636 N. East Avenue

19. H. C. Goodrich House
    534 N. East Av.

20. Edwin H. Cheney House
    520 N. East Av.

21. Rollin Furbeck House
    515 Fair Oaks Av.

22. William G. Fricke House
    540 Fair Oaks Av.

23. Charles E. Roberts Stable
    317 N. Euclid Av.

24. George Furbeck House
    223 N. Euclid Av.

25. George W. Smith House
    404 Home Av.

RIVER FOREST

26. William H. Winslow
    House & Stable
    515 Auvergne Pl.

27. Chauncey L. Williams House
    530 Edgewood Pl.

28. Isabel Roberts House
    603 Edgewood Pl.

29. J. Kibber Ingalls House
    562 Keystone Av.

30. E. Arthur Davenport House
    559 Ashland Av.

31. River Forest Tennis Club
    615 Lathrop Av.

Walk · 28

FRANK LLOYD WRIGHT IN
OAK PARK AND RIVER FOREST

WALKING TIME: 2 hours.   HOW TO GET THERE: Take a Lake Street CTA elevated train
headed for Oak Park at any of the Loop L stations, and get off at Oak Park Avenue. Walk 1
block north to Lake Street and then 2 blocks west to Kenilworth Avenue, where this
walk starts. If you drive, take the Eisenhower Expressway, turn off at Harlem Avenue, go
north about 1 mile to Lake Street, then 4 blocks east to Kenilworth Avenue.

We are indebted to the Oak Park Public Library and W. R.
Hasbrouck for most of the information and descriptions given for
this walk. The order chosen for viewing Wright's works follow
that given in a booklet issued by the Oak Park Library, *A Guide
to the Architecture of Frank Lloyd Wright in Oak Park and
River Forest, Illinois.* Since the booklet includes pictures of all
the buildings referred to, it would be an especially
appropriate souvenir of your walk. Stop at the Oak Park Library
if you would like to secure one. Copies are available for $1.00
each. Library hours are 9:00 A.M. to 9:00 P.M. Monday through
Friday; 9:00 A.M. to 5:00 P.M. Saturday.

Frank Lloyd Wright was one of 3 great Chicago architects who
turned their backs on the accepted style of classic design and
created new forms for people of the late 19th and early 20th
centuries. The 2 others, who preceded him and doubtless
influenced him in his earlier years, were Henry Hobson
Richardson and Louis H. Sullivan. All were men of great talent
and originality. Among these, Wright gave the most attention to
domestic architecture and over the years developed a quite new
style of home, now known worldwide as the "Prairie House."
The Robie House in Chicago (1909) (see Walk No. 18; Hyde
Park - University of Chicago) is probably the most familiar
example of the Prairie House design.

The Chicago area is incredibly fortunate in having a practically
complete record of Wright's progress toward the Prairie House—
in more than 20 houses that he built in the suburb of Oak Park
and 7 additional houses in nearby River Forest. The buildings

319

listed for this walk cover a period of only about 20 years in Wright's life. But the impact of the type of house he had developed by the end of that period continues to be felt today in house designs all over the world. Low roof lines, wide eaves, open planes, casement windows, and car ports—all are characteristics of the Prairie House.

You will be surprised at the designs of some of Wright's earlier products, especially those before 1900; steep gables and dormer windows have little resemblance to the style now associated with his name. If you could choose a chronological order—which is obviously impractical!—instead of the geographical order that must be followed, you would more easily observe the record of changes in Wright's style.

Unless otherwise indicated, the buildings listed here are *not* open to the public.

Unity Temple (a Universalist church) and Parish House—Lake Street and Kenilworth (1906)

The Unity Temple is Wright's only *public* building in Oak Park— except for the Memorial Fountain just across the street to the north, on Lake near Grove Avenue (1903). The Temple is an esteemed international architectural landmark. Building a church in cubic form, without a steeple, was a revolutionary step, but the symbolism of light from above (through skylight and windows under the eaves) is surely no less valid for worshiping human beings than the centuries-old symbolism of the church spire for human aspiration.

With this church Wright effectively paved the way for modern use of concrete poured into wooden forms. The church's washed pebble surface, which gives the concrete a granite-like appearance, was also an innovation of Wright's, which in modified forms is still used by many top-ranking architects. A common entrance unites the church and parish house, although each is independent for its separate uses. The auditorium inside the Temple is in a sense an actual revival of temple architecture. With the pulpit in front center, Wright located seats on 3 sides, so that minister and congregation are close to each other. (Years later Wright used a similar plan for the Greek Orthodox church in Milwaukee.) Koeper, referring to the design of Unity Temple, has paid special tribute to Wright in these words: "Like the music of Bach, the architecture of Wright develops magnificent variations on simple themes."[9]

Unity Temple may be visited on Tuesday, Thursday, Friday, and Saturday between 1:00 P.M. and 5:00 P.M. Entrance fee is $1.00.

The restoration of Unity Temple has been going on for 6 years. The congregation has been given a match fund grant from the Edgar Kaufman Memorial Foundation in the past three years for $75,000. They have matched $50,000 and the remaining $25,000 they are trying to match will go toward exterior restoration.

The specific items that have been restored are the front doors; as a consequence of a fire in January, 1971, the entire Unity Temple interior has been restored which is the south end of the building, including the architectural skylight overhead. Colors were selected by Lloyd Wright, the oldest son of the architect. The roof has been replaced throughout. Skylights have been added over the minister's study and the robe room which are directly over the lobby. The weather skylight over the temple has been restored.

The amount of money spent, including the fire restoration for about $20,000, is a total of about $110,000 on the above restoration projects.

The next priority for restoration is the exterior exposed aggregate concrete that should commence in spring of 1973.

Frank Lloyd Wright House—428 Forest Avenue, and
Frank Lloyd Wright Studio—951 Chicago Avenue.
(House, 1889; Studio, 1895)

Next is the Frank Lloyd Wright House, adjoining his Studio, which faces the street around the corner, at 951 Chicago Avenue. Wood shingles, brick and stone were used. Both buildings were remodeled by Wright into apartments (1911).

The house and studio of Frank Lloyd Wright may also be visited from Wednesday to Sunday from 11:00 A.M. to 5:00 P.M. Entrance fee here is $1.25.

Dr. W. H. Copeland House—400 Forest Avenue. (Remodeled, 1909)—The remodeling of this house was not entirely according to Wright's plans and was not done under his supervision.

Arthur Heurtley House—318 Forest Avenue. (1902)—Roman brick. Remodeled later into 2 apartments—all at ground level.

Mrs. Thomas H. Gale House—6 Elizabeth Court. (1909; renovated, 1962)—Elizabeth Court is half a block farther south. The facade of this house is stucco with wood trim. Roofs are flat, in the Prairie House style, and the various planes give this small house tremendous architectural interest.

H. P. Young House—334 North Kenilworth (1895)—This is an 1895 remodeling; it retains the old farmhouse (around which Wright built the newer home) as the kitchen area.

P. A. Beachy House—238 Forest Avenue (1906)—This also incorporates an earlier house. It is built of brick, stucco, and wood trim.

Frank Thomas House—210 Forest Avenue (1901)—Built of stucco on wood frame, this house has been resurfaced with wooden siding. All rooms are above grade, with no basement. Here you can see some resemblances to the later Prairie House.

E. R. Hills House—313 Forest Avenue (Remodeled by Wright, 1902)—Stucco exterior with wood trim.

Nathan G. Moore House and Stable—333 Forest Avenue (1895, rebuilt 1924)—Roman brick, stucco, and wood trim exterior. The rebuilding in 1924 was necessary because of a fire that had destroyed the upper floor.

Francis Wooley House—1030 Superior Street (1893)—This house has been resurfaced with imitation brick siding.

Walter Gale House—1031 Chicago Avenue (1892)—Clapboard exterior.

R. P. Parker House—1027 Chicago Avenue (1892)—Another clapboard exterior. Note the high-peaked circular roofs, both in this and in the next house, so different from Wright's later style.

Opposite, Frank Lloyd Wright home and studio.

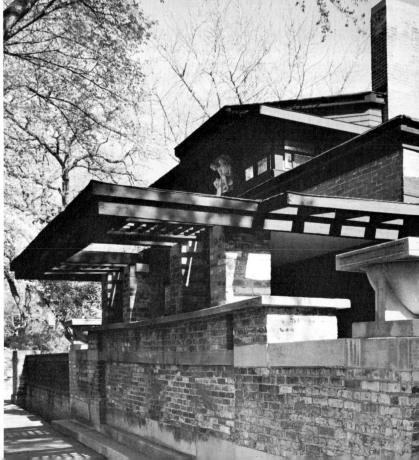

Thomas H. Gale House—1019 Chicago Avenue (1892)—Again, a clapboard exterior and high-peaked roofs.

O. E. Balch House—611 North Kenilworth (1911)—Stucco exterior with wood trim.

Harry S. Adams House—710 Augusta Boulevard (1913)—Brick and stucco exterior.

W. E. Martin House—636 North East Avenue (1903)—Stucco exterior with wood trim. This house has been converted into apartments.

H. C. Goodrich House—534 North East Avenue (1896)—Here we have another exterior of clapboards.

Edwin H. Cheney House—520 North East Avenue (1904)—This one-story brick house, set within gardens enclosed by brick walls, has a contemporary appearance, though it was built more than half a century ago. There are striking resemblances to the Robie House, which Wright built in Chicago 5 years later.

Rollin Furbeck House—515 Fair Oaks Avenue (1898)—The house here was expanded some years after its original constructions along with interior changes.

William G. Fricke House—540 Fair Oaks Avenue (1902; remodeled, 1907)—Stucco exterior with wood trim. A garage was added at the time of the remodeling.

Charles E. Roberts Stable—317 North Euclid Avenue (1896)—Originally built as a stable, this has now been converted into a house.

George Furbeck House—223 North Euclid (1897)—Brick with wood trim.

George W. Smith House—404 Home Avenue (1898)—Exterior of wood shingle. The high-peaked roofs are a sign of its early date.

The George W. Smith House is the last of the Oak Park houses by Wright that you are viewing on this walk. You go now to River Forest by walking West.

William H. Winslow House and Stable—515 Auvergne Place
(1893)—The exterior is Roman brick and stone, with terra-cotta
frieze above. Here you see many of the characteristics that will
be incorporated in Wright houses of a later date—wide eaves,
low roofs, a single chimney, and plain surfaces contrasting
with ornamented sections.

Chauncey L. Williams House—530 Edgewood Place (1895)—
Roman brick below the window sills and stucco above.

Above, Chauncey L. Willams
House.

325

Isabel Roberts House—603 Edgewood Place (1908; rebuilt, 1955)—This house, built in the form of a cross, is especially distinguished by a 2-story living room.

J. Kibben Ingalls House—562 Keystone Avenue (1909)—Stucco and painted wood trim.

E. Arthur Davenport House—559 Ashland Avenue (1901)—The building materials here are stained wood horizontal board and battened sheathing. This is the last of the homes to be viewed in River Forest.

River Forest Tennis Club—615 Lathrop Avenue (at Quick Street) (1906)—Here too the exterior is of stained wood and battened sheathing. Charles E. White, Jr., and Vernon S. Watson were associate architects.

This walk has taken you from Oak Park's Unity Temple to River Forest's Tennis Club. Between the 2 you have seen many examples of Wright's chief contribution to American architecture —buildings planned as individual homes, from some of his earliest to those of a later period in which he was working out various forms of the Prairie House.

Water Tower by
William LeBaron
Jenney.

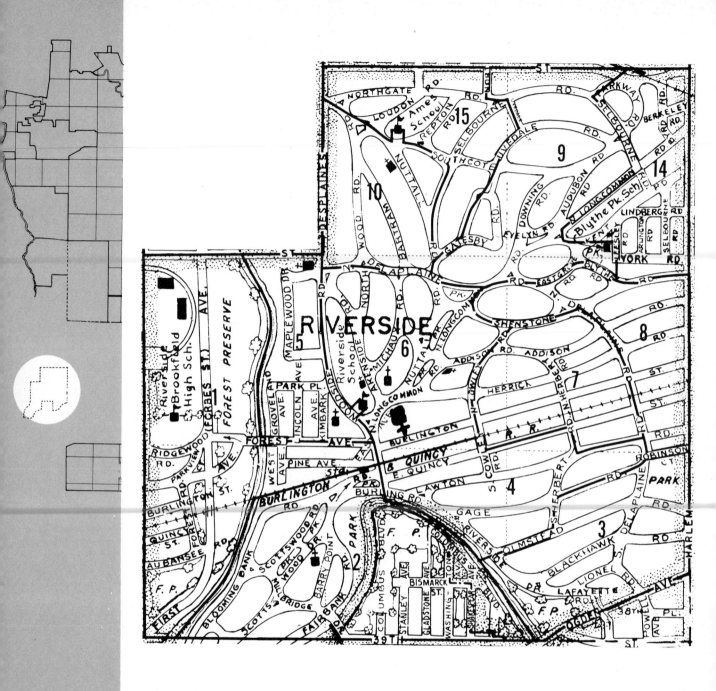

Walk · 29

RIVERSIDE OLD NEW TOWN

WALKING TIME: 1 hour.   HOW TO GET THERE: If you don't drive, take the Burlington
Commuter Railroad at Union Station. Train schedules are available by calling the
railroad offices at FR2-6700. The train trip takes about a half hour each way. If you drive from
downtown, take the Eisenhower Expressway west to Harlem Avenue (about 10 miles) turn
south on Harlem Avenue to Long Common Road (about 3 miles).

Riverside was planned in 1869 by the firm of Olmsted, Vaux and
Company, landscape architects. The two partners of this firm
that contributed greatly to the creation of two new professions—
landscape architecture and city planning—were Frederick Law
Olmsted, Sr. (1822-1903) and Calvert Vaux (1824-1895).
Frederick Law Olmsted was the principal planner of Riverside.

Olmsted set out to create for the Riverside Development
Association a community which represented "the best application
of the art of civilization to which mankind has yet attained."
With his partner, Calvert Vaux, Olmsted used careful planning
to make the Chicago suburb a place to foster the "harmonious
cooperation of men in a community and the intimate
relationship and constant intercourse and interdependence
between families."

Olmsted and Vaux designed many parks and communities
during their professional career. Outstanding were Central Park
in New York City; Fort Green Park, Brooklyn, New York;
Prospect Park, Brooklyn, New York; Park System, Boston,
Massachusetts; Jackson Park, Chicago; the world's Columbian
Exposition, Chicago; and Mount Royal, Montreal, Canada.
Olmsted and Vaux were given practically free rein by the
trustees of the Riverside Development Association. The site was
ideal and contained 1600 acres along both banks of the
Des Plaines River. The Burlington Railroad commuter service
was already in operation and offered excellent service between
Chicago's Loop and the western suburbs. The topography had
a gentle slope and was ripe for Olmsted's skills as a town
planner and landscape architect.

The plans called for interior curvilinear streets winding around natural features and focusing on the river. Trees were clustered in the parkways and were also located on the lawns of the houses—all well set back from the streets. The streets were curved for the first time in American suburban development. As Olmsted described them "to suggest and imply leisure, contemplativeness and tranquility." Some interior roads were deliberately depressed so that the sight lines would be directed towards the river.

It is a great tribute to Olmsted that the first of his suburbs has managed to maintain its rural character for over a century, despite the increase in automobiles and urban growth. It is also a tribute that Riverside has been the precursor of many similar developments in recent years.

The park along the Des Plaines River still remains as public recreation land for the entire community. The dam across the river has increased the expanse of water available for pleasure

100 Fairbank Road, Swiss cottage by Olmstead, Vaux and Co. *Opposite,* 185 Michaux Road.

331

boating. The trees and landscaping of the individual houses along the curvilinear streets have maintained the air of beauty and privacy.

As you wander through Riverside you will see every style of architecture. That is how it was supposed to be. The earliest Georgian style house, built in 1870, is located at 185 Michaux Road. Olmsted's Riverside was designed to provide a landscaped background to make each man's home "more beautiful by its surroundings." Architects, great and near great, came to Riverside to place their works in this romantic setting.

Frank Lloyd Wright built what he called his "best" home at 281 Bloomingbank Road and two others at 350 Fairbank Road and 150 Nuttal Road. No, the home at 283 Scottswood Road was not done by Frank Lloyd Wright but its designers Gruenzel and Drummond followed his tradition.

You've never heard of F. E. Withers but he has been discovered by college students. Withers did the town's first store building at 1 Riverside Road and the original portions of the Riverside Presbyterian Church at 116 Barrypoint Road.

Two Sullivan buildings of the Babson Estate still stand at 281 and 277 Gatesby Road. The chandelier from the main house hangs in the Riverside Museum.

H. H. Richardson, pace-setting architect of the 1880's, did not design any Riverside homes as far as is known but the style he set captured the imagination of many Riversiders. We can still enjoy the many relics of the 1880's. Three homes at 145, 157, and 165 Bartram Road were built for three grandchildren of Chicago's first settler, John Kinzie. The Town Hall at 27 Riverside Road and The Central School at 61 Woodside Road also have many of the features that Richardson made popular.

Oddly enough, the medieval style is represented by one of the newest buildings. The Riverside Public Library, 1 Burling Road, won an architectural prize when it was built in 1930.

No guide to Riverside would be complete without including Hoffman Tower. Everyone who sees it asks the inevitable question, "What is it?" The only certain answer is, "It's a tower." But the truth does not always satisfy man's inherent

Opposite, top, Coonly Playhouse by Frank Lloyd Wright, 350 Fairbank Road. *Bottom,* Garden at Babson Estate by Louis Sullivan, 272-281 Gatesby Road.

333

178 Michaux Road, by William
LeBaron Jenney.

curiosity, so through the years many stories have been told.
It was a toll gate for boats traveling up the river. Or a lookout to
spot any Riversiders that had fallen in through the ice on their
way to Lyons for a literal bucket of suds because they were
too impatient to wait for a good freeze. Perhaps Mr. Hoffman
simply missed the castles on the Rhine. Maybe you can conjure
up the real reason why Hoffman built his mystery tower and
the dam across the Des Plaines where Barrypoint Road
crosses the river.

Walk-30

Rebecca Crown Center.

FRANCES SEARLE BUILDING
(Communicative Disorders)

LINDHEIMER
ASTRONOMICAL
RESEARCH CENTER

TECHNOLOGICAL

O. T. HOGAN
BIOLOGICAL
SCIENCES

INSTITUTE

JAMES   ROSCOE   MILLER
CAMPUS

DEARBORN
OBSERVATORY

SHAKESPEARE
GARDEN

VOGELBACK
COMPUTING
CENTER

GARRETT
THEOLOGICAL
SEMINARY

SWIFT HALL

EDUCATION

NATHANIEL
LEVERONE
HALL

NORRIS UNIVERSITY
CENTER

Engelhart
Tower

Deering Library

NORTHWESTERN
UNIVERSITY
LIBRARY

Hermann Tower

Deering
Tower

SCENE
SHOP

UNIVERSITY
HALL

SPEECH

SPEECH
ANNEX

EMERSON ST

CAHN
AUDITORIUM

SCOTT
HALL

HARRIS
HALL

KRESGE
CENTENNIAL
HALL

OLD
COLLEGE

LOCY

UNIVERSITY PL

MILLAR
CHAPEL

FISK
HALL

SHERIDAN   RD

REBECCA
CROWN
CENTER

LEVERE

SHERIDAN ROAD

PARKES

CLARK ST

LAKE MICHIGAN

SHERMAN   AVE

ORRINGTON   AVE

CLARK ST

CHICAGO   AVE

HINMAN   AVE

JUDSON   AVE

SHERIDAN   RD

CHURCH ST

Start here

DAVIS STREET

Walk · 30

NORTHWESTERN UNIVERSITY— EVANSTON CAMPUS

WALKING TIME: About 1½ hours.   HOW TO GET THERE: Take a northbound CTA
Howard Street train in any subway station along State Street. Transfer at Howard Street to the
Evanston ''El'' train and get off at Davis Street. Walk east 2 blocks to Orrington and
1 block north to Clark and the Rebecca Crown Center. This is the central administrative
center of the university. Here you may make inquiries about guided tours or of any
particular department that interests you.

   If public transportation is not your mode, then drive by taking Lake Shore Drive north to
Hollywood and then follow Sheridan Road north to Evanston and the Northwestern Campus.
Driving or public transportation time should take about 45 minutes.

An arresting combination of architectural styles is transforming
the landscape on the Evanston campus of Northwestern
University on the Lake Michigan shoreline just north of Chicago.

To accommodate a long-range, unified campus plan, the
university created its J. Roscoe Miller campus with an 84-acre
landfill extending into Lake Michigan. This new landfill campus
is just east of the old campus, which, of course, is east of
Sheridan Road. The landfill runs north and south with a large
lagoon and is approximately between University Place on
the south and Central Street on the north.

Your first stop is at the north end of downtown Evanston, where
the business district and the university join at Clark and
Orrington. There is a municipal parking lot nearby, or one
provided by the university at the south end of the new campus.

Rebecca Crown Memorial Center
Architects: Skidmore, Owings and Merrill (1965)

This striking center is the "gateway" to the Evanston campus
and houses all the university administrative and business
officials. It was constructed with funds donated by Colonel
Henry Crown, a well-known Chicago financier and
philanthropist, and his sons along with a bequest by the late
John Hardin, tenth president of the university's
Board of Trustees.

337

The Center has three wings—executive wing, north wing, and east wing. The design is modern in concept and developed to blend with the varied architectural styles of the campus. The building's surface is Indiana limestone and embraces an open court paved with dark-toned brick.

A striking highlight of the Center is a 100-foot clock tower, also of limestone, that rises from the east end of the Center. A 60-car garage is located below the court.

Now, walk 1 block east and 1 block north to Chicago Avenue and Sheridan Road.

Alice Millar Chapel
Architects: Jense and Halstead (1964)

This chapel is the focal point of Protestant religious activities on the Evanston campus. The pedantic gray limestone structure is of a modified English-Gothic design. The interior consists principally of the Alice Millar Chapel which seats 720, the Jeanne Vail Meditation Chapel which seats 188, and Parkes Hall.

There are in all, 12 stained-glass windows. The great chancel window is at the north end of the chapel. Rising above the chancel floor, it measures 35 feet in width and 52 feet in height. The theme of the chancel window is Creation, Redemption, and Triumph. These windows of the chapel were designed and executed by the Willett Stained Glass Studios of Philadelphia.

Levere Memorial Chapel
Architect: Arthur Howell Knox (1930)

Just a few feet east at Sheridan and Hinman is the national headquarters and chapel of the Sigma Alpha Epsilon Fraternity. This is an authentic replica of a small twelfth-century English Gothic church, built as the national headquarters for the fraternity—an obvious example by the architect of care and attention to detail. Now, return to Sheridan Road intersection.

Women's Residences Quadrangle

Before crossing Sheridan Road on to the main campus, look northwest to the complex of English Gothic and Tudor Gothic residence halls built around two quadrangles. They were constructed in the 1930's for several women's residence halls and sororities. Facing Sheridan Road just east of the residence quadrangles is Scott Hall and Cahn Auditorium. Scott Hall, completed in 1940, is the student activities center. It contains lounge rooms, a student grill, and the offices of the deans of men and women. There are also many student organization offices located here.

Now, cross Sheridan Road and step on to the old campus and walk east up the tree-lined path to a cluster of respected and original main campus structures. They include Harris, University, and Kresge halls. The distinguished School of Speech and Speech Annex halls are part of this group of original main campus buildings. They are not distinguished as great architectural gems, but do present an authentic nineteenth-century scene of campus life in the Midwest—also characteristic of the traditional American eclectic architecture of that time. To the east are Fisk Hall, Locy Hall, and Old College.

Fisk Hall contains the Department of Home Economics and Medill School of Journalism. This red brick structure was designed by Burnham and Root in 1898.

Old College

We are told that back in 1855 when the campus was still a primitive forest, a neat frame building was erected as the temporary home for the new Northwestern University. It housed the entire college program and a preparatory school until 1869. When University Hall was built at that time, the Old College was moved to its present location. It now contains offices of nearby, overcrowded buildings.

The tall stone building with the spire is University Hall, second oldest on campus—completed in 1869. Directly south is Harris Hall, designed by Shepley, Coolidge, Bulfinch and Abbott of Boston in 1915.

Kresge Centennial Hall
Architects: Holabird and Root (1954)

This classroom building is similar in style to the Technological Institute, also designed by the same architects. The Institute

is farther north on the campus and will be viewed shortly. Kresge is a seriveable building but does not warrant any special attention.

By this time your eyes have been directed out to the exciting new Lindheimer Astronomical Research Center, located on a promontory in Lake Michigan. This building and several others are located in filled land named in honor of past president James Roscoe Miller. This in-fill came about when Northwestern needed to expand its campus and found it difficult, if not impossible, to acquire sufficient property west of Sheridan Road. It was then that the campus planners realized what a tremendous asset the lakeshore was. They quickly developed a plan to fill about 80 acres of lake with a lagoon, and proceeded with expansion.

The less said about the Old Campus, the better, because it is a potpourri of eclectic, unrelated designs and periods. If there were a plan, it is not apparent. However, the university has more than made up for this omission with its strikingly stunning new campus—its impact, the spirit of the future.

Lindheimer Observatory.

340

Turn east to Swift Hall, a brick building that is the first university structure in the U.S., designed especially for a theatre for the School of Speech.

Northwestern University Library
Architects: Skidmore, Owings and Merrill (1971)
Partner in Charge: Walter Netsch

This dramatic three-pavilion complex unites the university's entire collection by connecting with Deering Library, the original campus library structure constructed in 1932. The new complex has been named Deering Tower, Hermann Tower, and Englehart Tower. Physically a one-story transitional base connects the three towers to Deering Library and aesthetically acts as a nodal interchange on the main north-south campus walk. These massive structures act as a striking contrast to the passive meadows of the lagoon and lakefront campus. At this plaza entrance level, the entry lantern, benches, steps clerestories, nodal spaces, and columns supporting the three research towers, intermingle with the heavily-treed old campus and the lake views.

Northwestern University Library.

341

Nathaniel Leverone Hall.

These buildings were designed to be used as well as admired. Many well-designed facilities are available for students, faculty, and scholars. A walk through a portion of the complex will convince you of how well they are used.

The total library complex houses a 50,000 volume core collection of indispensable books for undergraduate study, a research collection of 1.2 million volumes, and seating for 3,500 students and 300 faculty members.

The architect handled the change in grade between the old campus and the new landfill campus by creating an extensive first floor to house the card catalog, reference, bibiography, periodicals, technical services, data processing, and administrative offices.

Construction is of poured-in-place reinforced concrete using board and plywood form finishes exposed. Exterior walls are floor height limestone with panels with a broached finish with painted wood and glass units.

342

Now walk a short distance northwest to the twin towers of
the Management and Education Schools.

Nathaniel Leverone Hall
Graduate School of Management
Architects: Loebl, Schlossman, Bennett and Dart (1972)
Partner in Charge: Edward Dart

This six-story reinforced concrete structure is the very epitome
of efficiency and discipline. The university has moved all of
its graduate programs in business to this new building.
This structure is joined with the twin six-story Graduate
School of Education.

Graduate School of Education
Architects: Loebl, Schlossman, Bennett and Dart (1972)
Partner in Charge: Edward Dart

This structure is the smaller of the twin six-story towers. It has
less classroom and office space but presents a similar facade
of simplicity and strength.

Both towers are constructed of reinforced concrete, some of
which is exposed and some clad with Indiana limestone. The
combination is one of particularly good design.

Garrett Theological Seminary

The French Gothic seminary, chapel spire, and residence hall
have long been a Northwestern landmark. The intricate tracery,
moldings, and Gothic arches have been faithfully copied
from some French abbey or seminary.

While at this location, be sure to see the Shakespeare Garden
and the Old Dearborn Observatory.

Technological Institute
Architects: Holabird and Root (1942)

The Institute contains the offices, classrooms, and laboratories
of 7 engineering departments, two interdisciplinary research
centers, and the departments of chemistry and physics. A
three-acre addition in 1963 increased the total size of the
Institute building to 13 acres. The new section provides
increased space for expanded research and graduate study.

This huge structure is modernized Gothic in spirit and presents a somewhat military appearance.

One hour tour every Saturday at 11:00 A.M. starts from 2145 Sheridan Road, 492-3365.

Norris University Center
Architects: Loebl, Schlossman, Bennett and Dart (1972)
Partner in Charge: Edward Dart

This handsome concrete and Indiana limestone structure is well suited to its location on the shore of the new lagoon. The site and building are on higher ground and command attention from every point of view.

This is Northwestern's first student union building and must be a most welcome addition to the campus. Lounges, dining halls, recreation rooms, meeting rooms, and study halls are an integral part of this fine facility.

Now, walk east a short distance.

Vogelback Computing Center
Architects: Skidmore, Owings and Merrill (1965)

This is one of the most modern computer installations in the United States. It is equipped with a Control Data Corporation 3400 computer, which is capable of 380,000 additions a second. Another computer of even greater capabilities is on order. The Center is an all-university facility, in that scholars in medicine, social science, and humanities are using it in their research as well as those in science and engineering.

The design of the structure is reinforced concrete and its straight-forward, horizontal lines express the precision of the mechanical interior presence.

O. T. Hogan Biological Sciences Research Building
Architects: Skidmore, Owings and Merrill (1971)
Partner in Charge: Walter Netsch

Just north of the Norris University Center is an equally impressive building by Walter Netsch. The strong vertical concrete and limestone lines of this structure make a fascinating contrast with Edward Dart's equally strong horizontal lines of

the student center. These and other similarly strong contrasts make for a fascinating new campus.

This structure is five stories in addition to a rooftop greenhouse. The vertical aluminum window walls have a glare-reducing glass. The building contains biological research laboratories, animal quarters, offices, and greenhouse.

Now, walk east a short distance.

Communicative Disorders Building
Architects: Skidmore, Owings and Merrill (1971)

This angular concrete three-story structure houses the Department of Communicative Disorders for the School of Speech. The three-story, reinforced-concrete structure is built in the new Science and Engineering Complex on the north campus.

The training offered is for teachers, clinicians, and researchers dealing with speech and hearing problems and with learning difficulties associated with speech, hearing, and language impairment.

The structure is in a roughly triangular shape with 141,000 square feet of floor space. The concrete frame has curtain walls

Communicative Disorders building.

of limestone panels spanning from floor to floor. It has reflective glass windows somewhat like one-way mirrors to reduce the solar load and effect savings in air conditioning.

The interior includes many special rooms and chambers for training and treating all phases of speech and hearing problems.

To the west of the Communicative Disorders Building lies an enormous complex of structures that make up the Men's Residences Area. Patten Gym is at the north end of this area. Dyche Stadium is located about one mile northwest of this point. It was constructed in 1926 and designed by Holabird and Root, architects. They also designed McGaw Memorial Hall in 1952. This is the major indoor athletic facility that is located just north of Dyche Stadium.

Lindheimer Astronomical Research Center
Architects: Skidmore, Owings and Merrill (1966)
Partner in Charge: Walter Netsch

This is easily the most spectacular structure on the campus and consists of a twin-tower observatory connected by a superstructure.

The observing level is elevated about sixty feet above the landfill and comprises three spaces; a 36-foot diameter dome-covered observing room for the 40-inch instrument, a control room, and a 24-foot diameter dome-covered space for the 16-inch telescope.

Immediately below the observing level are the instrument room, small dark room, and main meeting room. Stairs connect with the observing level and lower level, although major circulation to the lower level is by elevator.

The lower level surrounding an entry court provides space for a machine shop, dark room, offices, electronics shop, and building services. The floor level is six feet below grade, and the roof of this level is covered with 18 inches of earth to minimize heat transmission from the structure and solar absorption and re-radiation.

New 40-inch and 16-inch reflecting telescopes will be housed in a tower structure with ancillary facilities provided at ground

Opposite, top, O. T. Hogan Biological Sciences Research building. *Bottom*, Bahai House of Worship.

level. Site planning incorporates provision for a future new research building and a tower housing the 18-inch refracting telescope presently in Dearborn Observatory. Trees will be provided on the lake periphery to assist in maintaining optimum observing conditions. As a matter of fact, the landscaping of the entire new campus will, of course, change somewhat the rather stark appearance. This will take several years' time.

For information regarding visiting hours, call 492-7651 or 492-5300.

If you drove here, it is suggested that you return to your car and drive north on Sheridan Road to Linden Avenue, about one mile. If you came by public transportation, walk west on Central Avenue to the CTA station and ride the elevated train to Linden Avenue.

Bahai House of Worship—Sheridan Road at Linden Avenue, Wilmette. Architect: Louis Bourgeois (1929)

This is truly an outstanding structure that houses this international religious society. It is nine-sided with ornament carved in limestone over reinforced concrete.

The Bahai religion was founded in 1863 in Persia (now Iran) and has become an international organization involving people of many nations and racial groups. The great dome has stone tracery that brings the sky into this fascinating house of worship.

The combination of the garden and the stone tracery is reminiscent of ancient Persia.

To enter, one approaches from the entrance on Linden, up a series of stairs that lead to a lovely landscaped area and garden. One's eye is soon caught by the stone tracery of the facades crowned by the great dome. The ground floor entrance and nearby windows reveal a simple, single room or chapel for worshipping. By all means go inside, if possible. You will be entranced by the simplicity and quiet serenity of the interior. It is open daily from 10:00 A.M. to 9:00 P.M. For tours call 279-4100 Ext. 341.

This is the end of this walk and it is suggested that, if tired, this is a good place to rest and meditate before returning the way you came.

348

Walk-31

Subway entrance,
under the Chicago
Civic Center
building.

Clark

Dearborn

State

Randolph

Washington

Madison

Start here

Walk · 31

UNDERGROUND WALKWAYS

WALKING TIME: ½ hour (if you don't stop along the way to shop).   HOW TO GET THERE:
From Michigan and Randolph walk 1 block south and 1 block west to the southwest corner of
Wabash Avenue and Washington Street.

An all-weather walkway system underground, which is being
planned for Chicago's Loop, is partially completed and available
for a walking tour. When finished, the walkways will connect
the majority of the Loop buildings. Mail will be delivered by
postmen with pushcarts starting from the underground section
at the new loop post office, which will be in the Federal Center
(see Walk No. 4, Dearborn Street). Because of the outdoor
connotation of the term "walking tour," this suggestion for a
subterranean walk may seem odd. Yet one of Chicago's
fascinations is this underground walkway system, on a scale
that is rare today even in great urban centers like ours.

For a good sample walk, start in the basement of Marshall Field's
Men's Store, at Wabash and Washington. Walk north in the
basement through the tunnel under Washington Street that
connects this with Marshall Field's main store. You will know
you are on the other side of Washington when you come to
furniture and rugs in the Budget Basement of the main store.
Keep on walking in the same direction for about 6 aisles (through
the section for junior girls' clothing); then turn left (which will
be west) and walk on beyond the cafeteria (called "Budget
Dinette"). Just beyond the cafeteria turn right (north) and walk
past elevators and escalator, watching for a green light overhead
announcing "SUBWAY." When you see that sign, pointing to
your left, you can be sure you are on the right path. If you lose
your way *before* you reach this point, just ask an employee
how to get to the subway!

At the "SUBWAY" sign turn left—as it directs you—to reach
the entrance to the CTA subway. You will now be walking west.
The 2nd stretch of your underground walking begins at the

subway entrance and—continuing west—takes you through the State Street subway's Randolph-Washington station, past its ticket window and exits. Keep going west, following the large signs on the wall that read, "To Dearborn Street," but instead of stopping when you reach the Dearborn Street subway's Randolph-Washington station (for which the signs are primarily intended) continue walking west until you reach the lighted sign: "Chicago Civic Center." Here you will be entering the lower concourse of the Civic Center Building.

Now, instead of continuing west to the City Hall and County Building, as you could easily do, turn left (south) and walk by the offices of the Chicago Data Center. Through the glass walls, designed expressly to give sightseers the best possible view, you can see a number of modern machines with rows of tiny colored lights, flashing off and on constantly with a frantic sort of speed as they process data of various kinds for the city of Chicago. The *people* that you see working in these offices— there are not many of them—appear extraordinarily relaxed, whatever they happen to be doing, in comparison with the incessant, nervous-looking activity of the machines!

As you continue south now into the Brunswick Building (69 West Washington) you will be walking in a tunnel under Washington Street again, this time 2 blocks west of the first Washington tunnel. The Brunswick lower concourse is a complete shopping center.

When you finally come to a travel agency, you have reached the steps leading down to the Dearborn-Washington subway station and are headed east. Pass through the station and follow the tunnel into the State-Madison Building's lower concourse. Here you will pass a Stouffer's restaurant, several small shops, and a Walgreen's cafeteria. As you leave the building, you enter the State-Washington subway station. Beyond the ticket window you can go into the basement of Wieboldt's department store and take an escalator to the main floor, to go out onto State Street or Madison Street. Or you can end this subterranean trip by going instead into the basement of Stevens' women's specialty store. After taking the escalator there, you will exit on State Street.

Top, Sculpture by Zoltan Kemeny. *Bottom*, Museum of Contemporary Art.

Oak

Walton

Chicago

Superior

Ontario

Michigan

◀ Start here

Walk · 32

NEAR NORTH SIDE ART GALLERIES

WALKING TIME: 2 hours.   HOW TO GET THERE: Take any of the following northbound
CTA buses—No. 151 (Sheridan) on Michigan; 152 (Addison) or 153 (Wilson-Michigan) on
State; or 76 (Diversey) on Wabash. (Or walk north on Michigan to the first bus sign beyond
Lake Street, where all of these buses stop.) Get off at Michigan and Ontario, (628 N)
and walk 2 blocks east to the Museum of Contemporary Art, where this walk starts.
If you are driving, turn off the Outer Drive *onto the Inner Drive* at Ohio Street (600 N);
continue north just 1 block, to Ontario, then drive west to 237, the Museum of Contemporary Art.

Chicagoans quite justly take pride in the fact that some of the
country's best private art collections are located here, often
available for public viewing at the various galleries and museums
in the city. Chicago's considerable interest in art supports
numerous galleries in many parts of the city. The area of their
greatest concentration lies on Ontario and Oak streets and
on Michigan Avenue.

A substantial number of Chicago artists find their livelihood in
painting and sculpture. They would seem to have a ready market
through displaying their work in these various galleries.
Unfortunately for them, the majority of the art galleries in
Chicago, while generally interested in contemporary painting
and sculpture, apparently prefer showing the works of artists
of international stature and fame. Some, however, like the
Phyllis Kind Gallery and the Distelheim Galleries are especially
interested in Chicago and other midwest artists. And on
occasion Chicago artists are given prominent attention—as, for
example, in the joint venture November 2, 1968, of the galleries
listed here called "Response to Violence in Our Society," an
especially bitter attack by Chicago artists on the official handling
of demonstrators at the time of the 1968 Democratic
nominating convention in Chicago.

The places listed for this walk do not include all the art
galleries in the area; you may find others as you go along that
have equal interest for you. Yet even these are obviously more
than you can *visit* in the 2-hour period suggested, especially
since many of them are on the 2nd or 3rd floor. Just discovering
where all of these are, however, will be worthwhile, so that
you may return to them later one by one. And even on this

355

walk you might have time to browse a little in a few that attract you most.

You can generally visit the galleries weekdays from 10:00 A.M. to 5:00 P.M., some of them opening earlier, some later. Most of them are closed Sundays, a few both Sundays and Mondays. But of course their schedules are always subject to change. Instead of quoting precise hours, therefore, we recommend that whenever you count on visiting any given art gallery you check about its hours in advance.

Museum of Contemporary Art—237 East Ontario. Architects for Remodeling: Brenner, Danforth and Rockwell (1967)

In October 1967 the Museum of Contemporary Art opened in a building previously used by Playboy Magazine, remodeled for its present purpose. The building gains considerable distinction and strength from the sculpture attached to the facade, the last work of the late Zoltan Kemeny of Zurich, Switzerland. This red copper bas-relief, 50 feet long and 8 feet high, called "Interior Geography 2," was given to the museum by Mr. and Mrs. Maurice A. Lipschultz. It is the museum's only permanent work of art.

The Museum is unique in that it has no permanent collection. Rather it continues its support of avant-garde art by presenting a new show every 7 weeks. In its recent history it has acknowledged the importance of underground comics and presented Paoli Soleri's new world architectural designs. An exhibition of monumental fiber forms and a first photography show, the challenging psychological studies of Diane Arbus, continue its tradition of displaying every mode of current art expression. It has also organized surveys of important modern artists and movements as the recent "White on White Exhibition," a study of the white monochrome in twentieth-century art; "James Rosenquist," works from one of America's most noted pop artists, and "Chicago Imagist Art," a study of Chicago's own eccentric masters. If you are one who thinks that art consists only of oil paintings on canvas or representational statuary, you may find this museum disturbing. But you can't fail to find it exciting, and you shouldn't miss it.

356

Arts Club of Chicago—109 East Ontario, 2nd floor.
Architect for the Club's interior:
Ludwig Mies van der Rohe (1955)

The only other indispensable *inside* visit for this walk is the
Arts Club of Chicago. Quite aside from any exhibit there, the
interior of the Club is worth seeing, since it was designed by
Mies van der Rohe. Though private, the Club opens all its
exhibits to the public. And over the years it has a history of
most distinguished exhibits, many of them the first in Chicago—
or even in the country—of works by artists later recognized as
of world importance. Rodin, Picasso, Toulouse-Lautrec,
Vlaminck, Utrillo, and Brancusi, for instance, were given early
one-man showings by the Arts Club of Chicago.

Other art galleries of the area, in order, are listed here.
(Remember: For Ontario and Oak streets, the even numbers are
on the north side of the street, odd numbers on the south. For
Michigan Avenue, even numbers are on the west side of the
street, odd numbers on the east.)

East Ontario (east to west)

Michael Wyman Gallery, 233—special showings of
contemporary artists.

The Carlsan Gallery, 226—continuous showing of hand-woven
contemporary tapestries.

Richard Feigen Gallery, 226—specializes in showing "modern
and old masters."

Pro-Grafica Art, 226—specializing in the graphic arts.

Phyllis Kind, 226—local artists, painting and sculpture.

B. C. Holland Gallery, 224 (formerly at 155)—generally open to
the public with no changing exhibitions. Paintings of late
nineteenth- and twentieth-century artists.

Deson-Zaks, 226—Italian contemporary painters and sculptors
are represented here.

Sternberg Galleries, 140, second floor—showing oil paintings
and rare prints.

Welna Gallery, 105—chiefly American painting and sculpture.

357

Fairweather-Hardin Gallery, 101—showings of contemporary art.

North Michigan Avenue (south to north)

Merrill Chase Galleries, 620, second floor—oils, etchings, lithographs.

Allan Frumkin Gallery, 620, second floor—exhibits avant-garde sculpture and paintings.

Richard Gray Gallery, 620, third floor—works of twentieth-century masters and emerging younger talents.

Kazimir Gallery, 620, third floor—featuring contemporary European painters and sculptors, especially constructionists.

R. S. Johnson-International Gallery, 645—drawings, paintings, special showings. Leger, Matisse, Picasso, Villon.

Van Straaten Gallery, Inc. 664—oils, lithographs and posters.

Stuart Brent Books and Records, 672—selling old and new prints and lithographs.

Wally F. Findlay Galleries, 814—impressionists, post-impressionists.

Oak Street (1000 North, east to west)

Limited Image, 108—sales, exhibitions of fine art, photographic prints.

Frank J. Oehlschlaeger, 107—showing contemporary painting, sculpture, and prints.

Gilman Galleries, 103—with two stories of avant-garde art in all media and a small outdoor patio in the rear with sculpture on display.

Distelheim Galleries, 17—offering contemporary painting and sculpture with emphasis on Chicago artists.

Oak Street Book Store, 58—lithographs and prints.

Other East-West streets, between Ohio and Oak

Lo Guidice Gallery Ltd., 210 E. Ohio—modern painting, drawing, sculpture, and graphics are shown in the third and fourth floor showrooms.

Herbert Baker Gallery, John Hancock Center's Chicago Gallery, by appointment only. 642-2994—African, Oceanic, and archaic sculpture, jewelry, and artifacts.

Jacques Baruch Gallery, 900 N. Michigan—a gallery in an apartment, for which appointments are necessary, with a large stock of European and American oil paintings and sculpture, and such unusual items as icons and el fresco paintings.

Benjamin Galleries, 900 N. Michigan—oils, drawings, graphics.

Maurice Sternberg Galleries, 936 N. Michigan—post impressionist and modern masters.

Faulkner-Main Street Galleries, 100 E. Walton—19th and 20th century graphics and paintings.

Nationwide Art Center, 70 E. Walton (932 N)—carrying a large assortment of paintings and reproductions.

Arts International—Le Garage, 58 E. Walton—an enormous stock of paintings and reproductions.

Siegel Galleries Ltd., 43 E. Walton—monthly exhibits.

If you are still able to walk, look south into Ernst Court and see some interesting shops and architects at work. There are many fine restaurants and snack shops in this area.

Index

Notes

WALK NUMBER 3
1. Giedion, Sigfried, *Space, Time, and Architecture, Sixth Edition.* (Cambridge: The Harvard University Press, 1946), p. 311.
2. Frederick Koeper, *Illinois Architecture.* (Chicago: The University of Chicago Press, 1968), p. 64.
3. Giedion, op. cit., p. 310.

WALK NUMBER 12
4. Kogan, Herman and Lloyd Wendt, *Chicago: A Pictorial History.* (New York: E. P. Dutton and Company, 1958), p. 203.

WALK NUMBER 15
5. Kogan and Wendt, op. cit., p. 177.
6. Ibid.

WALK NUMBER 16
7. Graham, Jory, *Chicago: An Extraordinary Guide.* (Chicago: Rand McNally and Company, 1968), p. 343, note quoting part of John Crerar's will.

WALK NUMBER 18
8. Saarinen, Eero, "Campus Planning: The Unique World of the University." *Architectural Record,* November 1960.

WALK NUMBER 28
9. Koeper, op. cit., p. 204.